Interfaces on Trial 2.0

The Information Society Series

Laura DeNardis and Michael Zimmer, series editors

Jonathan Band and Masanobu Katoh, *Interfaces on Trial 2.0*

Interfaces on Trial 2.0

Jonathan Band and Masanobu Katoh

The MIT Press
Cambridge, Massachusetts
London, England

For information about quantity discounts, email special_sales@mitpress.mit.edu.

Set in Stone Sans and Stone Serif by the MIT Press. Printed and bound in the United States of America.

Library of Congress Cataloging-in-Publication Data

Band, Jonathan.
Interfaces on trial 2.0 / Jonathan Band and Masanobu Katoh.
    p. cm.— (Information society series)
Includes bibliographical references and index.
ISBN 978-0-262-01500-4 (hardcover : alk. paper)
1. Copyright—Computer programs. 2. Computer software industry—Law and legislation. I. Katoh, Masanobu. II. Title.
K1443.C6B363 2011
346.04'82—dc22
                                                                    2010017746

10 9 8 7 6 5 4 3 2 1

to David Louis Band

Contents

Foreword

In 1995, when Jonathan Band and Masanobu Katoh published *Interfaces on Trial*, the technology landscape was very different. But their vision and insights have proven to be timeless.

At the time, a gigabyte hard drive was unheard of and the Internet was unknown to many people. Now you can carry several gigabytes around in your pocket, and the Internet is the platform upon which a significant portion of global commerce occurs every day.

The early interoperability legal battles that Band and Katoh described so vividly in *Interfaces on Trial* highlighted devices like the Apple II and video game cartridges. Today, interoperability fights involve everything from word processing file formats to DVD encryption to the "jailbreaking" of Apple iPhones. While the underlying technology has advanced considerably, the legal issues have not changed, and many of the actors remain the same. Indeed, today interoperability is more important than ever, and the threats to its prevalence are greater than ever.

A legal regime that permitted technological interoperability has reinforced the open architecture of the Internet. This regime grew out of an intellectual-property framework that balanced the goals of protection with the goals of follow-on innovation—a framework that is well established in developed economies around the world. Nonetheless, some technology companies have sought to improve their positions in the marketplace by attempting to mold IP law through litigation and lobbying to exercise ever more restrictive control over who can interconnect with what. These demands are invariably presented with a self-interested, simplistic view that more protection of intellectual property is always better. But that isn't the case, and it never has been. IP policy must continue to give creators adequate incentives to innovate without enabling rightsholders to broadly foreclose competition. As the U.S. Supreme Court recognized in its *Grokster* decision, "[t]he more artistic protection is favored, the more technological innovation may be discouraged; the administration of copyright law is an exercise in managing the trade-off."

In the years since the enactment of the Digital Millennium Copyright Act in the United States, the difficulty of managing the interoperability trade-off has become evident. Even more troublesome, courts willingly entertain "clickwrap" licenses with provisions that are decidedly inimical to competition. Whether through technological control or contract, the ability to dictate how—and even whether—competitors can interoperate with a dominant software or hardware product represents a threat to the competitiveness of the technology industry.

As corporations and governments make billion-dollar investments in mainframe technology, and as consumers spend billions on digital media and devices, the question of whether a software or hardware provider can leverage its intellectual-property rights to dictate control over those investments looms large. If IP law prevents competitors from achieving interoperability, the competition landscape will be barren.

We can only hope that policy makers—armed with insights from authors such as Jon Band and Masanobu Katoh—will reject unbalanced intellectual-property policies and renew their commitment to openness and multifaceted innovation.

Ed Black
President, Computer & Communications Industry Association

Acknowledgments

Even it the Digital Age, it still takes a village to draft, edit, and publish a book. We would like to thank the following, in alphabetical order, for their significant contributions to this process: Margy Avery, Paul Bethge, Brandon Butler, Peter Choy, Laura DeNardis, Tricia Donovan, Andriani Ferti, Ben Grillot, Laura Iandoli, Taro Isshiki, Peter Jaszi, Masahiro Kamei, Makoto Kono, Mark Kurtz, Noah Levine, Michael Rodgers, Lowell Sachs, Josh Sarnoff, Matt Schruers, Thomas Vinje, and Lynda Wilkes. Without their help, this book would still be more than a dozen disconnected articles scattered among disparate, relatively inaccessible journals.

1   The Interoperability Debate

1.1   Introduction

We live in an interoperable world. Computer hardware and software products manufactured by different vendors can exchange data within local networks and around the globe via the Internet. Competition enabled by interoperability has led to innovation and lower prices, and this has placed extraordinary computing capacity in the hands of ordinary users.

This interoperable world represents a dramatic change from the computing environment of the 1970s. In those days, once a company purchased a computer system, the company was essentially "locked in" to that system: the system was not compatible with the products manufactured by other companies, and the conversion costs were high. Although "locking in" was extremely profitable for dominant vendors, such as IBM, competitors and users suffered from high prices, indifferent service, limited choice, and slow innovation.

Many factors have contributed to the transition from the locked-in environment of the 1970s to today's interoperable world, including consumer demand, business strategy, government policy, and the ideology of technologists. One factor that is often overlooked is the evolution of copyright law over the past 30 years. Because computer programs are copyrightable, copyright law determines the rules for competition in the information-technology industry. For this reason, there has been a 30-year debate concerning the application of copyright to software.

The parties to the debate are the dominant vendors (who want to lock in users and lock out competitors) and the developers of interoperable software products (who want to compete with the dominant vendors). The debate has occurred in courts in North America, Europe, and the Pacific Rim; in the U.S. Congress and the European Parliament; and in law schools, think tanks, and legal publications. It has centered on two related matters:

the scope of copyright protection for program elements necessary for interoperability and the permissibility of the reverse engineering necessary to uncover those elements in a competitor's program. Underlying these two matters is the central competitive issue confronting the software industry: Could one firm prevent other firms from developing software products that interoperated with the products developed by the first firm?

In 1995 we published *Interfaces on Trial: Intellectual Property and Interoperability in the Global Software Industry*. That 370-page book closely examined the interoperability debate in the United States, the European Union, and Japan. Its first chapter provided a general overview of computer technology, the structure of the computer industry, and the significance of intellectual-property protection to innovation and competition in the industry. Its second chapter reviewed the fundamentals of intellectual-property law, focusing on copyright and on the application of copyright to software. Its third chapter tackled the first controversy in the interoperability debate: copyright protection for interface specifications. It explored the early missteps in the 1980s by the U.S. Court of Appeals for the Third Circuit, and the Second Circuit's[1] 1992 landmark decision (rejecting the earlier rulings) in *Computer Associates v. Altai*. Its fourth chapter treated the second controversy in the interoperability debate: the permissibility of software reverse engineering. It reviewed the resolution of this controversy by the Ninth Circuit in *Sega v. Accolade*. The book then addressed the development of the EU Software Directive (in chapter 5) and the interoperability debate in Japan (in chapter 6).

To our pleasant surprise, *Interfaces on Trial* ran through three printings; to our great relief, it received very favorable reviews.[2]

At the time we published *Interfaces on Trial*, we thought that the interoperability debate was largely over. In the United States, several appellate courts had followed *Computer Associates* and *Sega*, so those decisions'

1. The U.S. federal court system has three levels: the federal district courts (which conduct trials), the intermediate U.S. Courts of Appeals (which hear appeals from the district courts), and the U.S. Supreme Court (which hears appeals from the U.S. Courts of Appeals and from state supreme courts). Most of the judicial decisions discussed in this book were issued by the U.S. Courts of Appeals. These courts are organized in eleven regional circuits. In addition, the U.S. Court of Appeals for the Federal Circuit has exclusive jurisdiction over patent appeals. In this book, "a decision by the Ninth Circuit," for example, means a decision by the U.S. Court of Appeals for the Ninth Circuit.
2. Robbie Downing, book review, 3 *International Journal of Law and Information Technology* 198 (1995); book review, 15 *Northwestern Journal of International Law and Busi-*

holdings seemed well entrenched. In the European Union, the member states had implemented the EU Software Directive's reverse-engineering exceptions with little difficulty.

Although the Software Directive ended the interoperability debate in the European Union, the debate continued in the United States and elsewhere. In the U.S., litigation proceeded on both the protectability of interface specifications and the permissibility of reverse engineering. Outside the Third Circuit, courts have issued decisions consistent with *Computer Associates* and *Sega*.

However, two new threats to interoperability emerged in the United States. First, several courts enforced contractual restrictions on reverse engineering, even when the vendors placed the restrictions in "shrinkwrap" or "click-on" licenses for widely distributed consumer software. Second, the World Intellectual Property Organization Copyright Treaty, adopted in December 1996, required signatories to take adequate measures to prevent the circumvention of copy-protection technologies for purposes of infringement. As Congress was implementing this requirement, developers of interoperable software recognized that the broad prohibition Congress was considering would allow dominant firms to frustrate interoperability by placing "locks" on their software. Accordingly, the developers lobbied for and secured an interoperability exception in the Digital Millennium Copyright Act (DMCA).

Significantly, the European Union anticipated both of these issues in its Software Directive, which contains provisions that expressly invalidate contractual restrictions on reverse engineering and that permit the circumvention of technological protection measures for the purpose of performing lawful reverse engineering.

The interoperability debate also continued in the Pacific Rim after 1995. Dominant U.S. companies, with the assistance of the U.S. Trade Representative, vigorously opposed the adoption of reverse-engineering exceptions based on the EU Software Directive in Australia, Hong Kong, Korea, and the Philippines.

This book picks up the story where *Interfaces on Trial* left off. Sections 1.2 and 1.3 of this chapter provide a quick review of the interoperability debate in the European Union and the United States before 1995. Chapter

---

ness 707 (1995); Book review, 20 *New Matter* 35 (1995); Zack Higgens, book review, 9 *Harvard Journal of Law and Technology* 585 (1996); Robert Brookshire, book review, 7 *Law and Policy Book Reviews* 206 (1997).

2 discusses the U.S. copyright cases since 1995 addressing the protectability of interface specifications and the permissibility of reverse engineering, and closes by noting that the executive and legislative branches have finally endorsed this pro-interoperability case law. Chapter 3 looks at the legislative history of the interoperability exception in the DMCA, as well as the interoperability cases decided under the DMCA. Chapter 4 examines the enforceability of contractual restrictions on reverse engineering, including the treatment of this issue in the context of the Uniform Computer Information Transactions Act (UCITA). Chapter 5 reviews the interoperability debate in the Pacific Rim, with stops in Australia, Singapore, Hong Kong, South Korea, and the Philippines. Chapter 6 briefly considers issues that may have more impact on interoperability in the future.

In this book, certain terms have the same meanings as in *Interfaces on Trial*:

• "Interoperability" is synonymous with "compatibility" and has two dimensions: interchangeability and connectability. "Interchangeability" refers to the degree to which one product can substitute for or compete with another product. "Connectability" refers to the degree to which a product can participate in a joint activity with another product.

• "Interface" means a functional characteristic of an element's interaction with other elements of the computer system, i.e., a permissible input, output, or control. This book focuses on interfaces between software and hardware, or between two software elements. This book does not examine user interfaces—that is, the interfaces between users and computers.

• "Interface specifications" are the rules of interconnection between two program elements. An interface specification can have different implementations—e.g., it can be encoded in different ways. A programming language or particular commands can be a form of interface specification.

• "Disassembly" and "decompilation" refer to the translation of machine-readable object code into a higher-level, human-readable format. "Disassembly" is the term usually used in the U.S. legal context; "decompilation" typically is used outside the United States. Accordingly, we will use "disassembly" when discussing the activity in the context of U.S. legal developments, and "decompilation" when referring to the activity in the international policy context.

• "Black-box reverse engineering" means observing the externally visible characteristics of a program as it operates, without looking into the program itself.

These terms, and computer technology generally, are discussed in much greater detail in *Interfaces on Trial*.

The present volume is intended to connect to, and not substitute for, *Interfaces on Trial*. Thus, it does not repeat the earlier volume's background information on computer technology, the structure of the computer industry, intellectual-property law, and the economics of standardization. Additionally, since the publication of *Interfaces of Trial* there has been a profusion of scholarly writings concerning the complex interaction between copyright and digital technology.[3] This book does not attempt to address this vast academic literature. Rather, it provides the second volume of the history of an ongoing legal debate.

Although we attempt to present contentious issues in a balanced manner, the reader should be forewarned that we are hardly objective observers in this debate. Rather, we have devoted significant time and energy over the past 20 years to advocating the views of developers of interoperable software. We believe that the triumph of interoperability will benefit both the information-technology industry and computer users around the world.

1.2 The Interoperability Debate in the European Union before 1995

In 1991, after a vigorous debate (described in detail in *Interfaces on Trial*), the European Union adopted its Software Directive.[4] During the three-year process that led up to the promulgation of the directive, dominant firms, developers of interoperable software, and computer users battled over the protectability of interface specifications and the permissibility of reverse engineering. The directive that emerged from this political process reflects a policy judgment that copyright should not interfere with interoperability. The Software

---

3. See, e.g., Pamela Samuelson and Suzanne Scotchmer, "The Law and Economics of Reverse Engineering," 111 *Yale Law Journal* 1575 (2002); Peter Menell, "Envisioning Copyright Law's Digital Future," 46 *New York Law School Law Review* 63 (2002–03); Douglas Lichtman, "Property Rights in Emerging Platform Technologies," 29 *Journal of Legal Studies* 615 (2000); Peter Menell, "An Epitaph for Traditional Copyright Protection of Network Features of Computer Software," 43 *Antitrust Bulletin* 651 (fall-winter 1998); Dennis Karjala and Peter Menell, "Applying Fundamental Copyright Principles in *Lotus Development Corp. v. Borland International Inc.*," 10 *High Technology Law Journal* 177 (1995); Pamela Samuelson, Randall Davis, Mitchell Kapor, and Gerald Reichman, "A Manifesto Concerning the Legal Protection of Computer Programs," 94 *Columbia Law Review* 2308 (1994); Andrew Johnson-Laird, "Software Reverse Engineering in the Real World," 19 *University of Dayton Law Review* 843 (1994); Dennis Karjala, "Copyright Protection of Computer Software, Reverse Engineering, and Professor Miller," 19 *University of Dayton Law Review* 975 (1994).
4. Council Directive 91/250/EEC, 1991 O.J. (L 122).

Directive has been implemented by all 27 member states of the European Union, and also by Croatia, Norway, Russia, Switzerland, and Turkey.

Article 5(3) of the Software Directive provides a broad exception from liability for "black-box reverse engineering"—activities such as observing the behavior of a program as it runs, input/output tests, and line traces. Article 6 provides a narrower exception for decompilation. Decompilation or disassembly involves translating machine-readable object code into a higher-level, human-readable form. Article 6 permits decompilation for purposes of achieving interoperability when the information has not previously been made available, when the decompilation is limited to those parts of the program necessary for interoperability, and when the final product created by the reverse engineer does not infringe on the copyright of the original product. There has been extensive debate on exactly what these provisions mean,[5] but to date there has been no copyright litigation concerning article 6.[6]

One particularly enigmatic provision is article 6(1)(b), which requires that "the information necessary to achieve interoperability has not previously been readily available" to the reverse engineer. One commentator has stated that "since the information must be 'readily' available, third parties would have no duty to ask for information if it is not contained in generally available documentation. Nor can it be said that interface information is 'readily' available if the rightholder is only willing to disclose it upon payment of a license fee, since this would undermine the very purpose of limited, but reliable access to interface information."[7] Others have interpreted this provision as requiring the reverse engineer to request the interface information from the developer of the target software before decompilation. The reverse engineer obviously would prefer not to have to make such a request, because the request would alert the first developer to the reverse engineer's business plans and would delay the decompilation.

5. See Jonathan Band and Masanobu Katoh, *Interfaces on Trial: Intellectual Property and Interoperability in the Global Software Market* (Westview, 1995), at 246–255. The governmental bodies of the European Union were lobbied heavily concerning the Software Directive. The Business Software Alliance attempted to limit the article 5 and 6 exceptions as much as possible. The European Committee for Interoperable Systems, led by Olivetti, Fujitsu Espana, and Bull, lobbied for broad exceptions. See id. at 230–241.

6. As will be discussed below, the European Court of First Instance interpreted the word "interoperability" in the directive during the course of the European Commission's competition case against Microsoft.

7. Thomas Drier, "The Council Directive of 14 May 1991, on the Legal Protection of Computer Programs," 9 *European Intellectual Property Review* 319, 324 (1991).

Article 9(1) of the Software Directive provides that any contractual restriction on the reverse-engineering exceptions in articles 5 and 6 is "null and void." Similarly, article 7 contains a reverse-engineering exception to the directive's prohibition on the circumvention of technological protection measures.

Thus, since 1991 there has been a high degree of certainty and predictability in Europe concerning the lawfulness of reverse engineering. The reverse engineer incurs no copyright liability for black-box reverse engineering for any purpose, nor for decompilation for purposes of achieving interoperability. The reverse engineer can ignore with impunity a contractual term prohibiting reverse engineering, presumably even in a negotiated contract. Further, the reverse engineer can circumvent a technological protection measure for purposes of engaging in other lawful reverse engineering.

The Software Directive does not address with any specificity the question of the scope of copyright protection: To what extent could the reverse engineer use what he learned through his reverse engineering? Rather, article 1(2) provides that "[i]deas and principles which underlie any element of a computer program, including those which underlie its interfaces, are not protected by copyright."[8] Commentators have interpreted this to mean that interface information necessary to achieve interoperability must fall on the idea side of the idea/expression dichotomy; otherwise the detailed decompilation provision in article 6 would be of little utility. Once again, there has been no copyright litigation in Europe concerning this.

In sum, the Software Directive settled the copyright issues relating to interoperability within the European Union in 1991. Indeed, in 2000 the European Commission issued a report on the implementation and effects of the Software Directive which concluded that "the objectives of the Directive have been achieved and the effects on the software industry are satisfactory (demonstrated for example by industry growth and decrease in software piracy)."[9] Accordingly, "there appears to be no need to amend the Directive."

Since 1991, the legal battle in the European Union concerning interoperability has centered on a competition-law (antitrust, in U.S. terminology) complaint brought by the European Commission against Microsoft.

8. The directive's eleventh "Whereas" clause defines interfaces as "the parts of the program which provide for . . . interconnection and interaction between elements of software and hardware."

9. Report from the Commission to the Council, the European Parliament and the Economic and Social Committee on the implementation and effects of Directive 91/250/EEC on the legal protection of computer programs, COM(2000) 199 final, at 2.

Though significant, this litigation is beyond the scope of this book because of its basis in competition law rather than copyright law.

However, the European Court of First Instance (CFI) did interpret the meaning of the word "interoperability" in the directive during the course of the litigation. This interpretation ratified the European Commission's long-standing view of the scope of the article 6 decompilation exception.

The case concerned Microsoft's alleged abuse of its dominant position by withholding interface information necessary for Sun Microsystems to make its Solaris operating system fully compatible with technologies based on Microsoft Windows.[10] In 2004, after an investigation, the European Commission found that Microsoft had abused its dominant position and ordered it to provide the necessary specifications to Sun and other companies on reasonable and nondiscriminatory terms. Microsoft appealed the Commission's decision to the CFI, arguing *inter alia* that the Commission's order was inconsistent with the legislative policy of the Software Directive. Specifically, Microsoft asserted that "interoperability" in the directive meant only the ability of one computer program to connect to another program. Because Microsoft licensed interface information to developers of application programs designed to run on Windows, Microsoft claimed that it satisfied the directive's objectives and thus did not abuse its dominant position.

The Commission, on the other hand, interpreted "interoperability" in the directive more broadly to mean the ability to connect to *or* substitute for another program. Because Microsoft refused to license interface information to Sun, whose Solaris operating system competed with Windows, the Commission argued that Microsoft frustrated the directive's intent and thereby abused its dominant position.

In 2007, the CFI ruled as follows:

> [W]hat is at issue in the present case is a decision adopted in application of Article 82 [of the European Community Treaty], a provision of higher rank than [the Software Directive]. The question in the present case is not so much whether the concept of interoperability in the contested decision is consistent with the concept envisaged in that directive as whether the Commission correctly determined the degree of interoperability that should be attainable in the light of the objectives of Article 82 EC.[11]

Nonetheless, the CFI held that the Commission's "two-way" interpretation of "interoperability" as including the ability to connect to and substitute

---

10. For a more detailed discussion of the case, see Pamela Samuelson, "Are Patents on Interfaces Impeding Interoperability?" 93 *Minnesota Law Review* 1943, 1989–1996 (2009).

11. Case T-201/04, *Microsoft Corp. v. Comm'n*, 2007 E.C.R. II-3601 ¶ 227.

for computer programs "is consistent with that envisaged in" the Software Directive.[12]

By interpreting the word "interoperability" in the directive as it did, the CFI eliminated any possible ambiguity concerning the scope of article 6's permitting decompilation "to obtain the information necessary to achieve the interoperability of an independently created computer program with other programs." Without question, article 6 allows the reverse engineer to decompile an existing computer program for the purpose of developing his own connecting *or* competing computer program. The Commission has consistently understood article 6 in this manner since 1991.[13] The CFI decision thus finally laid to rest the argument that article 6 permits decompilation only for the purpose of developing connecting products.[14]

The CFI decision also strongly implied that article 1(2) of the directive excludes copyright protection for interface specifications. As was noted above, article 1(2) provides that "[i]deas and principles which underlie any element of a computer program, including those which under lie its interfaces, are not protected by copyright." The CFI stated:

In requiring, by way of remedy, that an undertaking in a dominant position disclose the interoperability information, the Commission refers to a detailed technical description of certain rules of interconnection and interaction that can be used within the work group networks to deliver work group services. That description does not extend to the way in which the undertaking implements those rules, in particular, to the internal structure or to the source code of its products.

The degree of interoperability thus required by the Commission enables competing operating systems to interoperate with the dominant undertaking's domain architecture on an equal footing in order to be able to compete viably with the latter's operating systems. It does not entail making competitors' products work in exactly the same way as its own and does not enable its competitors to clone or reproduce its products or certain features of those products.[15]

---

12. Id. at ¶ 225.

13. Commission of the European Communities, Twentieth Report on Competition Policy (1991); Michael Sucker, "The Software Directive—Between the Combat Against Piracy and the Preservation of Undistorted Competition," in *A Handbook of European Software Law* (Oxford University Press, 1993).

14. During the drafting of the directive, BSA attempted to limit the decompilation exception to the development of connecting products. See Band and Katoh, *Interfaces on Trial* at 237–240. Similarly, as other countries have considered reverse-engineering exceptions, BSA has argued that article 6 applies only to the development of connecting products. See chapter 5 below.

15. Case T-201/04, *Microsoft Corp. v. Comm'n*, 2007 E.C.R. II-3601 Summary of Judgment ¶4.

The distinction the CFI drew between the "detailed technical description of certain rules of interconnection and interaction" and the way in which a company "implements those rules" in "the internal structure" or "the source code of its products" parallels the idea/expression dichotomy embodied by article 1(2).

Although the Software Directive resolved the copyright issues relating to interoperability within Europe, since 1995 fierce legislative wars have been waged in several Pacific Rim countries over the adoption of the Software Directive's exceptions for reverse engineering. These wars are described in chapter 5.

1.3   The Interoperability Debate in the United States before 1995

In the United States, the story before and after 1995 is much more complex for both of the central questions of the interoperability debate. This is because both questions were resolved in the United States in a common-law, case-by-case manner by the federal courts, rather than by the legislative process of the Software Directive.

1.3.1   The Unprotectability of Interface Specifications

Between 1983 and 1995, U.S. courts became increasingly sophisticated in their understanding of the unique characteristics of computer programs. The courts became more aware that, although the copyright law classifies programs as literary works, they in fact are functional works operating in highly constrained environments. Accordingly, by 1995, courts understood that many program elements should not receive copyright protection, particularly the information necessary for achieving interoperability.

When courts first looked at the issue of interoperability, they favored protection of interface information. In 1983, for example, the U.S. Court of Appeals for the Third Circuit suggested that compatibility was a "commercial and competitive objective which does not enter into the somewhat metaphysical issue of whether particular ideas and expression have merged."[16] Under this reasoning, copyright could protect interface specifications. Three years later, the Third Circuit reinforced this protectionist trend in *Whelan v. Jaslow*.[17]

16. *Apple Computer, Inc. v. Franklin Computer Corp.*, 714 F.2d 1240, 1253 (3d Cir. 1983), *cert. dismissed*, 464 U.S. 1033 (1984).
17. *Whelan Associates, Inc. v. Jaslow Dental Laboratory, Inc.*, 797 F.2d 1222 (3d Cir. 1986), *cert. denied*, 479 U.S. 1031 (1987).

1.3.1.1   *Whelan v. Jaslow* (1987)

Jaslow, the owner of a dental laboratory, hired Whelan, a computer programmer, to develop a computer program to run his business. They agreed that Whelan would retain the copyright in the program and that Jaslow would try to market the program to other dental laboratories. Jaslow soon realized that the Whelan program, written in Event Driven Language (EDL) for an IBM Series One computer, was not compatible with the computers many dental laboratories already possessed. Jaslow then developed a dental lab program in BASIC, which could run on these computers. Whelan sued for copyright infringement.

At trial, Jaslow's expert testified that he compared the source and object code of the two programs, and found "substantive differences in programming style, in programming structure, in algorithms and data structures."[18] Whelan's expert agreed that the Jaslow program was not a simple translation of the Whelan program, but stated that the programs were similar in several respects. The file structures and screen outputs, for example, were virtually identical. Further, five important subroutines "performed almost identically within both programs."[19] Even Jaslow's expert confirmed that the programs had "overall structural similarities."[20]

The district court ruled for Whelan. Jaslow appealed. Jaslow's primary argument on appeal was that copyright protected only the literal elements of a computer program—the actual lines of source or object code—and not the non-literal elements such as program structure. In a lengthy opinion, the U.S. Court of Appeals for the Third Circuit rejected Jaslow's argument and held that copyright could program the non-literal elements of a computer program, including its "structure, sequence, and organization." The reasoning and language used by the Third Circuit, however, went much farther than necessary to reach this conclusion.

Upon completing a background discussion on the basic principles of copyright law applicable to the case, the Third Circuit turned to "whether a program's copyright protection covers the structure of the program or only the program's literal elements, *i.e.*, its source and object codes."[21] The court observed that "computer programs are classified as literary works for the purposes of copyright," and that "[o]ne can violate the copyright of a play or book by copying its plot or plot devices." Accordingly, the court reasoned that copyright protection should extend to a computer program's structure.

18. Id. at 1228.
19. Id.
20. Id.
21. Id. at 1234.

The court then formulated the following rule for separating idea from expression in utilitarian works:

[T]he purpose or function of a utilitarian work would be the work's idea, and everything that is not necessary to the purpose or function would be part of the expression of the idea. Where there are various means of achieving the desired purpose, then the particular means chosen is not necessary to the purpose; hence, there is expression not idea.[22]

The court defined the idea in the case before it as "the efficient management of a dental laboratory."[23] It then went on to say that "[b]ecause that idea could be accomplished in a number of different ways with a number of different structures, the structure of the [Whelan] program is part of the program's expression, not its idea."[24]

The *Whelan* court's reasoning contained two related flaws. First, the *Whelan* court identified a single, highly abstract idea in the entire computer program. Second, the court incorrectly reduced the idea/expression dichotomy to the merger doctrine. In the court's view, if several means existed for performing the program's basic function (its idea), then the means did not merge with the function and thus were protected expression. The court failed to understand that each means of performing the function could in its own right be unprotected under section 102(b) as a procedure, process, system, method, or operation. Patents, not copyrights, protect "the means for carrying the idea out."[25] By protecting the means for performing a function, the *Whelan* court in effect used copyright to protect patentable subject matter.[26]

The *Whelan* decision contained two justifications for this extreme result. First, because Congress classified computer programs as literary works, the court treated them as traditional literary works, comparable to novels and plays, without recognizing their utilitarian nature.[27] Second, the *Whelan* court noted that "the coding process is a comparatively small part of programming,"[28] whereas "among the more significant costs in computer

22. Id.
23. Id. at n. 28.
24. Id.
25. *Kruger v. Whitehead*, 153 F.2d 238, 239 (9th Cir. 1946), *cert. denied*, 332 U.S. 774 (1947).
26. See Arthur J. Levine, "Comment on Bonito Boats Follow-Up: The Supreme Court's Likely Rejection of Nonliteral Software Copyright Protection," *The Computer Lawyer* 29, 30 (July 1989).
27. *Whelan*, 797 F.2d at 1237 (citations omitted).
28. Id. at 1231.

programming are those attributable to developing the structure and logic of the program."[29] It observed that "[t]he rule proposed here . . . would provide the proper incentive for programmers by protecting their most valuable efforts, while not giving them a stranglehold over the development of new computer devices that accomplish the same end."[30] The court evidently believed that a programmer's method for solving a program deserved protection—so long as other methods for solving the program existed—because the method was the most valuable part of the program.

In other words, *Whelan* suggested that, in the computer context, the court need only assess whether alternative methods of accomplishing the basic ideas exist to determine whether the elements the defendant copied constitute protected expression. This truncated protected expression analysis invariably affords programs "thick" copyright protection—indeed, thicker protection than is accorded traditional literary works such as novels and plays, which undergo a complete protected expression analysis. Although *Whelan* did not specifically concern interoperability, its reasoning inevitably led to the conclusion that detailed program elements such as interface specifications received copyright protection.

The *Whelan* decision was controversial from the moment it was issued. Just five months later, the Fifth Circuit rejected its reasoning in a case involving programs with similar design specifications that assisted cotton farmers in growing and marketing their product (*Plains Cotton Co-Op Ass'n v. Goodpasture Computer Serv., Inc.*).[31] Nonetheless, lower courts followed *Whelan* until 1992, when the Second Circuit revealed its serious flaws in a case that did involve interoperability: *Computer Associates Int'l, Inc. v. Altai, Inc.*[32]

1.3.1.2 *Computer Associates v. Altai* (1992)

Computer Associates developed an application program with a component, ADAPTER, that permitted the application to run on different IBM mainframe operating systems. Altai developed a similar application designed to run on a single IBM operating system. Altai then decided to develop a component that allowed its program to run on other IBM operating systems. Computer Associates filed suit, alleging that Altai's component, OSCAR 3.4, infringed the copyright in ADAPTER. Altai determined that 30 percent of the OSCAR 3.4 code was copied from ADAPTER, and it conceded

29. Id.
30. Id. (footnotes omitted).
31. 807 F.2d 1256 (5th Cir.), *cert. denied*, 484 U.S. 821 (1987).
32. 982 F.2d 693 (2d Cir. 1992).

liability with respect to OSCAR 3.4. Altai then rewrote its component in a clean room, without access to ADAPTER. Computer Associates amended its complaint to allege that the new version, OSCAR 3.5, also infringed its copyright.

The district court rejected *Whelan* as simplistic and as leading to excessively broad protection for computer programs. The court then compared the two programs. Because of the use of the clean room, the code was completely different. The parameter lists and macros of the programs were similar, but the court determined that these similarities were dictated by the IBM operating systems with which the programs were designed to interoperate. There was overlap in the list of services, but this too was dictated by function. Finally, the court found similarity in the programs' organization charts, but the charts were "simple and obvious" and of *de minimus* importance. Accordingly, the district court concluded that the programs were not similar in protected expression.

Computer Associates appealed. After reviewing the principles of computer program design and the facts of the case, the U.S. Court of Appeals for the Second Circuit acknowledged the "essentially utilitarian nature of a computer program."[33] Identifying the seminal U.S. Supreme Court decision in *Baker v. Selden* as the "doctrinal starting point in analyses"[34] of the scope of protection for computer programs, the Second Circuit emphasized that "compared to aesthetic works, computer programs hover even more closely to the elusive boundary line described in Section 102(b)."[35]

The Second Circuit rejected the principles for analyzing computer programs offered in *Whelan*, holding that "[t]he crucial flaw in [*Whelan's*] reasoning is that it assumes that only one 'idea' in copyright law terms, underlies any computer program."[36] It also agreed with the district court that a computer program's "ultimate function or purpose is the composite result of interacting sub-routines."[37] The Second Circuit wrote: "[S]ince each sub-routine is itself a program, and thus, may be said to have its own 'idea,' *Whelan's* general formulation that a program's overall purpose equates with the program's idea is descriptively inadequate."[38] The Second Circuit further agreed with the district court's rejection of *Whelan's*

33. *Computer Associates,* 982 F.2d at 704.
34. Id.
35. Id.
36. Id. at 705 (citations omitted).
37. Id.
38. Id.

terms "structure, sequence and organization," observing that they were based on a "somewhat outdated appreciation of computer science."[39]

Noting that "*Whelan*'s approach to separating idea from expression in computer programs relies too heavily on metaphysical distinctions and does not place enough emphasis on practical considerations,"[40] the Second Circuit proposed a three-part procedure for determining whether an allegedly copied program is "substantially similar" to another copyrighted program:

In ascertaining substantial similarity under this approach, a court would first break down the allegedly infringed program into its constituent structural parts. Then, by examining each of these parts for such things as incorporated ideas, expression that is necessarily incidental to those ideas, and elements that are taken from the public domain, a court would then be able to sift out all non-protectable material. Left with a kernel, or perhaps kernels, of creative expression after following this process of elimination, the court's last step would be to compare this material with the structure of an allegedly infringing program.[41]

The Second Circuit based its first step—abstraction—on Judge Learned Hand's famous test in *Nichols v. Universal Pictures Corp.*[42] The court explained:

In a manner that resembles reverse engineering on a theoretical plane, a court should dissect the allegedly copied program's structure and isolate each level of abstraction contained within it. This process begins with the code and ends with an articulation of the program's ultimate function.[43]

The discussion of the second step—filtration—is perhaps the most significant part of the opinion. The court adopted the "successive filtering method" proposed by the well-respected treatise *Nimmer on Copyright*, which "entails examining the structural components at each level of abstraction to determine whether their inclusion at that level was 'idea' or was dictated by considerations of efficiency, so as to be necessarily incidental to that idea; required by factors external to the program itself; or taken from the public domain and hence is nonprotectable expression."[44]

The "successive filtering method" is a refinement of Judge Hand's abstractions test. In its classical formulation, the abstractions test calls for a court to analyze a work's levels of abstraction and to then draw a line above

39. Id. at 706.
40. Id.
41. Id.
42. 45 F.2d 119 (2d Cir. 1930), *cert. denied*, 282 U.S. 902 (1931).
43. Id. at 707.
44. Id.

which everything is idea and below which everything is expression. Here, the Second Circuit suggested that idea and expression may be present at each level of abstraction.

The court then provided additional detail on the non-protectability of elements dictated by efficiency and by external factors. It observed that "[e]fficiency is an industry-wide goal,"[45] and that "[w]hile, hypothetically, there might be a myriad of ways in which a programmer may effectuate certain functions within a program—i.e., express the idea embodied in a given subroutine—efficiency concerns may so narrow the practical range of choice as to make only one or two forms of expression workable options."[46] Under these circumstances, the expression would merge with the idea and would not receive copyright protection.

Discussing external factors, the Second Circuit stated that "in many instances it is virtually impossible to write a program to perform particular functions in a specific computing environment without employing standard techniques."[47] The Second Circuit went on to hold that under the doctrine of *scènes à faire* copyright protection should not extend to those program elements in which a programmer's "freedom of design choice"[48] is "circumscribed by extrinsic considerations such as (1) mechanical specifications of the computer on which a particular program is intended to run; (2) compatibility requirements of other programs with which a program is designed to operate in conjunction; (3) computer manufacturers' design standards; (4) demands of the industry being serviced; and (5) widely accepted programming practices within the computer industry."[49] Applying these principles to the facts before it, the Second Circuit affirmed the district court and held that Altai had not copied protected expression.

Thus, relying on the *scènes à faire* doctrine, the Second Circuit held that similarities resulting from the need to interoperate with other components of a computer system did not constitute copyright infringement.[50]

---

45. Id. at 708.
46. Id.
47. Id. at 709 (quotation omitted).
48. Id.
49. Id. at 709–710.
50. Under the *scènes à faire* doctrine, courts "deny protection to those expressions that are standard, stock or common to a particular topic or that necessarily follow from a common theme or setting. Granting copyright protection to the necessary incidents of an idea would effectively afford a monopoly to the first programmer to express those ideas." *Gates Rubber Co. v. Bando Chem. Indus., Inc.*, 9 F.3d 823, 838 (10th Cir. 1993) (citations omitted).

In essence, the Second Circuit ruled that interface specifications were not protected expression, and that a competitor could conform to the rules of intercommunications developed by another vendor without infringing that vendor's copyright.

The reasoning of the *Computer Associates* decision was so powerful that many courts throughout the United States and abroad adopted it rapidly.[51] *Whelan* was thoroughly repudiated, and courts began applying the abstraction-filtration-comparison methodology in a wide range of copyright cases, including cases that did not involve computer programs. Additionally, other courts soon followed *Computer Associates'* specific rulings concerning interoperability.

1.3.1.3   *Atari v. Nintendo* and *Sega v. Accolade* (1992)

Just three months after the Second Circuit issued *Computer Associates*, the U.S. Court of Appeals for the Federal Circuit relied upon it in *Atari Games Corp. v. Nintendo of America, Inc.*, stating that "the court must filter out as unprotectable . . . expression dictated by external factors (like the computer's mechanical specifications, compatibility with other programs, and demands of the industry served by the program)."[52] In *Atari*, both the district court and the Federal Circuit extended protection to Nintendo program elements that currently had no purpose but that Atari argued would be necessary for Atari to achieve compatibility in the future with Nintendo products not yet on the market. The Federal Circuit stated that "[t]he district court did not abuse its discretion by refusing to allow Atari to rely on speculative future events to justify inclusion of unnecessary [Nintendo] program elements in the [Atari] program."[53] The Federal Circuit made it clear, however, that it would not protect program elements needed to achieve compatibility at the time of the writing of the compatible program.

A month later, the U.S. Court of Appeals for the Ninth Circuit, also relying on *Computer Associates*, expressly recognized, in *Sega Enters. Ltd. v. Accolade, Inc.*, that computer programs "contain many logical, structural, and visual display elements that are dictated by . . . external factors such as compatibility requirements and industry demands," and that "[i]n some

51. To get the full flavor of the *Computer Associates* tidal wave, see Band and Katoh, *Interfaces on Trial* at 131–150.
52. 975 F.2d 832, 839 (Fed. Cir. 1992).
53. Id. at 845.

circumstances, even the exact set of commands used by the programmer is deemed functional rather than creative for purposes of copyright."[54]

1.3.2 The Permissibility of Reverse Engineering

Following *Computer Associates*, the *Sega* court had little trouble concluding that copyright did not protect program elements necessary for interoperability. A trickier issue for the *Sega* court was the permissibility of the copying that occurred while examining a competitor's product to uncover these program elements. To be sure, the U.S. Supreme Court has long recognized that there is nothing inherently wrong with studying a competitor's product to understand how it works and to figure out how to make a better product. For example, in *Kewanee Oil Co. v. Bicron Corp.*[55] the Supreme Court stated that "trade secret law . . . does not offer protection against discovery by fair and honest means, such as . . . by so-called reverse engineering, that is by starting with a known product and working backward to divine the process which aided in its development or manufacture."

The Supreme Court has also recognized the benefits of reverse engineering: "Reverse engineering . . . often leads to significant advances in technology."[56] Further, the Supreme Court has noted that "the competitive reality of reverse engineering may act as a spur to the inventor, creating an incentive to develop inventions that meet the rigorous requirements of patentability."[57]

Copyright law, however, has the potential of raising obstacles to reverse engineering of software. Because of the nature of computer technology, reverse engineering of software almost always requires the making of a reproduction or derivative work. For example, the reverse-engineering method of disassembly or decompilation involves "translating" the publicly distributed, computer-readable program into a higher-level, human-readable form. This act of translation could be considered the preparation of a derivative work.[58] Black-box reverse engineering is less intrusive than disassembly because an engineer observes the program's behavior and interaction with its environment without looking at the program itself. Although less intrusive than disassembly, black-box reverse engineering requires that the program be copied into the computer's random-access memory (RAM)

54. 977 F.2d 1510, 1524 (9th Cir. 1992) (citations omitted).
55. 416 U.S. 470, 476 (1974).
56. *Bonito Boats, Inc., v. Thunder Craft Boats, Inc.*, 489 U.S. 141, 160 (1989).
57. Id.
58. See 17 U.S.C. §106(2).

as the computer runs the program. Such copying arguably infringes the reproduction right.[59] As was noted above, the European Union, in its 1991 Software Directive, established a statutory copyright exception excusing the copying that occurs during reverse engineering. In contrast, in the early 1990s U.S. courts employed the doctrine of fair use, codified at 17 U.S.C. §107, to permit reverse engineering.

The first thorough judicial consideration of software reverse engineering occurred in 1992 in *Sega Enters. v. Accolade Inc.*[60] Accolade, a developer of computer games, decompiled software in the Sega video console and in Sega-compatible games in order to learn the interface specifications that would enable it to port its games to the Sega console. Sega sued for copyright infringement, and the district court issued a preliminary injunction against Accolade. The U.S. Court of Appeals for the Ninth Circuit reversed, finding that "where disassembly is the only way to gain access to the ideas and functional elements embodied in a copyrighted computer program and where there is a legitimate reason for seeking such access, disassembly is a fair use of the copyrighted work, as a matter of law."[61] In the *Sega* case, the court concluded that achieving interoperability between the Accolade games and the Sega game console was such a legitimate reason.

Much of the *Sega* court's fair-use analysis centered on the second of the four fair-use factors: the nature of the copyrighted work. The court recognized the unique characteristics of software and understood that if reverse engineering were not permitted the developer would receive *de facto* protection over uncopyrightable ideas. In *Atari Games Corp. v. Nintendo of America, Inc.*[62] the Federal Circuit reached the same conclusion for the same reason.

In sum, by 1995 courts in the United States had ruled that copyright did not protect interface specifications and that the copying incidental to the reverse engineering necessary for interoperability did not infringe copyright. But, as we shall see, the interoperability debate was far from over.

59. The Ninth Circuit in *MAI Systems Corp. v. Peak Computer, Inc.*, 991 F.2d 511 (9th Cir.), *cert. denied*, 510 U.S. 1033 (1993), found that the loading of a program into a computer's RAM constituted a copy for purposes of the Copyright Act. However, as we discuss below in section 2.5, the Second Circuit's decision in *Cartoon Network LP v. CSC Holdings, Inc.*, 536 F.3d 121 (2d Cir. 2008), *cert. denied*, 129 S. Ct. 2890 (2009), suggests that not all temporary copies are fixed within the meaning of the Copyright Act.

60. 977 F.2d 1510 (9th Cir. 1992).

61. Id. at 1527–1528.

62. 975 F.2d 832 (Fed. Cir. 1992).

2 Copyright Cases in U.S. Courts

By the mid 1990s, U.S. courts had ruled on the two copyright issues critical to interoperability. First, following the Second Circuit's methodology
in *Computer Associates Int'l, Inc. v. Altai, Inc.*,[1] several courts had refused to
extend copyright protection to interface specifications. Second, both the
Ninth Circuit and the Federal Circuit had found the copying incidental
to reverse engineering permitted by the fair-use doctrine. In the ensuing
decade, courts continued to reach similar conclusions. Additionally, both
the executive branch and the legislative branch had endorsed this case law.
Thus, the unprotectability of interface specifications and the permissibility
of software reverse engineering are well established in U.S. copyright law.

2.1 The Unprotectability of Interface Specifications

In July of 1992 (only a month after the issuance of *Computer Associates*), in
Lotus v. Borland,[2] a district court narrowly construed the Second Circuit's
withholding of copyright protection from interface specifications. In effect,
the district court found that copyright *did not* protect the interface specifications necessary to attach to an existing product, but that copyright *did*
protect the specifications necessary to replace the existing product. In 1995,
the U.S. Court of Appeals for the First Circuit reversed the district court,
finding that Lotus's command structure was an unprotectable method of
operation. Lotus appealed the decision to the U.S. Supreme Court, which
affirmed the First Circuit's ruling in a 4–4 ruling (Justice Stevens having
recused himself). Since *Lotus v. Borland*, courts have withheld copyright
protection from interface specifications under several different theories,
including variations of the idea/expression dichotomy and the fair-use

1. 982 F.2d 693 (2d Cir. 1992).
2. *Lotus Development Corp. v. Borland Int'l Inc.*, 799 F. Supp. 203 (D. Mass. 1992), *rev'd,*
49 F.3d 807 (1st Cir. 1995), *aff'd by an equally divided Court*, 516 U.S. 233 (1996).

doctrine. These decisions have helped to alleviate the concerns of many developers regarding their exposure to copyright-infringement liability for their interoperable products.

2.1.1 *Lotus v. Borland* (1995)

During its pendency, *Lotus v. Borland* was characterized in both the popular press and the computer press as a "look and feel" case.[3] Indeed, District Court Judge Keeton, although he criticized the term "look and feel," largely viewed the case as such. His focus on the user interface was completely understandable: in the forerunner to *Lotus v. Borland*—*Lotus v. Paperback*[4]— the Paperback and Lotus user interfaces shared many features. Further, at the outset of *Lotus v. Borland*, Lotus alleged that Borland International Inc. had copied a number of user-interface features. By the time the case got to the First Circuit, however, the only similarity at issue was the command structure of Lotus 1-2-3. Free from the baggage of the *Paperback* decision and the early complaint against Borland, the First Circuit correctly perceived that this case did not concern the "look and feel" of the user interface at all, but instead concerned interoperability. And once the First Circuit understood the role of the command structure in achieving interoperability, it had little difficult reversing the lower court.

2.1.1.1 The Factual Background

In the late 1970s, Visicalc developed the first computerized spreadsheet, which ran on Apple II computers. Soon after the introduction of the IBM PC, Lotus Development Corporation released Lotus 1-2-3, a spreadsheet program that was compatible with the IBM PC. Lotus 1-2-3 soon dominated the spreadsheet market, eclipsing Visicalc, and its popularity contributed to the success of the IBM PC.

Although Lotus 1-2-3 incorporated some of Visicalc's commands in its user interface, it had an original menu tree structure in which more than 400 commands were arranged in a clearly defined hierarchy. Using different code, Paperback Software developed a program that re-created the entire Lotus 1-2-3 command structure and other features of the Lotus 1-2-3 user interface. Lotus sued for copyright infringement, and prevailed in 1990.[5] Paperback did not have the resources to appeal the judgment.

---

3. This subsection is based on Jonathan Band, *"Lotus v. Borla*nd Viewed through the Lens of Interoperability," *The Computer Lawyer*, June 1995, at 1.

4. *Lotus Development Corp. v. Paperback Software Int'l*, 740 F. Supp. 37 (D. Mass. 1990).

5. Id. After Lotus's victory, 300 picketers protested Lotus's litigation strategy outside Lotus's headquarters in Cambridge. See Michael Alexander, "Lotus Litigation Draws Protest," *Computer World*, August 6, 1990, at 6.

Another Lotus competitor, Borland International, sensed that it was next in line, so it initiated a declaratory judgment action against Lotus in what it hoped would be a more hospitable forum in California. Lotus then filed suit against Borland in Massachusetts, where it had brought the *Paperback* action. The case was assigned to the same judge who had decided in Lotus's favor in *Paperback*: Judge Robert Keeton, a former Harvard Law School professor. A jurisdictional tussle between the federal district courts in California and Massachusetts ensued, and Lotus succeeded in having the two cases consolidated before Judge Keeton in Massachusetts.

Borland's Quattro Pro could operate in two different modes: a native mode (which was completely different from Lotus 1-2-3) and a 1-2-3 mode (which offered the user the same command structure as Lotus 1-2-3).[6] As in *Paperback*, there was no allegation that Borland copied any Lotus code. In contrast with *Paperback*, however, the Borland user interface, even when in the 1-2-3 mode, looked completely different from Lotus 1-2-3. Despite this absence of visual similarity, Lotus claimed that Borland infringed its copyright by copying the 1-2-3 command structure.

Although familiarity with the technical facts is important in every software copyright case, it is particularly important in this case because of the dual function of the Lotus 1-2-3 command structure. First, the Lotus commands appear on the screen in a logical order to inform the user about the available options at that stage of operation, and the user invokes a sequence of the commands to instruct the program directly to perform certain spreadsheet functions. In this role, the commands act as an interface between the user and the program. Second, the spreadsheet user can employ the Lotus commands to write a "macro"—a program that employs a sequence of menu commands to perform a series of spreadsheet operations in a particular order. In this role, the command structure acts as an interface between the spreadsheet program and the user-written macro.

Although Lotus 1-2-3, taken as a whole, is an application program, it assumes some of the characteristics of an operating system with respect to the user-written application programs—the macros—that attach to it. In other words, Lotus 1-2-3 serves as a platform upon which the macros run. The syntax and the semantics of the communication between a macro and the Lotus platform are those of the Lotus commands.

Lotus users had invested substantial time and resources in developing libraries of customized macros appropriate to their business needs. Because of this, the Lotus users were "locked in" to the Lotus environment; as they

---

6. Borland's 1-2-3 mode also offered the user additional commands not found in Lotus 1-2-3.

expanded their operations, they simply would not purchase spreadsheet programs developed by a Lotus competitor such as Borland unless the Borland spreadsheet could execute their macros.[7]

The most basic form of macro-compatibility required the Borland platform to have the ability to translate the user-written macros instructions into instructions intelligible to the Borland platform, and vice versa. Because the set of instructions used by the macro was a subset of Lotus's commands, the Borland platform had to translate those instructions from the macros by means of a file that replicated the Lotus 1-2-3 command structure, syntax, and semantics. Borland called this file the Key Reader.

2.1.1.2 The District Court Decisions

In finding for Lotus, Judge Keeton primarily considered the Lotus command structure in its user-interface role.[8] Relying heavily on the Third Circuit's decision in *Whelan v. Jaslow*,[9] he found the command structure to be protected expression. Although Judge Keeton rejected *Whelan*'s simplistic one-idea-per-program rule, he nonetheless adopted *Whelan*'s abbreviated copyright analysis, in which the idea/expression dichotomy was reduced to the merger doctrine. In Judge Keeton's view, if an author had alternatives available to him, there was no merger, and if there was no merger, there was protected expression. Because a programmer theoretically could construct many different spreadsheet command structures, copyright protected the Lotus 1-2-3 command structure. Accordingly, the Borland user interface in the 1-2-3 mode infringed Lotus's copyright.

In one of his four decisions in the case, Judge Keeton specifically addressed the Key Reader and macro-compatibility. Keeton ruled that the Key Reader infringed Lotus's copyright just as the Borland user interface did. Keeton acknowledged that under *Computer Associates v. Altai*,[10] issued only a month before his macro-compatibility ruling, "aspects of computer software cannot be subject to copyright if they are greatly circumscribed by the hardware or software with which they are designed to interact."[11] Nonetheless, Keeton concluded that this proposition did not apply to the

---

7. Neil Gandal, "Hedonic Price Indexes for Spreadsheets and an Empirical Test for Network Externalities," 25 *Rand Journal of Economics* 160 (spring 1994).

8. *Lotus Development Corp. v. Borland Int'l Inc.*, 799 F. Supp. 203, 206 (D. Mass. 1992), *rev'd*, 49 F.3d 807 (1st Cir. 1995), *aff'd by an equally divided Court*, 516 U.S. 233 (1996).

9. 797 F.2d 1222 (3d Cir. 1986), *cert. denied*, 479 U.S. 1031 (1987).

10. 982 F.2d 693 (2d Cir. 1992). Judge Keeton issued his decision on July 31, 1992; the Second Circuit issued *Computer Associates* on June 22, 1992.

11. *Borland*, 799 F. Supp. at 212.

Key Reader. He reached this result by limiting *Computer Associates'* rejection of copyright protection for interface specifications to situations where "what the program was designed to fit was already in existence before the program was designed to fit."[12] In other words, whether a program characteristic received protection turned on the constraints existing at the time of that program's creation, and not on the constraints existing at the time of the allegedly infringing program's creation.

Under Judge Keeton's reasoning, a second programmer writing a new application program could copy the interface specifications of an earlier application program designed to run on a pre-existing operating system, because those interface specifications had been constrained by the operating system and thus did not receive copyright protection. A second programmer writing a new operating system, however, could not copy the pre-existing operating system's interface specifications to permit the new operating system to run the two application programs, because the interface specifications of the first operating system were not constrained at the time of their creation and thus *did* receive copyright protection. This result would have effectively eliminated competition in operating systems or any software product that functions as a platform for other software products. Judge Keeton, therefore, interpreted *Computer Associates* as permitting only the development of products that attached to, but did not compete with, a pre-existing platform. A developer of interoperable software could write programs to run on the opposite side of the interface from the pre-existing platform, but not on the same side.

In the *Paperback* decision, Judge Keeton had articulated an interesting policy rationale that appears to underlie this outcome. *Paperback*, like *Borland*, had raised the issue of macro-compatibility. Paperback argued that because the Lotus command structure had become a *de facto* standard among spreadsheet users, Paperback should be free to copy it. Judge Keeton responded by attributing Lotus's *de facto* standard status to the creativity of the Lotus programmers. In his view, it would be perverse for the command structure somehow to lose its copyright protection simply because the Lotus programmers had done such a good job that they had established a *de facto* standard that now constrained competitors.[13] Had the Lotus programmers been less creative, and had 1-2-3 been less successful, it would

---

12. Id. at 213. The similarities between the Computer Associates and Altai programs resulted in large part from constraints imposed by the pre-existing IBM operating systems with which they interoperated.

13. *Paperback*, 740 F. Supp. at 79.

not have become a *de facto* standard and Paperback would not seek to use it. Copyright should reward creativity, he argued, not penalize it.

Judge Keeton's narrow reading of *Computer Associates* flowed directly from this analysis. From his perspective, it would have been perverse to allow Borland to copy the Lotus command structure in order to compete with Lotus 1-2-3; Lotus should not be disadvantaged by the fact that its innovative product became as popular as it did. This reasoning reveals that, at bottom, Judge Keeton still viewed the case in terms of "look and feel" rather than interoperability. That is, he viewed Borland as trying to free ride on a popular product developed by Lotus, much as a maker of jeans or tennis shoes tries to sell products that look like those of the market leader. He saw only two parties in the copyright calculus: Lotus and Borland. Almost completely absent from his analysis were users, without question the most important party from the perspective of the U.S. copyright system. Had he looked at the case through interoperability lenses, he would not have committed this error.

The scant attention Judge Keeton gave users is visible in three distinct ways. First, he failed to take the user-written macros seriously. In the decision he used trivial examples of macros involving only a handful of steps. In the business world, however, a macro could have thousands of steps, and could represent a significant investment by the user. Second, Judge Keeton's decision gave no meaningful weight to the problem of user lock-in. Because of their significant investment in the macros, users were not willing to switch to a rival platform, even if it were technologically superior. Third, Judge Keeton did not acknowledge the users' contribution to the *de facto* standardization of the Lotus command structure. Lotus 1-2-3 became the standard in large measure because of users' significant investment in macros.[14] To be sure, Lotus 1-2-3 contained many innovative features when it hit the market, but its success was at least partly attributable to many other causes, most notably the development by users of macros dependent on 1-2-3.

Judge Keeton did not fully appreciate the interoperability dimension of the case, but the First Circuit did. Unlike Judge Keeton, the First Circuit was aided by *amicus* briefs emphasizing interoperability. These briefs were filed by the Software Entrepreneurs Forum (an organization of more than 1,000 independent software developers, consultants, and providers), by a group of 27 leading computer scientists, by a collection of 20 groups of personal

14. See Frederick R. Warren-Boulton, Kenneth C. Baseman, and Glenn A. Woroch, "Copyright Protection For Software Can Make Economic Sense," *The Computer Lawyer*, February 1995.

computer users, and by the American Committee for Interoperable Systems (whose 30 members include Sun Microsystems, Storage Technology, Bull HN, Amdahl, and Broderbund).

2.1.1.3 The First Circuit's Opinion

On March 9, 1995, the First Circuit reversed Judge Keeton.[15] The opinion of the court, written by Judge Stahl, focused on interoperability from the outset. Judge Stahl described the macro-compatibility function of the command structure in the third paragraph of the opinion. In the fifth paragraph, he addressed Borland's motivation for copying the 1-2-3 command structure in terms of interoperability: "Borland included the Lotus command hierarchy in its programs to make them compatible with Lotus 1-2-3 so that spreadsheet users who were clearly familiar with Lotus 1-2-3 would be able to switch to the Borland programs without having to learn new commands or rewrite their Lotus macros."[16]

The court defined the question before it very narrowly: "whether a computer menu command hierarchy constitutes copyrightable subject matter." It then opined that this was a question of first impression. With no hesitation, the court proceeded to conclude that the Lotus command structure was a method of operation not protected under section 102(b) of the Copyright Act. "The Lotus menu command hierarchy," the court explained, "provides the means by which users control and operate Lotus 1-2-3. . . . Users must use the command terms to tell the computer what to do. Without the menu command hierarchy, users would not be able to access and control, or indeed make use of, Lotus 1-2-3's functional capabilities."[17]

The First Circuit rejected the district court's argument that copyright protected the Lotus command structure because Borland could—and did —develop its own command structure using different terms and a different arrangement. "If specific words are essential to operating something," the First Circuit stated, "then they are part of a 'method of operation' and, as such, are unprotectable."[18] This is true even if a parallel set of words could operate a parallel program. That is, the mere fact that a programmer could construct other methods of operation in no way renders a given method of operation protected expression.

The court then turned to the underlying theme of interoperability:

---

15. *Lotus Development Corp. v. Borland Int'l Inc.*, 49 F.3d 807 (1st Cir. 1995), *aff'd by an equally divided Court*, 516 U.S. 233 (1996).
16. Id. at 810.
17. Id. at 815.
18. Id. at 816.

That the Lotus menu command hierarchy is a "method of operation" becomes clearer when one considers program compatibility. Under Lotus's theory, if a user uses several different programs, he or she must learn how to perform the same operations in a different way for each program used. . . . We find this absurd. The fact that there may be many different ways to operate a computer program, or even many different ways to operate a computer program using a set of hierarchically arranged command terms, does not make the actual method of operation chosen copyrightable; it still functions as a method for operating the computer and as such is uncopyrightable.[19]

The court amplified this theme in the context of macro-compatibility:

Under the district court's holding, if the user wrote a macro to shorten the time needed to perform a certain operation in Lotus 1-2-3, the user would be unable to use that macro to shorten the time needed to perform that same operation in another program. Rather, the user would have to rewrite his or her macros using that other program's menu command hierarchy. This is despite the fact that the macro is clearly the user's own work product. We think that forcing the user to cause the computer to perform the same operation in a different way ignores Congress's direction in Section 102(b) that "methods of operation" are not copyrightable.[20]

The opinion closed by proclaiming its consistency with the Supreme Court's decision in *Feist v. Rural Telephone*[21] and by paraphrasing the policy embodied by *Feist*:

We also note that in most contexts, there is no need to "build" upon other people's expression, for the ideas conveyed by that expression can be conveyed by someone else without copying the first author's expression. In the context of methods of operation, however, "building" requires the use of the precise method of operation already employed; otherwise, "building" would require dismantling, too. Original developers are not the only people entitled to build on the methods of operation they create; anyone can. Thus, Borland may build on the method of operation that Lotus designed and may use the Lotus menu command hierarchy in doing so.[22]

2.1.1.4 Judge Boudin's Concurring Opinion

Judge Boudin[23] wrote a concurring opinion that delved even deeper into the economic and policy ramifications arising from the interoperability dimension of the case. He noted that most of the law of copyright had developed in the context of literary works, such as novels, plays, and films.

19. Id. at 817–818.
20. Id. at 818.
21. 499 U.S. 340 (1991).
22. *Borland*, 49 F.3d at 818 (footnote deleted).
23. Judge Boudin replaced Judge Breyer on the panel after Breyer was elevated to the Supreme Court.

He explained that "to assume that computer programs are just one more new means of expression, like a filmed play, may be quite wrong," and that "[a]pplying copyright law to computer programs is like assembling a jigsaw puzzle whose pieces do not quite fit."[24] Judge Boudin observed that, because of the utilitarian and functional nature of a computer, the danger of over-protection is greater than in the case of traditional literary works: "[A] 'mistake' in providing too much protection [for traditional works] involves a small cost: subsequent authors treating the same themes must take a few more steps away from the original expression."[25] But in the case of computer programs, the improper grant of copyright protection "can have some of the consequences of patent protection in limiting other people's ability to perform a task in the most efficient manner."[26]

Turning to the facts before him, Judge Boudin remarked that "the present case is an unattractive one for copyright protection."[27] He noted that "the menu commands . . . are largely for standard procedures that Lotus did not invent and are common words that Lotus cannot monopolize."[28] Further, if Lotus could receive a copyright in its command structure, users who invested in learning Lotus 1-2-3 and writing macros compatible with it would be "locked" into Lotus, and the copyright would preclude competitors from developing products capable of interoperating with the installed base. Judge Boudin wrote:

Requests for the protection of computer menus present the concern with fencing off access to the commons in an acute form. A new menu may be a creative work, but over time its importance may come to reside more in the investment that has been made by users in learning the menu and in building their own mini-programs—macros—in reliance on the menu.[29]

If Lotus could obtain a monopoly in the 1-2-3 command structure, users who have learned the command structure of Lotus 1-2-3 or devised their own macros are locked into Lotus. . . . Apparently, for a period Lotus 1-2-3 has had such sway in the market that it has represented the de facto standard for electronic spreadsheet commands. So long as Lotus is the superior spreadsheet—either in quality or in price—there may be nothing wrong with this advantage.

But if a better spreadsheet comes along, it is hard to see why customers who have learned the Lotus menu and devised macros for it should remain captives of Lotus because of an investment in learning made by the users and not by Lotus. Lotus has

24. *Borland*, 49 F.3d at 820 (Boudin, J., concurring).
25. Id. at 819.
26. Id.
27. Id. at 821.
28. Id.
29. Id.

already reaped a substantial reward for being first; assuming that the Borland program is now better, good reasons exist for freeing it to attract old Lotus customers: to enable the old customers to take advantage of a new advance. . . .[30]

In view of the obvious benefits to the user resulting from withholding copyright protection from program elements necessary for interoperability, the question for Judge Boudin "is not whether Borland should prevail but on what basis."[31] The judge identified two possible bases. The first of these was the basis articulated by Judge Stahl: viewing the command structure as an unprotected method of operation. The second was permitting Borland's use under the fair-use doctrine. Judge Boudin candidly acknowledged that the majority's "formulation is as good, if not better, than any other that occurs to me now as within the reach of courts."[32] Nonetheless, Judge Boudin explored the concept of fair use further. Borland's use here would be privileged because "it is not seeking to appropriate the advances made by Lotus' menu; rather, having provided an arguably more attractive menu of its own, Borland is merely trying to give former Lotus users an option to exploit their own prior investment in learning or in macros."[33]

Judge Boudin emphasized that the privilege would be available only because Borland was providing the user with additional functionality; had it simply copied the menu using different code, but contributed nothing significant of its own, Judge Boudin would not have permitted the use.

Judge Boudin conceded that Borland's use might not fit squarely within the fair-use doctrine under its current formulation, but added that "the doctrine of fair use was created by the courts and can be adapted to new purposes."[34] He further acknowledged that widespread application of the fair-use doctrine for purposes of achieving interoperability "would entail a host of administrative problems that would cause cost and delay, and would also reduce the ability of the industry to predict outcomes."[35]

Judge Boudin's reasoning is unabashedly oriented toward results. The fair-use doctrine, however, encourages precisely such reasoning. As the Supreme Court stated in *Stewart v. Abend*, the fair-use doctrine is an "equitable rule of reason which permits courts to avoid rigid application of the copyright statute when, on occasion, it would stifle the very creativity

30. Id. at 821.
31. Id.
32. Id. at 822.
33. Id.
34. Id.
35. Id. at 821–822.

which the law is designed to foster."[36] Judge Boudin recognized that preventing interoperability invariably stifles creativity; new firms cannot introduce new products for the locked-in base, and the monopolist has little incentive to innovate—and innovation is the ultimate goal of the intellectual-property system. Interoperability, conversely, permits competition, which stimulates innovation—the ultimate good of the intellectual-property system.

2.1.1.5 The Treatment of *Computer Associates*

Much of the briefing before the First Circuit centered on how the Second Circuit's decision in *Computer Associates* should be applied to the facts of the case at hand. Interestingly, Judge Stahl, in a section devoted entirely to *Computer Associates*, concluded that the *Computer Associates* abstraction-filtration-comparison test was "of little help." He explained that the *Computer Associates* test might be useful in cases involving non-literal copying, but that this case involved "Borland's deliberate, literal copying of the Lotus menu command hierarchy."[37] Judge Stahl further stated that the *Computer Associates* test in this context might actually be "misleading" because it could cause the identification of expression at a low level of abstraction while obscuring the fact that the expression may be part of a method of operation at a higher level of abstraction. In other words, Judge Stahl flipped the standard critique of the *Computer Associates* test on its head. Tony Clapes (then an intellectual-property lawyer with IBM) and others have argued that the *Computer Associates* test could lead to the "atomization" of a computer program, thereby obscuring expression in the selection, coordination, and arrangement of non-protectable elements.[38] For Tony Clapes, atomization leads to under-protection; for Judge Stahl, it leads to over-protection!

To be sure, the sloppy application of the *Computer Associates* test can lead to either over-protection or under-protection. Although *Computer Associates* and its progeny (notably *Gates v. Bando*[39]) have crafted a highly structured legal test, the test still is only as good as the judge applying it. Thus, careful application of the *Computer Associates* test to the facts of this case would not mislead a court.

36. 495 U.S. 207, 237 (1990) (citations omitted).
37. *Borland*, 49 F.3d at 814.
38. Anthony L. Clapes and Jennifer M. Daniels, "Revenge of the Luddites: A Closer Look at *Computer Associates v. Altai*," *The Computer Lawyer*, November 1992, at 4.
39. 9 F.3d 823 (10th Cir. 1993).

Indeed, one could argue that, even though Judge Stahl stated that *Computer Associates* was of little help, both he and Judge Boudin applied the *Computer Associates* test successfully. Because the case involved literal copying, the First Circuit could skip the abstraction step altogether and focus on filtration—that is, on determining whether copyright protected the element Borland had copied word for word (the Lotus command structure). In performing the filtration step, the First Circuit appears to have been informed by the teachings of *Computer Associates* and its progeny on the utilitarian nature of computer programs. It appears to have been similarly informed by these cases that copyright should not be applied in a manner that hinders interoperability.[40] Accordingly, even though the First Circuit seemed to distance itself from *Computer Associates*, its decision falls squarely within the *Computer Associates* tradition.

2.1.1.6   *Lotus v. Borland* before the Supreme Court

Lotus petitioned the U.S. Supreme Court to review the First Circuit's decision, and the Supreme Court granted its request. Because *Lotus* was to be the first software copyright case ever decided by the Supreme Court, the industry expected final resolution of the scope of protection question generally and the interoperability debate in particular.

In its petition for writ of certiorari, Lotus argued that the First Circuit's decision was a "jarring departure" from the recent decisions in the other circuits.[41] Lotus contended that under the First Circuit's reasoning the user interface of a computer program would always constitute an unprotectable method of operation. Lotus contrasted this result with other courts' grants of protection to user interfaces. Lotus further argued that, by the First Circuit's logic, "it is unclear what, if any, elements of computer program would merit protection, because all programs to some degree described a 'method of operation' for a machine."[42] *Amicus* briefs filed by the Intellectual Property Owners and the Information Technology Industry Council in support of Lotus echoed the criticism that First Circuit's ruling "contains no limiting principle by which to differentiate the aspects of a program that are copyrightable from those that are not protectable."[43]

40. See, e.g., *Atari Games Corp. v. Nintendo of America, Inc.*, 975 F.2d 832 (Fed. Cir. 1992); *Sega Enterprises Ltd. v. Accolade, Inc.*, 977 F.2d 1510 (9th Cir. 1992).
41. Brief of Lotus Development Corp. in support of Petition for Writ of Certiorari, *Lotus v. Borland*, 516 U.S. 233 (1996) (No. 94-2003), at 22.
42. Id.
43. Brief *Amicus Curiae* of Information Technology Industry Council, *Lotus v. Borland*, 516 U.S. 233 (1996) (No. 94-2003), at 11.

In response, Borland contended that it was Judge Keeton, rather than the First Circuit, who was in conflict with the other circuits. Borland then demonstrated that the First Circuit's decision was in fact consistent with the recent decisions in other circuits. Finally, Borland argued that the First Circuit's clear exclusion of menu command hierarchies from protection would enhance productivity in the software industry by providing developers with much-needed certainty.

On September 27, 1995, the Supreme Court agreed to review the First Circuit's decision. In its opening brief, Lotus sharpened its criticism of the First Circuit's methodology. Lotus contended that the First Circuit had agreed with Judge Keeton that the Lotus 1-2-3 command structure contained expression that was separable from its idea and functionality, but that the First Circuit nonetheless refused to extend copyright protection to this expression because it was an element of the program's method of operation. Lotus also repeated its earlier arguments that, under the First Circuit's reasoning, no copyright protection remained for any element of a computer program, because all such elements were ultimately part of a method of operation. Heavy lobbying by Borland stopped both the Intellectual Property Owners and the Information Technology Industry Council from filing *amicus* briefs on the merits in support of Lotus. Nonetheless, Intel, DEC, Xerox, and Gates Rubber filed a joint *amicus* brief in favor of Lotus. Moreover, the American Intellectual Property Law Association filed a brief that officially was "in support of neither party" but which in fact made the same arguments as the Lotus brief, only more persuasively.[44] Significantly, neither Lotus nor its *amici* addressed the question of macro-compatibility in any detail.

In its answering brief, Borland did not respond directly to Lotus's specific attacks on the First Circuit's methodology. Instead, it explained that the First Circuit had reached the correct result, and that the Lotus command structure could be protected only by the patent laws. A torrent of *amicus* briefs supported Borland, three of them filed by groups of law professors and others by economists, computer scientists, users of personal computers, and software entrepreneurs. Many of these briefs addressed macro compatibility and the dire consequences of protecting program elements necessary for interoperability.

Only one brief, filed jointly by the American Committee for Interoperable Systems (ACIS) and the Computer & Communications Industry

---

44. Brief *Amicus Curiae* of American Intellectual Property Law Association, *Lotus v. Borland*, 516 U.S. 233 (1996) (No. 94-2003), at 1.

Association (CCIA), attempted to defend the First Circuit's methodology in addition to its result.[45] ACIS and CCIA contended that the First Circuit never conceded that the command structure contained separable expression. To be sure, the First Circuit had acknowledged that the Lotus developers had made some expressive choices when selecting and arranging the command terms. But the appellate court made it clear that those choices had merged with the command structure. The question thus became whether the command structure, as a whole, was idea or expression. According to ACIS and CCIA, the answer to this question turned on the definition of a phrase used by Lotus in its brief: "same functionality." If a command structure with the "same functionality" as the 1-2-3 structure could offer exactly the same selection of functions as 1-2-3, but with different terms in a different sequence, then Lotus should prevail. Conversely, if a command structure with the "same functionality" as 1-2-3 meant one which was completely compatible with 1-2-3, then Borland should prevail. Not surprisingly, ACIS and CCIA argued that "same functionality" meant complete compatibility.

Although on January 8, 1996 the federal government was closed down by one of the worst blizzards in Washington's history, Chief Justice Rehnquist ordered that the oral arguments scheduled for that day, including those in the *Lotus v. Borland* case, proceed as planned.[46] All the justices and the lawyers participating in the case succeeded in reaching the Supreme Court—even Justice Souter, whose car reportedly got stuck in a snowbank and who had to be rescued by the Supreme Court police. Justice Stevens's flight back from his home in Florida was canceled, but he would not have participated in the oral argument; he had recused himself from the case for undisclosed reasons.

Henry Gutman of the New York office of Baker & Botts, representing Lotus, argued first.[47] He contended that the First Circuit had erred in failing to separate the expression in the selection and arrangement of the words of the 1-2-3 command structure from the underlying functionality of the program. At this juncture, Justice Souter asked whether the case really was an "analysis" case, as Lotus suggested, or a "choice" case. In other words,

45. Brief *Amicus Curiae* of American Committee for Interoperable Systems and Computer & Communications Industry Association, *Lotus v. Borland*, 516 U.S. 233 (1996) (No. 94-2003).

46. This subsection is based on Jonathan Band, "Oral Argument in Lotus Foreshadows Outcome," *Intellectual Property Strategist*, January 2006, at 8.

47. The transcript of the oral argument can be found at 51 *Patent, Trademark & Copyright Journal* 381 (January 18, 1996).

Justice Souter was suggesting that the issue before the Supreme Court was not so much whether the First Circuit had employed the correct method of analysis in separating idea from expression as whether it had made the correct choice in determining that the Lotus command structure fell on the idea side of the idea/expression dichotomy. Soon thereafter, Justice Ginsburg expressed concern for users who had invested substantial time and effort in creating macros with the 1-2-3 command structure, and wondered whether Borland's copying of the command structure should be excused because it enabled the users to take full advantage of their own investment. Gutman, in perhaps the most significant development of the argument, conceded that there might be a legal difference between Borland's using the Lotus command structure in the Quattro Pro user interface and Borland's using the command structure in the "Key Reader" file (which allowed Quattro Pro to execute user-written macros). Gutman stated that the infringement claim was "weaker" in the case of the Key Reader. The justices asked no more questions concerning the Key Reader and macro-compatibility, focusing instead on the command structure in the user-interface mode. Justice Breyer, for example, used the analogy of a department store's "system," in which departments are arranged in a particular order on particular floors, and suggested that a department store's owner should not be able to use a copyright in the arrangement of the names of the departments to prevent others from copying the system. Justice Breyer further suggested that the names of the departments might "merge" into the system of the arrangement of the departments.

Arguing on behalf of Borland, Gary Reback of the Silicon Valley law firm Wilson, Sonsini emphasized that what Lotus sought to protect via copyright could be protected only by patent. Justice Ginsburg stated that it appeared that the First Circuit had concluded that the command structure was a method of operation, and then had made no effort to determine whether it contained separable expression. Justice O'Connor appeared dismayed that Borland had made an identical copy of all 469 terms in the Lotus command structure. Justice Scalia disagreed with Reback that Borland had to use the same words on the screen display as Lotus to provide the user with the same functions. He contended that Borland did not have to use any words at all; rather, its program simply had to be able to interpret the user's keystrokes. Balancing these hostile questions, Justice Breyer added the analogy of an airplane cockpit with a control panel of 469 buttons, each with a label. He indicated that copyright would not protect the layout of the buttons nor the labels. Justice Souter seemed to accept Reback's description of the command structure as a language.

In sum, Justices Breyer and Souter leaned toward Borland, while Justices O'Connor and Scalia leaned toward Lotus. Justice Ginsburg leaned toward Borland with respect to the Key Reader, but toward Lotus with respect to the user interface. The other justices' questions did not reveal their sympathies or their thinking.

Just a week after the oral argument, on January 16, 1996, the Supreme Court surprised the software industry by issuing a two-sentence *per curiam* order affirming the First Circuit's decision with a vote of 4–4.[48] (As has already been noted, Justice Stevens recused himself.) The quick affirmance reflected the division within the panel that was apparent during the oral arguments. However, because the Court's *per curiam* order did not disclose how the justices voted, there is no way to determine whether they voted consistent with their questioning at oral argument. Although the four votes to reverse the First Circuit's ruling evidence concern with aspects of the appellate court's decision, the flow of the oral argument suggests that none of the justices was troubled by the First Circuit's refusal to extend copyright protection to program elements necessary for software interoperability.

2.1.1.7 Significance of *Lotus v. Borland*

Technically, the affirmance by an equally divided Supreme Court left the *Borland* decision as binding authority only in the First Circuit. Thus, the *per curium* order did not provide the industry with the definitive, sweeping resolution it had sought. Nonetheless, the Supreme Court's affirmance of *Borland* allowed the trend throughout the circuit courts toward excluding copyright protection for function-dictated aspects of programs, particularly those elements necessary for interoperability, to continue unchecked.

Although the *Computer Associates* decision held that program elements constrained by interoperability requirements—interface specifications—could not receive copyright protection, Judge Keeton's Key Reader decision limited that holding to the specifications necessary to attach to the pre-existing platform, excluding those necessary to compete with it. Because of the large concentration of software-development activity in Massachusetts, and because of Judge Keeton's scholarly reputation, the Key Reader decision had the potential to retard the development of interoperable software products significantly. The First Circuit's reversal of Judge Keeton lifted the cloud of uncertainty that had been hanging over developers of interoperable software products and their many customers. The First Circuit ruled unambiguously that program elements necessary to achieve interoperability—to

---

48. *Lotus v. Borland*, 516 U.S. 233 (1996).

attach as well as to compete—were, by definition, methods of operation not protected by copyright. Judge Boudin further suggested that, to the extent such elements were not methods of operation, their use should be permitted under the fair-use doctrine.

The First Circuit also expanded the concept of interoperability to include not only the ability of different products to work together, but also the ability of a user to employ the same skill set with different products. The court essentially reasoned that a method of operation is a method of operation, whether it is performed by a person or by a program.

Notwithstanding the First Circuit's ruling, many program elements remain subject to copyright protection. The First Circuit specifically stated that the screen displays (apart from the command structure), and the computer code implementing the command structure in both its user-interface and macro-compatibility roles, could still receive copyright protection.[49] This combination of proprietary and non-proprietary elements meets the copyright imperative of balancing the need to provide incentives to the developers of new technologies with the need to permit competition through interoperability.

2.1.2 Protectability of Interface Specifications after *Lotus v. Borland*

As discussed above, one of the central issues in *Lotus v. Borland* was the protectability under copyright of elements necessary to achieve interoperability.[50] Judge Keeton of the U.S. District Court for Massachusetts had ruled that such elements did receive protection. The First Circuit, however, reversed Judge Keeton on this point and withheld protection from the Key Reader file that allowed macros compatible with Lotus 1-2-3 to run on Borland's spreadsheet program. Although Lotus did not specifically appeal the First Circuit's ruling on the Key Reader file, Borland and its *amici* emphasized to the Supreme Court that interoperability was central to the case.

Had the Supreme Court decided the case on the merits, we would have definitive answers to whether copyright protects interface specifications, and, if it doesn't, under what theory it doesn't. But the Court did not reach the merits, and thus the law continued to evolve in the lower courts. Four courts subsequently refused, under a variety of different theories, to extend protection to interface specifications. They continued the lower courts' pro-interoperability tilt, but did so in a way that did not endanger copyright

---

49. *Borland*, 49 F.3d, at 815–816.
50. This subsection is based on Jonathan Band, "Interoperability after Lotus v. Borland: The Ball Is in the Lower Courts Again," *The Computer Lawyer*, March 1996, at 11.

protection for those program elements that deserve it under law. The Third Circuit, however, found that the reproduction necessary for interoperability infringed copyright.

2.1.2.1   *Bateman v. Mnemonics* (1995)

Brian Bateman developed a single-board computer for use in automated parking systems. A subsidiary of Mnemonics, Inc. purchased the Bateman computers and developed compatible application programs. After Bateman and Mnemonics had conducted business with each another for several years, Mnemonics began experiencing difficulties with the Bateman computers. When Bateman could not correct the problem, Mnemonics disassembled[51] the Bateman operating system to discern the interfaces necessary for compatibility with the existing application programs, then developed its own compatible operating system. Bateman filed suit for, among other things, copyright infringement of its operating system. After trial, a jury found for Bateman.

The appeal centered on the jury instructions. Mnemonics claimed that the district court had committed reversible error by instructing the jury to filter out only nonliteral similarities when applying the Second Circuit's "abstraction-filtration-comparison" test and by failing to instruct the jury on the legal consequences of copying elements dictated by compatibility requirements.

Application of Abstraction-Filtration-Comparison Test

Mnemonics had asked the trial judge to instruct the jury to filter out unprotected features appearing in literal as well as nonliteral elements of the Bateman program before comparing it to the Mnemonics program.[52] The trial judge, however, instructed the jury to filter out only non-literal elements, thereby allowing comparison of unprotected literal elements. According to Mnemonics, this "effectively rendered futile [Mnemonics'] efforts to rebut Bateman's evidence of literal similarity with regard to elements of the work for which copyright was claimed, thereby nullifying several of [Mnemonics'] key defenses, including compatibility, efficiency, and standard programming techniques."[53]

---

51. Disassembly is a form of software reverse engineering that involves translating machine-readable object code into a higher-level, human-readable form. The *Bateman* court's treatment of reverse engineering is discussed below.

52. In computer programs, "literal elements" refers to the source and object code; "non-literal elements" refers to the program's structure and organization.

53. *Bateman v. Mnemonics*, 79 F. 3d 1532, 1544 (11th Cir. 1996).

In its decision on the appeal, the U.S. Court of Appeals for the Eleventh Circuit acknowledged that the Second Circuit, in *Computer Associates v. Altai*,[54] had fashioned the abstraction-filtration-comparison methodology to address the copying of nonliteral elements, and that the First Circuit, in *Lotus v. Borland*,[55] had suggested that this methodology might be of "little help" when considering the copying of literal elements. The Eleventh Circuit observed, however, that this disagreement was "more a matter of semantics than substance."[56] "Even if the Altai test is limited to nonliteral copying," the Eleventh Circuit stated, ". . . a parallel type of analysis must be undertaken in examining alleged instances of literal copying of computer code. . . . Whether one chooses to call the consideration of such generally recognized challenges to literal code copying as merger and efficiency 'filtration' is of little consequence; what matters is that these well-established 'defenses' are considered."[57] The trial judge, in essence, instructed the jury not to consider these "defenses" with respect to the instances of literal copying. This was "a manifest distortion and misstatement of the law,"[58] and sufficient grounds for a new trial insofar as much of Bateman's evidence concerned literal copying.

In a footnote, the Eleventh Circuit explained the critical significance of separating idea from expression in the context of computer programs:

It is particularly important to exclude methods of operation and processes from the scope of copyright in computer programs because much of the contents of computer programs is patentable. Were we to permit an author to claim copyright protection for those elements of the work that should be the province of patent law, we would be undermining the competitive principles that are fundamental to the patent system.[59]

In support of this proposition, the Eleventh Circuit cited the U.S. Supreme Court's decisions in *Baker v. Selden*[60] and *Bonito Boats v. Thunder Craft Boats*[61] and the Federal Circuit's decision in *Atari v. Nintendo*.[62] The Eleventh Circuit signaled that it viewed computer programs as utilitarian literary works

54. 982 F.2d 693 (2d Cir. 1992).

55. 49 F.3d 807, 815 (1st Cir. 1995), *aff'd by an evenly divided Court*, 516 U.S. 233 (1996).

56. *Bateman*, 79 F.3d at 1545.

57. Id.

58. Id.

59. Id. at 1541, n. 21.

60. 101 U.S. 99 (1879).

61. 489 U.S. 141 (1989).

62. 975 F.2d 832 (Fed. Cir. 1992).

that should receive "thinner" copyright protection than more expressive literary works such as novels and plays.

Copying Dictated by Compatibility Requirements

The trial judge had instructed the jury that computer programs are utilitarian articles that contain elements that may be dictated by external factors, "such as compatibility requirements." Mnemonics, on appeal, argued that this instruction, though technically correct, did not go far enough, because it failed to direct the jury to filter out those portions of the Bateman operating system dictated by the interface with the Mnemonics program.

The Eleventh Circuit concluded that if Mnemonics was arguing that interface specifications are not copyrightable as a matter of law, it was wrong: "It is an incorrect statement of the law that interface specifications are not copyrightable as a matter of law."[63] The Eleventh Circuit hastened to add, however, that the trial court had erred "in not instructing the jury on the legal consequences of copying dictated by compatibility requirements."[64] The appellate court then explained what it meant. It reviewed the decisions from other circuits, including *Sega v. Accolade, Computer Associates v. Altai, EDI v. SSI,*[65] and *Atari v. Nintendo*, which found "that external factors such as compatibility may work to deny copyright protection to certain portions of a computer program."[66] Next, it stated that "[w]hether the protection is unavailable because these factors render the expression unoriginal, nonexpressive per 17 U.S.C. § 102(b), or whether these factors compel a finding of fair use, copyright estoppel, or misuse, the result is to deny copyright protection to portions of the computer program."[67]

The Eleventh Circuit emphasized in a footnote that it was merely holding that external factors such as compatibility "*may* negate a finding of infringement."[68] "Such a finding," the court noted, "will depend on the particular facts of a case, and thus it would be unwise for us to formulate a bright line rule to address this issue, given the importance of the factual nuances of each case."[69]

In sum, the Eleventh Circuit refused to issue a *per se* rule that interface specifications cannot receive copyright protection. At the same time,

63. *Bateman*, 79 F.3d at 1547.
64. Id.
65. 26 F.3d 1335 (5th Cir. 1994).
66. *Bateman*, 79 F.3d at 1547.
67. Id.
68. Id. at 1548, n. 33 (emphasis added).
69. Id.

the court provided five different theories under which such specifications would not receive protection.[70] *Borland* addressed two of these theories: the majority relied on the idea/expression dichotomy in section 102(b), whereas Judge Boudin relied on fair use under section 107.

Further, by ordering the district court in the new trial to instruct the jury on "the legal consequences of copying dictated by compatibility requirements," the Eleventh Circuit presumably insisted that the district court enumerate these theories to the jury.[71] Thus, although the Eleventh Circuit refused to draw a permanent "bright line" around interface specifications, it certainly penciled a line in.

The Eleventh Circuit's reluctance to categorically exclude interface specifications from copyright protection makes sense when one recognizes that "interface specification" is a programming term, not a legal term of art. The *Bateman* decision does not define "interface specification," and also refers to "interface commands" and "operating system interface" in the same section. The Eleventh Circuit correctly recognized that it would be reckless for it to attach legal results to terms whose meaning and technological significance may change over time. Instead, it provided a framework within which elements related to interoperability should be examined. The wisdom of retaining the freedom to look at "the factual nuances of each case" is demonstrated by the decision in *Compaq v. Procom*.

2.1.2.2 *Compaq v. Procom* (1995)

The Compaq servers at issue in this litigation held several "hard drives" (i.e., hard disk drives). The server contained the Compaq Insight Manager program (CIM), which, among other things, monitored the operation of the hard drives and generated a pre-failure warning when a hard drive's performance fell below a certain level. Compaq then replaced the hard drive free of charge. The CIM thus helped effectuate Compaq's warranty to its customers.

What the CIM actually monitored were five parameters contained in the Monitor and Performance (M&P) partition of the hard drive. The M&P partition appeared to be firmware. For each parameter there was a threshold value; if that value was exceeded, the CIM generated a pre-failure warning.

Procom sold Compaq-compatible hard drives. The Procom hard drives could interoperate with the Compaq server even if they did not contain

70. By including copyright misuse in this list, the Eleventh Circuit breathed new life into this theory, which until then had not gained much legitimacy outside of the Fourth Circuit.

71. *Bateman*, 79 F.3d at 1547.

any of the parameters in the M&P partition; the CIM simply would never issue a pre-failure warning. Moreover, the CIM could function if the Procom parameters contained different threshold values; the CIM would then just issue its pre-failure warning at a different time from when it would have had a Compaq hard drive been used. The CIM could not work properly, however, if the M&P partition contained different parameters (i.e., monitored different functions).

According to the decision, Procom never completely understood how the M&P partition worked. Thus, it simply copied the parameters and the threshold values from the Compaq M&P partition. Compaq sued for infringement.

The district court ruled on a motion for preliminary injunction that the five threshold values constituted a protectable compilation. According to the court, the values were not empirically verifiable facts, but rather resulted from Compaq's decision-making process. First, Compaq had to make a prediction when the disk drive would actually fail. Then, Compaq had to make a business decision as to when—before that actual point of failure—it was willing to replace the disk drive under its warranty. "In making this decision," the court ruled, "Compaq must weigh several considerations such as the cost of replacing drives too early in their life versus the risk of waiting too long to replace the drive and having it fail while in use. It seems unlikely that other drive manufacturers, facing different economic considerations and different customer expectations, would choose the exact same point in time to replace a drive that Compaq chose."[72] In other words, the court did not view the parameter values as dictated by function. That court acknowledged, however, that merger would be implicated if the values were solely engineering predictions of when the drives would fail.

Though the court extended copyright protection to the set of particular parameter values established by Compaq, it refused to protect the parameters themselves:

. . . to obtain prefailure warnings through CIM, the drive must have the five numbers representing the five parameters monitored by the program. A third party attempting to gain access to CIM has no choice but to also select those five parameters for observation. If a third party selected other parameters, then any warnings that CIM issued would be meaningless.[73]

The court likewise recognized that the CIM would not function properly if the parameters appeared in the M&P partition in a different sequence.

72. *Compaq v. Procom*, 908 F. Supp. 1409, 1418 (S.D. Tex. 1995).
73. Id. at 1419.

Accordingly, the parameters and their sequence were not protected as a system or under the merger and scènes à faire doctrines.

The court also rejected Procom's fair-use argument on the basis that Procom had no real need to copy the values of the parameters. The court distinguished this case from *Sega v. Accolade*[74] by emphasizing that, whereas Accolade sought to understand how Sega's product worked and took only what was necessary to achieve interoperability, Procom never really understood Compaq's product and thus took more than was necessary.[75]

This decision demonstrates the importance of courts' understanding the "factual nuances" of the cases before them. Had it reviewed the facts in a cursory manner, it might have concluded that, because business judgments went into the selection of the parameter values, the parameters as well as the set of values should receive copyright protection. Alternatively, the court might have decided that both the parameters and the values were related to interoperability and thus that neither the parameters nor the values deserved protection. By closely examining the facts, however, the court succeeded in drawing a line between interface specifications and implementations: the parameters and their sequence are the specifications; the values are the implementations. Therefore, it was possible for the court to withhold copyright protection from the interface specifications under section 102(b) but still give meaningful copyright protection to the implementations.

Because the Procom hard drive could function in the Compaq server even if the CIM did not function properly, the court could have concluded that the parameters were not really necessary for interoperability. The court understood, however, that Procom hard drives would not be as desirable to customers if they were not CIM compatible. In other words, the court recognized that there were degrees of interoperability, and allowed Procom to perform the copying necessary to achieve complete interoperability.

2.1.2.3 *Softel v. Dragon Medical* (1996)

In 1996, the U.S. Court of Appeals for the Second Circuit had the opportunity to revisit the methodology it had articulated in *Computer Associates v. Altai*. Although the case did not involve interoperability, the court did

---

74. 977 F.2d 1510 (9th Cir. 1992).

75. The *Procom* court interpreted *Sega* as permitting disassembly for purposes of developing a product that competed with the target of the disassembly. Some commentators have incorrectly suggested that *Sega* permitted disassembly only for purposes of developing products that *attached* to the target of the disassembly.

clarify some features of the abstraction-filtration-comparison methodology; for that reason, the case merits a brief discussion.

Softel developed for Dragon's computer programs certain modules that demonstrated medical conditions and procedures. After a business dispute between the companies, Dragon replaced the Softel modules with its own. Softel alleged that Dragon's new modules infringed its copyright in its modules. The district court concluded that Dragon's modules were not similar to Softel's in protected expression. Softel appealed to the Second Circuit, arguing that "its software combined certain computer programming design elements in an expressive way and that Dragon had copied that expression."[76] Specifically, Softel contended that the integration of four elements—an external file structure, English-language commands, functional modules, and hierarchical menus—constituted protected expression. It claimed that "[t]he genius of the structure, sequence, and organization of plaintiff's program is in the way it receives, assembles, calculates, retains, correlates, and produces information on screen," and that "[s]ince there are other ways of performing those functions to achieve the same purpose as the Softel program, plaintiff's copyrighted work is a protectable expression of ideas."[77]

Reviewing *Computer Associates* and other copyright precedents, the Second Circuit concluded that "an allegation of infringement based on similarities in architecture cannot be ignored merely because many or all the design elements that make up that architecture are not protectable when considered at a lower level of abstraction."[78] The court quoted Harvard Law School professor Arthur Miller: "Individual program elements that are 'filtered' out at one level may be copyrightable when viewed as part of an aggregate of elements at another level of abstraction."[79]

Turning to the facts before it, the Second Circuit stated that "Softel presented an argument, supported by some evidence, that the manner in which it had combined certain computer design elements was expressive for purposes of copyright law."[80] Further, the Second Circuit found that the district court had "either ignored or misanalyzed Softel's argument, and consequently failed to perform the *Altai* analysis at the highest level of abstraction—here, the interrelationships among the four identified

76. *Softel, Inc., v. Dragon Medical and Scientific Communications, Inc.*, 118 F. 3d 955, 963 (2d Cir. 1996), *cert. denied*, 523 U.S. 1020 (1998).
77. Id.
78. Id. at 964.
79. Id. at 966.
80. Id.

elements."[81] The Second Circuit observed that the district court "credited Dragon's expert testimony that each of the four design elements was pervasively used in the computer industry, but did not address the issue of whether the choice and manner of combination of the four elements was commonplace."[82] Expressing no opinion as to the merits of Softel's claim, the Second Circuit remanded the case to the district court, instructing it to determine "whether the manner in which Softel combined the various design elements in its software was protectable expression."[83] There is no reported decision on remand.

2.1.2.4 *Mitel v. Iqtel* (1997)

This case involved simple codes programmed into communications hardware for facilitating functions such as speed dialing. Mitel was the dominant company in the industry, and the technicians who installed the hardware and software were familiar with Mitel's sixty commands. Iqtel developed competitive hardware with its own command system. The Iqtel software was capable of understanding the Mitel commands via a translation module, which contained a copy of the Mitel commands. The Iqtel manual also contained a listing of the Mitel commands with a cross index to the Iqtel commands. The district court, following the First Circuit in *Lotus v. Borland*, held that the Mitel command set was an unprotected method of operation. The court also rested its decisions on grounds that Mitel's commands codes were not original, were dictated by external factors, and were not protectable under the scènes à faire doctrine.

The U.S. Court of Appeals for the Tenth Circuit affirmed the district court's ruling.[84] But instead of following *Borland* directly, the Tenth Circuit applied the Second Circuit's abstraction-filtration-comparison test. After applying this test, it found that all Mitel's commands were unprotected. The Tenth Circuit ruled that most of the commands were unoriginal because they were either arbitrary or simply sequential. The court found the few commands that were slightly original to be unprotected under the scènes à faire doctrine. Under this doctrine, a court excludes from protection those elements of a work that necessarily result from external factors inherent in the subject matter of the work. The Tenth Circuit listed the external factors set forth in *Computer Associates v. Altai* and *Gates v. Bando Chemical*[85]:

81. Id.
82. Id. (citation omitted).
83. Id.
84. *Mitel v. Iqtel*, 124 F.3d 1366 (10th Cir. 1997).
85. 9 F.3d 823 (10th Cir. 1993).

hardware standards and mechanical specifications, software standards and compatibility requirements, computer manufacturers' design standards, the software industry's programming practices, and the practices and demands of the industry being served.

2.1.2.5 Fly in the Ointment? *Dun & Bradstreet v. Grace Consulting* (2002)

In 2002, in *Dun & Bradstreet Software Servs. v. Grace Consulting, Inc.*,[86] the U.S. Court of Appeals for the Third Circuit issued a decision that cited the then-25-year-old opinion in *Apple v. Franklin*[87] and appeared to take a different tack from the decisions discussed above. Perhaps because the decision emerged from an appeal of a jury verdict, the facts in the opinion are incomplete and hard to follow. It seems that Dun & Bradstreet developed a suite of business programs that included software for payroll and other personnel functions. Former D&B employees developed a W-2 program based on D&B's W-2 program and sold it to Grace. Grace, in turn, marketed the program to D&B customers for a price lower than that of the new release of D&B's W-2 program. It appears that the Grace program sat on top of the D&B program, and, when it ran, called and copied various routines from the D&B program. "Grace admitted that the installation, testing, compiling and link editing of its W-2 programs required copying [D&B's] software and link editing the [D&B] code."[88] Thus, when the Grace program ran, 43 percent of its compiled code derived from the D&B program.

Grace argued that calling and copying D&B routines was necessary to achieve interoperability between the Grace and D&B program and therefore did not infringe copyright. The Third Circuit rejected this argument, citing its decision in *Apple v. Franklin* that compatibility was a "commercial and competitive objective which does not enter into the somewhat metaphysical issue of whether particular ideas and expression have merged."[89] Additionally, the Third Circuit found that any elements copied from the D&B program were still protected by copyright because those elements were not constrained by compatibility requirements. The Third Circuit noted that the question was not whether Grace needed a particular element to achieve compatibility with the D&B product but whether D&B was constrained by compatibility requirements when it created the element Grace sought to copy. The court concluded that D&B was not so constrained.

86. 307 F.3d 197 (3d Cir. 2002), *cert. denied*, 538 U.S. 1032 (2003).
87. 714 F.2d 1240, 1253 (3d Cir. 1983), *cert. dismissed*, 464 U.S. 1033 (1984).
88. *Grace Consulting*, 307 F.3d at 213.
89. *Franklin*, 714 F.2d at 1253.

It could very well be that D&B did not design its W-2 program as a platform for other applications, and that Grace copied unconstrained elements.
But the Third Circuit's logic is flawed if applied to platforms. The court
assumes that a developer designs a platform in a vacuum. In fact, the developer designs a platform precisely so that it can interoperate with applications. In other words, when writing a platform, the developer creates a
system for communication between diverse elements. When he designs the
hooks in the platform, he simultaneously designs the eyelets in the applications. The shape of the hook is constrained by the shape of the eyelet, and
vice versa.[90]

Grace Consulting raises issues that are beyond the scope of copyright protection for interface specifications. Applications often call on routines or
libraries in the platform it runs upon, and these elements are compiled
together with the application in the computer's RAM when the user runs
the program. *Grace Consulting* suggests that calling on these elements without the platform developer's authorization might constitute infringement.
To be sure, it could be that Grace copied such large amounts of the D&B
program because Grace was, in essence, marketing a later release of the D&B
program. Nonetheless, *Grace Consulting* remains a troubling precedent.[91]

The *Grace Consulting* decision is a marked departure from the direction
of the other circuits. Not only does it resurrect the *Apple v. Franklin* decision
(a decision that other courts rejected), it also repeats arguments, made by
the district court in *Lotus v. Borland*, that were subsequently repudiated by
First Circuit. Because the *Grace Consulting* decision conflicts with decisions
made by other circuit courts, and because the facts are incomplete, other
circuit courts are not likely to follow it. Nonetheless, it is the law in the
Third Circuit.

2.1.2.6   *Lexmark v. Static Control Components* (2004)
In 2004, the U.S. Court of Appeals for the Sixth Circuit ruled in one of the
more notorious Digital Millennium Copyright Act (DMCA) cases. In what
was widely viewed as an abuse of the DMCA, Lexmark had tried to use the
statute to prevent competition in the market for printer toner. (The Sixth

90. An advantage of treating interface specifications as methods of operation, rather
than analyzing them under the merger or scènes à faire doctrines, is that one avoids
this "which came first, chicken or egg" discussion.
91. From the decision it is clear that the Third Circuit believed that Grace Consulting
was beneath contempt. It breached an array of license agreements with D&B, and it
induced D&B customers to breach their agreements with D&B.

Circuit's rejection of this claim is discussed in greater detail in chapter 3.) The Sixth Circuit also considered the scope of copyright protection in one of Lexmark's computer programs—the toner loading program (TLP).

Lexmark designed the software embedded in its printer—the printer engine program (PEP)—to permit the printer to operate only if it recognized an authentication sequence from the TLP, which was embedded in the toner cartridge. Lexmark did this to prevent users from using less expensive toner cartridges in its printers. Static Control Components (SCC) manufactured the Smartek chip and sold it to manufacturers of replacement toner cartridges. The Smartek chip contained a copy of the Lexmark TLP so that the replacement toner cartridges could operate in Lexmark printers. Lexmark sued SCC for infringing the copyright in the TLP and for violating the DMCA by circumventing the technological measures that protected access to the TLP and the PEP. The district court found that Lexmark was likely to prevail on the merits of both claims, and entered a preliminary injunction in its favor.

The Sixth Circuit reversed with respect to both the copyright claim and the DMCA claim.[92] Much of the decision focused on whether the TLP was protectable under copyright law. The district court found that the TLP could have been written in different ways, and therefore contained protectable expression. The Sixth Circuit rejected this analysis, noting that external constraints may limit a programmer's choices as a practical matter. The Sixth Circuit emphasized that lock-out codes are particularly constrained:

Generally speaking, "lock-out" codes fall on the functional-idea rather than the original expression side of the copyright line. Manufacturers of interoperable devices such as computers and software, game consoles and video games, printers and toner cartridges, or automobiles and replacement parts may employ a security system to bar the use of unauthorized components. To "unlock" and permit operation of the primary device (i.e., the computer, the game console, the printer, the car), the component must contain either a certain code sequence or be able to respond appropriately to an authentication process. To the extent compatibility requires that a particular code sequence be included in the component device to permit its use, the merger and *scènes à faire* doctrines generally preclude the code sequence from obtaining copyright protection.[93]

The Sixth Circuit found that the district court had failed to consider the external constraints that limited the practical options available to the Lexmark programmers. The Sixth Circuit was persuaded by the testimony

92. *Lexmark Int'l, Inc. v. Static Control Components, Inc.*, 387 F.3d 522 (6th Cir. 2004).
93. Id. at 536.

of SCC's expert witness that the TLP "as it is written is the most 'straightforward, efficient, natural way to express the program.'"[94] A critical element in the Sixth Circuit's analysis was that the TLP was a short, simple program, with only 45 commands using 55 bytes of memory. In distinguishing the Third Circuit's decision in *Apple v. Franklin*, the Sixth Circuit observed that the Apple operating system's "size and complexity is to the Toner Loading Program what the Sears Tower is to a lamppost."[95]

Moreover, the district court had erred in assessing whether the TLP functioned as a lock-out code. The Sixth Circuit found that the PEP used every data byte of the TLP as input in a calculation that had to produce a certain result before the PEP would allow the printer to operate: "If a single byte of the [TLP] is altered, the checksum value will not match the checksum calculation result."[96] The Sixth Circuit agreed with the testimony of SCC's expert witness that it was "computationally impossible" to modify the checksum value without other information, which SCC did not possess (and which it could not have gathered through a reasonable amount of reverse engineering). The Sixth Circuit distinguished the facts in this case from those in *Atari v. Nintendo*.[97] In *Atari*, different programs could produce the same data stream that unlocked the console. In *Lexmark*, the program itself was the data stream that unlocked the console. As an example, the court noted that "a poem in the abstract could be copyrightable, but that does not mean that the poem receives copyright protection when it is used in the context of a lock-out code."[98] (The court took this example, without attribution, from an *amicus* brief filed by the Computer & Communications Industry Association.)

Because the more complete record at the permanent-injunction phase might have demonstrated that the TLP was copyrightable, the Sixth Circuit also addressed SCC's fair-use defense. In looking at the first factor (the purpose of the use), the Sixth Circuit found that "it was far from clear that SCC copied the [TLP] for its commercial value as a copyrighted work."[99] Rather, SCC had copied the TLP to permit printer functionality. Accordingly, the first factor tipped toward SCC. With respect to the fourth factor (the effect of the use on the market for the copyrighted material), the Sixth Circuit

---

94. Id. at 540.
95. Id. at 539.
96. Id. at 541.
97. 975 F.2d 832 (Fed. Cir. 1992).
98. *Lexmark*, 387 F.3d at 543.
99. Id. at 544.

stated that the district court had focused on the wrong market. The district court had looked at the impact on toner cartridge market, when it should have looked at the impact on the market for TLPs. Of course, it appears that there is no market for Lexmark's TLP.

Judge Feikens dissented from the Sixth Circuit's finding that the TLP was not copyrightable. He thought that there was evidence in the record indicating that the TLP was not as constrained as found by the majority. Likewise, the judge felt that there was evidence in the record suggesting that the printer could run if the TLP were switched off, and that SCC could have determined this through a reasonable amount of reverse engineering. If so, the TLP really wasn't a lock-out code, in which case the scènes à faire and merger doctrines shouldn't have come into play. Accordingly, the dissenting judge would have remanded the issue to the district court for further fact finding.

2.1.3   Different Approaches, Same Result

Long before the emergence of the Law and Economics movement at the University of Chicago Law School or the emergence of Critical Legal Theory at the Harvard Law School, professors at the Yale Law School taught Legal Realism.[100] The Legal Realists argued that judges typically reached a result in a case on the basis of their idiosyncratic notion of which side deserved to win, and then found a legal rationale justifying that result.[101] Indeed, Critical Legal Theory arguably is just a refinement—or a perversion—of Legal Realism.

The decisions concerning the protectability of interface specifications discussed above—*Lotus v. Borland, Bateman v. Mnemonics, Compaq v. Procom, Mitel v. Iqtel,* and *Lexmark v. SCC*—can be best explained by Legal Realism. In all five decisions, the courts concluded that the defendant software developers should be permitted to make copies of the plaintiffs' programs to the extent necessary to achieve interoperability. Once they had reached that same conclusion, they selected different legal theories justifying how they got there.

This interpretation does not suggest that the courts were unprincipled in any way. Rather, it simply acknowledges that until the law in a particular

---

100. This subsection is based on Jonathan Band and Noah Levine, "You Say Misuse, I Say Fair Use," *The Computer Lawyer*, November 1996, at 10.

101. See Karin Wentz, 1987 Survey of Books Relating to the Law, 85 *Michigan Law Review* 1105 (1987); Joseph W. Singer, "Legal Realism Now," 76 *California Law Review* 465, 471–472 (1988) (both reviewing Laura Kalman, *Legal Realism at Yale, 1927–1960* (1986)).

area is well settled, almost any result can be justified by several plausible legal theories. Under those circumstances, there is nothing unprincipled about a court's selecting a victor on the basis of notions of fairness and consumer welfare, then finding the strongest legal basis for reaching that result. In all these cases, the courts recognized the importance of interoperability to competition in the software industry, and therefore interpreted the Copyright Act in a manner that did not conflict with interoperability.

In other words, Judge Birch, the author of the Eleventh Circuit's decision in *Bateman*, like Judge Boudin before him, first identified his concern— that the copying necessary to the development of interoperable computer software should not necessarily be precluded by copyright law—and only then proposed various alternatives for reaching such a conclusion through accepted forms of legal reasoning. And by listing five alternatives, Judge Birch made clear that he did not much care which legal theory the lower court used, so long as it reached the right result.

From a strict Legal Realist perspective, it makes little difference whether a judge selects misuse, fair use, or a variant of the idea/expression dichotomy. The result is the same: the copying is excused. But the selection does make a difference in the signal the decision sends to other courts and to the software industry. The fair-use defense focuses on the actions of the defendant—that is, on whether the defendant's use was justified. Similarly, a defense predicated on section 102(b) focuses on whether the defendant is entitled to copy the work that is at issue. The misuse defense, by contrast, focuses on the actions of the plaintiff—that is, on whether the plaintiff overreached. In *Borland, Bateman, Computer Associates*, and *Sega*, the court, in essence, asked whether the defendant was permitted to make the copies that were necessary to achieve interoperability. But Judge Birch in *Bateman* also suggested an altogether different question: Was the plaintiff permitted to use his copyright to frustrate interoperability? Judge Birch's mention of

Table 2.1

Case	Basis for Withholding Protection
Borland majority	Method of operation (§ 102(b))
Judge Boudin (*Borland*)	Fair use
Bateman	Unoriginal, nonexpressive (§ 102(b)), fair use, copyright estoppel, misuse
Procom	Scènes à faire (§ 102(b))
Mitel	Unoriginal, scènes à faire (§ 102(b))

misuse, and the resulting focus on the actions of the plaintiff, may indicate the judiciary's deepening commitment toward software interoperability.

However, developers of interoperable products should not overlook the Third Circuit's decision in *Grace Consulting*. Although it may have been wrongly decided, it still is a decision from a U.S. circuit court of appeals.

2.2   The Permissibility of Reverse Engineering

The preceding section looked at the case law concerning the protectability of program elements necessary for interoperability. The other copyright concern of developers of interoperable software is that of potential liability for infringements committed in the process of uncovering these elements. Because software firms typically distribute their software only in machine-readable object code, a developer of an interoperable program often can uncover the target program's interface specifications only by reverse engineering the program. This reverse engineering could involve the developer observing the program's behavior while running it, or in translating the object code into a higher-level, human-readable form. In 1992, the Ninth Circuit in *Sega v. Accolade* ruled that copyright's fair-use doctrine permitted this translation or disassembly to gain access to the unprotectable elements of the program. Subsequent courts permitted reverse engineering under theories of fair use or copyright misuse.

2.2.1   *Bateman v. Mnemonics* (1995)

As was discussed earlier in this chapter, Bateman developed a computer with an operating system for use in automated parking systems.[102] Mnemonics purchased the Bateman computers and developed compatible application programs. When Mnemonics began experiencing difficulties with the Bateman computers, Mnemonics disassembled the Bateman operating system to discern the interfaces necessary for interoperability with the existing application programs, then developed its own interoperable operating system. Bateman filed suit for copyright infringement of its operating system. A jury found for Bateman.

Mnemonics' appeal to the U.S. Court of Appeals for the Eleventh Circuit centered on the judge's instructions to the jury concerning the scope of copyright protection for the operating system. But before reaching the issues on appeal, the Eleventh Circuit, in a footnote, discussed the lawfulness of Mnemonics' disassembly. Although disassembly was not before the

---

102. See subsection 1.2.1 of chapter 1 above.

Eleventh Circuit, and indeed it appears that disassembly had not been an issue at trial, the Eleventh Circuit elected to provide the district court with guidance, noting that the lawfulness of disassembly "likely will appear on remand."[103] After briefly discussing the Ninth Circuit's decision in *Sega v. Accolade* and the Federal Circuit's decision in *Atari v. Nintendo*, the Eleventh Circuit stated: "We find the *Sega* opinion persuasive in view of the principal purpose of copyright—the advancement of science and the arts."[104] In effect, the Eleventh Circuit directed the district court to find Mnemonics' disassembly for purposes of achieving interoperability to be a fair use.

2.2.2 *DSC v. DGI* (1996)

Both DSC and DGI manufactured various forms of telecommunications equipment, including microprocessor cards for phone-switching systems. The conflict between the companies arose when DGI began developing a microprocessor card that would be compatible with the DSC-manufactured phone switch and thus would be substitutable for the card produced by DSC.

DSC moved for a preliminary injunction with respect to three distinct sets of copies. First, DGI purchased some of DSC's microprocessor cards on the open market and disassembled the programs embedded on those chips ("firmware") into human-readable form. Relying on *Sega v. Accolade*, the district court found this copying likely to be a fair use because the disassembly was "the only way to understand the functional elements of DSC's firmware."[105] Second, DGI made removable, identical copies of the operating system in the DSC phone switch at a customer's facility and brought the copies back to the DGI laboratories for study. Because DGI had obtained access to the operating system without DSC's permission, the district court found this to be actionable infringement and granted DSC's motion for a preliminary injunction enjoining such copying.[106] Third, in order for any microprocessor card to operate in the DSC phone switch, the card had to download DSC's copyrighted operating system into the card's random-access memory. Thus, for DGI to successfully test and run its product, it had to place its microprocessor cards in the DSC phone switch and thereby cause the making of a RAM copy of the DSC operating system. The district court implicitly found this form of copying to be permitted. It did so

103. *Bateman v. Mnemonics*, 79 F. 3d 1532, 1539 n. 18 (11th Cir. 1996).
104. Id.
105. *DSC Communications Corp. v. DGI Technologies, Inc.*, 898 F. Supp. 1183, 1190 (N.D. Tex. 1995), *aff'd*, 81 F.3d 597 (5th Cir. 1996).
106. See id. at 1193–1196.

by limiting the preliminary injunctive order such that it did not prohibit "downloading into dynamic RAM on a microprocessor or test microprocessor card which is incidental to the testing or operating of a compatible [microprocessor] card so long as the copy is not capable of being removed from the customer location and transported to any other location."[107]

The issue on appeal to the U.S. Court of Appeals for the Fifth Circuit concerned only the last form of copying. DSC argued that the preliminary injunction was too narrowly drawn because it did not also prohibit the copying incidental to testing or operating of DGI's newly created microprocessor cards. Because DGI conceded that a RAM copy of the DSC operating-system software was made whenever the microprocessor cards were booted up, DGI relied on the copyright-misuse defense.[108]

Judge Garza, writing for the Fifth Circuit, expressed the same concern as Judges Boudin and Birch: that copyright law might be construed to bestow patent-like protection in the computer software context. He noted:

DSC seems to be attempting to use its copyright to obtain a patent-like monopoly over unpatented microprocessor cards. Any competing microprocessor card developed for use on DSC phone switches must be compatible with DSC's copyrighted operating system software. In order to ensure that its card is compatible, a competitor such as DGI must test the card on a DSC phone switch. Such a test necessarily involves making a copy of DSC's copyrighted operating system, which copy is downloaded into the card's memory when the card is booted up. If DSC is allowed to prevent such copying, then it can prevent anyone from developing a competing microprocessor card, even though it has not patented the card.[109]

Seeking to prevent this result, Judge Garza argued that the copyright-misuse theory "forbids the use of the copyright to secure an exclusive right or limited monopoly not granted by the Copyright Office."[110]

107. Id. at 1197.
108. The Fifth Circuit appeared to accept the Ninth Circuit's ruling—in *MAI Sys. Corp. v. Peak Computer, Inc.*, 991 F.2d 511 (9th Cir. 1993), *cert. dismissed*, 510 U.S. 1033 (1994)—that a RAM copy is a "copy" within the meaning of the Copyright Act.
109. *DSC Communications Corp. v. DGI Technologies, Inc.*, 81 F.3d 597, 601 (5th Cir. 1996). For similar concerns expressed by Judges Birch and Boudin, see *Bateman*, 79 F.3d at 1547 n. 33 ("In no case, however, should copyright protection be extended to functional results obtained when program instructions are executed and such results are processes of the type better left to patent and trade secret protection."); *Borland*, 49 F.3d at 819 (Boudin, J., concurring) ("Granting protection, in other words, can have some of the consequences of *patent* protection in limiting other people's ability to perform a task in the most efficient manner.").
110. *DSC Communications*, 81 F.3d. at 601, quoting *Lasercomb America v. Reynolds*, 911 F.2d 970, 977 (4th Cir. 1990).

What is distinctive about *DSC Communications* is that Judge Garza chose to act on his concern about *de facto* patent protection through the affirmative defense of copyright misuse. In *Lasercomb America v. Reynolds*,[111] the Fourth Circuit based its misuse finding on the fact that Lasercomb—by the terms of its copyright license agreement—was attempting to monopolize something that clearly was not part of the bundle of rights granted by copyright: the right to develop competing software utilizing the same ideas. Lasercomb could not make even a plausible argument that a copyright holder could effectively prevent other parties from creating a computer program that would be similar to the copyright holder's program only in that it would accomplish the same task.

Although DSC prohibited customers by license from running its operating-system software on non-DSC equipment,[112] Judge Garza did not rest his decision on that license agreement. He instead found that the attempt by DSC to prevent the making of identical copies by another party to constitute copyright misuse. This clearly extends the reasoning of *Lasercomb*. The right to create a program implementing only the same ideas—the activity Lasercomb sought to control—is not among the copyright holder's exclusive rights under the act. Conversely, the right to reproduce the program in question—which DSC sought to control—is an exclusive right of the copyright holder.[113]

What is even more remarkable about Judge Garza's choice of copyright misuse as the basis for his decision is that he preferred the new and not widely accepted misuse defense over the venerable fair-use defense, which also was available to him. As was noted above, the district court found DGI's disassembly of DSC's firmware to constitute fair use under *Sega Enterprises Ltd. v. Accolade, Inc.*[114] It could be that Judge Garza was reluctant to rely on *Sega* because the reproduction before him was a verbatim copy made by DGI while it was testing its product, rather than a translation DGI made in the course of reverse engineering. However, DGI arguably had a stronger fair-use argument than Accolade had in the *Sega* case. Whereas DGI's RAM copy of the DSC operating system could not impair the market for the operating system in any way, Accolade's disassembly of Sega products could have led to the development of Accolade products that might have diminished the sales of Sega products.

At trial, DSC presented evidence that its license to its customers prohibited the running of the DSC operating system on non-DSC cards. The

111. 911 F.2d 970, 977 (4th Cir. 1990).

112. See *DSC Communications*, 81 F.3d at 600.

113. See 17 U.S.C. § 106(1).

114. 977 F.2d 1510 (9th Cir. 1992).

jury found that DSC's license agreement constituted copyright misuse. On appeal, the Fifth Circuit agreed: "DSC has used its copyright to indirectly gain commercial control over products DSC does not have copyrighted, namely its microprocessor cards."[115] On this basis, the Fifth Circuit denied DSC a permanent injunction. The Fifth Circuit thus established misuse as an alternative theory for excusing copying done during the development of interoperable products.

It should be noted that in a case brought by DSC against Pulse Communications (another developer of interoperable cards) the Federal Circuit rejected Pulse's assertion of fair use with respect to Pulse's loading of DSC's software onto Pulse's cards:

Rather than being a part of an attempt at reverse engineering, the copying appears to have been done after Pulsecom had determined how the system functioned and merely to demonstrate the interchangeability of the Pulsecom cards with those made and sold by DSC.[116]

Here the Federal Circuit drew a clear distinction between product development and product demonstration.

2.2.3   *United States v. Microsoft* (1999)
Once in a while, a passage appears in a judicial opinion that succinctly captures the essence of an exceedingly complex issue. Paragraph 52 of U.S. District Court Judge Jackson's findings of fact in the U.S. government's antitrust action against Microsoft is such a passage.[117] In this one paragraph, Judge Jackson laid to rest many of the vexing factual questions relating to software interoperability in general and reverse engineering in particular. Because interoperability plays a crucial role in permitting competition in the networked environment, these insights are of growing importance as electronic commerce expands.

2.2.3.1   The Context of Paragraph 52
Judge Jackson's lengthy Findings of Fact, issued on November 5, 1999, center on Microsoft's efforts to protect the Application Program Interface (API) barrier to entry.[118] According to Judge Jackson, the large number of

115. *Alcatel U.S.A., Inc., v. DGI Techs., Inc.* 166 F.3d 772, 793 (5th Cir. 1999).
116. *DSC Communications Corp. v. Pulse Communications*, 170 F.3d 1354, 1363 (Fed. Cir. 1999).
117. This subsection is based on Jonathan Band, "Paragraph 52: A Window into Judge Jackson's Findings of Fact," *The Computer Lawyer*, March 2000, at 3. The copyright arguments advanced by the Department of Justice in this case are discussed below in subsection 2.3.1.

application programs written to the APIs exposed by Windows hindered competition from rival operating systems, such as Apple's Mac OS, which could not run these applications. The Findings of Fact recite in great detail Microsoft's efforts to preserve the API barrier to entry by preventing the broad adoption of "middleware," such as Netscape's Navigator, which would run on top of Windows and expose a different and attractive set of APIs to independent software developers.

A critical element in Judge Jackson's analysis was the inability of a competitor to develop an operating system that exposed the same APIs as Windows. In paragraph 46, Judge Jackson recounted IBM's unsuccessful effort: "In late 1994, IBM introduced its Intel-compatible OS/2 Warp operating system and spent millions of dollars in an effort to attract independent software vendors (ISVs) to develop applications for OS/2 and *in an attempt to reverse engineer, or 'clone,' part of the Windows API set*. Despite these efforts, IBM could obtain neither significant market share nor ISV support for OS/2 Warp."[119] In paragraph 52, Judge Jackson drew conclusions from IBM's experience on the feasibility of reverse engineering Windows to uncover the APIs and then replicating them in a competing operating system—a process he referred to as "cloning."

2.2.3.2   The Text of Paragraph 52
Paragraph 52 reads as follows:

Theoretically, the developer of a non-Microsoft, Intel-compatible PC operating system could circumvent the applications barrier to entry by cloning the APIs exposed by the 32-bit versions of Windows (Windows 9x and Windows NT). Applications written for Windows would then also run on the rival operating system, and consumers could use the rival system confident in that knowledge. Translating this theory into practice is virtually impossible, however. First of all, cloning the thousands of APIs already exposed by Windows would be an enormously expensive undertaking. More daunting is the fact that Microsoft continually adds APIs to Windows through updates and new versions. By the time a rival finished cloning the APIs currently in existence, Windows would have exposed a multitude of new ones. Since the rival would never catch up, it would never be able to assure consumers that its operating system would run all of the applications written for Windows. IBM discovered this to its dismay in the mid-1990s when it failed, despite a massive investment, to clone a sufficiently large part of the 32-bit Windows APIs. In short, attempting to clone the 32-bit Windows APIs is such an expensive, uncertain undertaking that it fails to present a practical option for a would-be competitor to Windows.[120]

118. *United States v. Microsoft Corp.*, 84 F. Supp. 2d 9 (D.D.C. 1999).
119. Id. at 22 (emphasis added).
120. Id. at 24.

2.2.3.3   The Lessons of Paragraph 52

As was noted above, Judge Jackson understood the "cloning" of the Windows APIs to include the reverse engineering of Windows to uncover its APIs. Accordingly, in paragraph 52 Judge Jackson stated that the process of reverse engineering Windows to uncover its APIs, and their subsequent incorporation in a competing operating system, was expensive and time consuming—so time consuming, in fact, that the competitor could never keep up with Microsoft. This seemingly simple observation contains many implicit and explicit lessons for the continuing debate about interoperability and competition in the information-technology industry.

The Availability of Interface Information

In numerous forums, Microsoft and other large software companies argued that reverse engineering was not necessary for achieving interoperability, because all the needed interface information could easily be licensed.[121] As IBM's experience recounted in paragraph 52 clearly demonstrates, this information is not made available to would-be competitors. Microsoft may have been willing to license some of this information to an ISV developing an application program designed to run on Windows, but it was not willing to license the full API set to the developer of a competing product—in this case, IBM.

Reverse Engineering Is Expensive

In the global debates over reverse engineering, opponents of the practice argued that it could be accomplished by the push of a button.[122] Indeed, these opponents contended that reverse engineering was so easy that it facilitated "disguised piracy." A pirate could "decompile" the object code of the program into a higher-level language, rename the variables and make other slight alterations, and then recompile the program.[123] This recompiled program would look sufficiently different from the original program to defeat claims of copyright infringement. Paragraph 52 debunks this "disguised piracy" myth. Reverse engineering is so time consuming and expensive that it would never be employed for disguised piracy. In fact, in IBM's case, it was so costly that it prevented IBM from developing a fully compatible operating system.

121. On the Business Software Alliance's presentation to Hong Kong's Legislative Council in 1997, see section 5.3 below.
122. We discuss these global debates in chapter 5.
123. Id.

Legitimate Developers Engage in Reverse Engineering
In the late 1980s and the early 1990s, IBM was one of the major opponents of the legalization of reverse engineering.[124] Yet, as paragraph 52 shows, in 1994 it reverse engineered Windows. Further, there is ample evidence that Microsoft has reverse engineered competitors' products, including America Online's Instant Messaging protocols.[125] Reverse engineering is a basic tool of software development.

Copyright Law Does Not Prevent Reverse Engineering
As important as what Judge Jackson said in paragraph 52 is what he did not say. Specifically, he did not say that copyright law prevented the "cloning" of the Windows APIs. This, of course, is consistent with the Ninth Circuit's ruling in *Sega v. Accolade*[126] that the copying incidental to decompilation was a fair use so long as the decompilation was the only way to uncover the information and the decompilation was performed for a legitimate purpose. It is also consistent with the line of cases, following the Second Circuit's *Computer Associates v. Altai*,[127] that refused to extend copyright protection to interface specifications. (Judge Jackson relied on these cases in an opinion rejecting the motion for summary judgment in which Microsoft argued that its copyright in Windows entitled it to impose whatever terms it wished in its Windows license agreements.[128])

Interface Information Is Essential to Competition
Although Judge Jackson devoted only one paragraph to "cloning," without question that paragraph formed a critical factual predicate for the entire case. "Theoretically," Judge Jackson noted, "the developer of a non-Microsoft, Intel-compatible PC operating system could circumvent the applications barrier to entry"[129] and thereby undermine Microsoft's monopoly. However, "[t]ranslating this theory into practice is virtually impossible"[130] because of the difficulty of reverse engineering a program as complex as

---

124. For example, IBM's opposition to reverse engineering in Australia is discussed below in section 5.1. See also Band and Katoh, *Interfaces on Trial*, at 18–28.
125. Saul Hansell, "In Cyberspace, Rivals Skirmish over Messaging," *New York Times*, July 24, 1999.
126. 977 F.2d 1510 (9th Cir. 1992).
127. 982 F.2d 693 (2d Cir. 1992).
128. *U.S. v. Microsoft*, 1998 U.S. Dist. LEXIS 14231 (D.D.C. September 14, 1998).
129. *Microsoft*, 84 F. Supp. 2d at 24.
130. Id.

Windows. In other words, Microsoft's monopoly in Windows is sustained largely by the difficulty of uncovering information about the Windows APIs. Interface information is the key to competitiveness in the information-technology industry, and there is no competition in the market for PC operating systems because Microsoft maintains tight control over the needed information.

It is interesting to consider how different the computer industry would be today had IBM succeeded in its Windows reverse-engineering effort. For a historical precedent, one can consider Phoenix Technologies' reverse engineering of the IBM PC's basic input/out system (BIOS) in the 1980s. With the information it obtained, Phoenix developed a compatible BIOS, which it then made available to other hardware manufacturers. This contributed significantly to the emergence of the IBM-compatible-PC industry and to the rise of Dell and Gateway.[131]

2.2.4 *Sony v. Connectix* (2000)

As technology has become more pervasive, lawmakers have felt increasing pressure from certain industries and from segments of the public to impose new regulations in an effort to limit technology's perceived harmful affects.[132] Such regulation could be too broad and could have the unintended consequence of frustrating the growth of useful technologies. To avoid that result, lawmakers would be well advised to follow the example of the U.S. Court of Appeals for the Ninth Circuit in *Sony v. Connectix*.[133]

The case concerned Connectix's development of software that emulated the Sony PlayStation. This emulator, called the Virtual Game Station (VGS), enabled a user to run a PlayStation-compatible game on a Macintosh computer. To ensure compatibility between the emulator and the PlayStation games, Connectix had to reverse engineer the Sony PlayStation. One step in the process of reverse engineering involved loading the PlayStation's basic input/output system into a computer and running it repeatedly as Connectix engineers developed software that interacted with it. Once they had completed this software, the Connectix engineers developed their own BIOS to interact with the software. The repeated running of the BIOS caused the making of numerous temporary copies of the BIOS

---

131. See Band and Katoh, *Interfaces on Trial*, at 29–32.

132. This subsection is based on Jonathan Band, "Rules to Live By: The Ninth Circuit's Decision in *Sony v. Connectix*," *Stanford Technology Law Review* (June 2000).

133. *Sony Computer Entertainment, Inc. v. Connectix Corp.*, 203 F.3d 596 (9th Cir.), *cert. denied*, 121 S. Ct. 172 (2000).

in the computer's random-access memory. Sony asserted that these copies infringed its copyright in the BIOS. The district court agreed and issued a preliminary injunction.

Following its decision in *Sega Enters., Ltd., v. Accolade, Inc.*, the Ninth Circuit reversed the district court's decision. It found that the temporary copies were excused under the doctrine of fair use because they were necessary for the uncovering of elements not protected by Sony's copyright—specifically, the BIOS's interface specifications.

Sony suggested that *Sega* applied to disassembly, but not to the making of RAM copies while observing the program's operation. The Ninth Circuit found no reason to distinguish between the different techniques of reverse engineering. Because both methods require intermediate copying, the court reasoned, "we find no reason inherent in these methods to prefer one as a matter of copyright law."[134] The Ninth Circuit also dismissed the district court's finding that Connectix went beyond *Sega* in not only studying the BIOS but also using the BIOS to develop the interoperable software. Reverse engineering, the Ninth Circuit observed, "is a technically complex, frequently iterative process. Within the limited context of a claim of intermediate infringement, we find the semantic distinction between 'studying' and 'use' to be artificial, and decline to adopt it for purposes of determining fair use."[135]

Sony argued that Connectix could have avoided making the RAM copies of the BIOS had it followed a different development process. Connectix could have developed its own BIOS at the beginning, and used that BIOS in the development of the interoperable software, rather than use the Sony BIOS in the development of the interoperable software and then develop its own BIOS.

The Ninth Circuit rejected Sony's argument out of hand:

Even if we were inclined to supervise the engineering solutions of software companies in minute detail, and we are not, our application of the copyright law would not turn on such a distinction. . . . [T]he rule urged by Sony would require that a software engineer, faced with two engineering solutions that each require intermediate copying of protected and unprotected material, often follow the least efficient solution. . . .This is precisely the kind of 'wasted effort that the proscription against the copyright of ideas and facts . . . [i]s designed to prevent.'[136]

The court further observed:

134. *Connectix*, 203 F.3d at 604.
135. Id.
136. Id. at 605 (citations omitted).

Such an approach would erect an artificial hurdle in the way of the public's access to the ideas contained within copyrighted software programs. . . . We decline to erect such a barrier in this case. If Sony wishes to obtain a lawful monopoly in the functional concepts in its software, it must satisfy the more stringent standards of the patent laws.[137]

In the same pro-competition vein, the Ninth Circuit rejected the district court's finding that the Connectix VGS was not transformative under the first fair-use factor because it merely supplanted Sony's PlayStation console. The court noted that the VGS was "a wholly new product" that "afforded game play in new environments, specifically anywhere a Sony PlayStation console and television are not available, but a computer with a CD-ROM drive is."[138]

The Ninth Circuit acknowledged that the VGS might cause Sony to lose some sales of consoles. "But," it noted,

because the Virtual Game Station is transformative, and does not merely supplant the PlayStation console, the Virtual Game Station is a legitimate competitor in the market for platforms on which Sony and Sony-licensed games can be played. For this reason, some economic loss by Sony as a result of this competition does not compel a finding of no fair use. Sony understandably seeks control over the market for devices that play games Sony produces or licenses. The copyright law, however, does not confer such a monopoly.[139]

In sum, the Ninth Circuit refused to supervise the engineering solutions of software companies in minute detail. It declined to force engineers to follow inefficient procedures. Instead, the court focused on the big pic-ture—what Connectix was trying to do, and how that comported with the objectives of the copyright law.

At an even higher level of generality, the court seemed to say that we should be concerned not with the process but with the end result (unless, of course, a process patent is involved). In other words, our laws should not restrict intermediate steps or products. Instead, our laws should pro-hibit only finished products that infringe intellectual-property rights, or the harmful use of non-infringing products (e.g., using a personal computer to upload infringing material onto the Internet). The Ninth Circuit fol-lowed this approach in *Kelly v. Arriba Soft*,[140] finding that fair use permitted

137. Id.
138. Id. at 606.
139. Id. at 607 (citations omitted).
140. 336 F.3d 81 (9th Cir. 2003).

the copying performed by a search engine in the course of developing its search database.

2.2.5 *Cartoon Network v. CSC Holdings* (2008)

The parties in *Connectix*, as well as the Ninth Circuit, assumed that all the RAM copies Connectix made while reverse engineering the Sony PlayStation were copies that could infringe the reproduction right. The U.S. Court of Appeals for the Second Circuit's decision in *Cartoon Network LP v. CSC Holdings, Inc.*[141] requires a reevaluation of that assumption.

Cablevision introduced a network digital video recording (DVR) service whereby users could direct the recording of a television program for later viewing. Rather than program his own DVR, the user would use a remote control to program a server at Cablevision's facility to record the show and store it until the user retrieved it. The server could store the programs recorded by thousands of subscribers. The motion picture studios sued Cablevision for copyright infringement. By stipulation, the parties agreed to focus the litigation on whether Cablevision engaged in direct infringement. The studios agreed to waive arguments that Cablevision was secondarily liable, and Cablevision agreed to waive any fair-use arguments.

The district court found that Cablevision directly infringed in three ways. First, it infringed the reproduction right when it made a temporary buffer copy from which a user could program a copy to be made. Second, Cablevision infringed the reproduction right when it made the copy on its server at the user's direction. Third, Cablevision infringed the performance right when it allowed users to watch the shows they had stored on the Cablevision server.

The Second Circuit reversed the district court on all three issues, but only the first is relevant here. The Second Circuit ruled that the buffer copy Cablevision made did not meet the statutory definition of fixation and thus did not infringe the reproduction right. Section 106(1) of the Copyright Act grants the copyright owner the exclusive right "to reproduce the copyrighted work in copies." Section 101 defines copies as material objects "in which a work is fixed by any method now known or later developed, and from which the work can be perceived, reproduced, or otherwise communicated, either directly or with the aid of a machine or other device." Section 101 also provides that "[a] work is 'fixed' in a tangible medium of expression when its embodiment in a copy . . . , by or under the authority of the author, is sufficiently permanent or stable to permit it to be perceived,

---

141. 536 F.3d 121 (2d Cir. 2008), *cert. denied*, 129 S. Ct. 2890 (2009).

reproduced, or otherwise communicated for a period of more than transitory duration."

In *MAI Systems Corp. v. Peak Computer, Inc.*,[142] the Ninth Circuit found that an operating system loaded into RAM was "fixed" when the operating system's error log was sufficiently permanent or stable to enable an independent service organization to view it in order to identify a computer malfunction. Based on this holding, most courts have assumed that all RAM copies met the statutory definition of fixation.[143] However, the Second Circuit in *Cartoon Network* examined the statutory definition closely and concluded that the buffer copy's 1.2-second existence was too short to satisfy the requirement of being perceptible for "a period of more than transitory duration." The Second Circuit distinguished *MAI* from the other cases involving RAM copies on the ground that in the other cases the copies lasted significantly longer than 1.2 second.

The *Cartoon Network* case did not involve reverse engineering. However, it suggests that some of the RAM copies made during the course of black-box reverse engineering might be so temporary as not to satisfy the statutory definition of fixation. Thus, *Cartoon Network* provides an alternative theory to fair use for permitting at least some of the "copies" made in the course of black-box reverse engineering. Even so, this alternate theory probably cannot be applied to disassembly, which involves the creation of a derivative work, not a copy.

2.3   The Executive Branch's Endorsement of Copyright Case Law

U.S. courts have wrestled with the application of copyright protection to computer programs for more than 20 years.[144] As we have seen, two issues in particular have received great attention in the courts because of their impact on competition in the software industry: the protectability of interface specifications and the permissibility of software reverse engineering. While the courts examined these issues, the executive and legislative branches of the U.S. government largely remained on the sidelines. But

142. 991 F.2d 511 (9th Cir.), *cert. denied*, 510 U.S. 1033 (1993).
143. For a more detailed discussion of temporary copies before the *Cartoon Network* decision, see Jonathan Band and Jeny Marcinko, "A New Perspective on Temporary Copies: The Fourth Circuit's Opinion in *CoStar v. LoopNet*," *Stanford Technology Law Review* (April 2005).
144. This subsection is based on Jonathan Band and Taro Isshiki, "Peace at Last? Executive and Legislative Branch Endorsement of Recent Software Copyright Case Law," *The Computer Lawyer* (February 1999).

once the courts finally reached a consensus on these issues favoring software interoperability, the executive branch and the legislative branch ratified the courts' conclusions.

2.3.1 The Department of Justice

When the Second Circuit in 1992 issued *Computer Associates v. Altai*, the leading decision on the scope of protection for computer programs, the decision provoked extensive discussion in copyright circles and in the software industry. The executive branch, however, remained mum, even as circuit after circuit voiced agreement with the *Computer Associates* court that copyright protection did not extend to the interface specifications of computer programs. However, in *U.S. v. Microsoft*, one of the most important antitrust cases of the 1990s, the executive branch relied heavily on *Computer Associates* and its progeny.[145] This reliance signaled the executive branch's agreement with the reasoning and the results in those cases.

In the antitrust case against Microsoft, the Antitrust Division of the U.S. Department of Justice and nineteen state governments (collectively "the Government") objected to Microsoft's insertion in its licensing agreements of restrictions requiring the pre-installation and display of Internet Explorer and preventing PC manufacturers from utilizing preferred means of developing and installing their own add-on programs or customizing the user interface. In its motion for summary judgment, Microsoft defended this practice on the ground that its copyright in Windows 95 and Windows 98 programs entitled it to impose whatever terms it wished in its Windows license agreements. On August 31, 1998, the Government filed a response that rested heavily on the interoperability cases in its rejection of Microsoft's contentions.

The district court agreed with the Government's arguments and denied Microsoft's motion.[146] But more important than the district court's agreement with the arguments is the fact the Government made them at all. It is now the official policy of the U.S. government that copyright law should be construed narrowly so as not to impede the interoperability of software.

2.3.1.1 No Moral Right In Software

The Government first rejected Microsoft's claim that it had a "moral right" in its software. Recognizing that "moral right" is a European concept largely

---

145. We discuss Judge Jackson's findings in the case concerning reverse engineering in subsection 2.2.3.

146. *U.S. v. Microsoft*, 1998 U.S. Dist. LEXIS 14231 (D.D.C. September 14, 1998).

foreign to American jurisprudence, the Government went on to assert that "whatever policy justifications might exist for a moral right in the integrity of works of art, they are substantially weaker when the work at issue is a computer program."[147] It then proceeded to discuss the functional nature of programs—particularly operating systems—and to note that numerous cases have allowed defendants to make alterations to plaintiffs' programs. In the course of this discussion, the Government cited with approval six of the most important software copyright cases that created the contours of today's software protection: *Lotus v. Borland, DSC v. DGI, Mitel v. Iqtel, Mitek v. Arce, Sega v. Accolade,* and *Vault v. Quaid.*[148]

2.3.1.2   The Limited Scope of Copyright Protection

The Government next refuted Microsoft's argument that it is free to do whatever it wishes in licensing its copyrighted works. Citing *Computer Associates v. Altai* and two Supreme Court cases,[149] the Government argued that copyright does not provide an unbounded property right but rather is a limited power designed to encourage the creation of new works of authorship.

Discussing the limits of copyright with respect to computer programs, the response states that "it is by now well established that the copyright in a computer program cannot extend to the functional aspects of that computer program; to design choices dictated by necessity, cost, convenience or consumer demand."[150] To support this statement, the Government turned to the Tenth Circuit's decision in *Mitel v. Iqtel,* which it summarized as follows: "[I]nterface specifications of a communications protocol are freely copiable because they are functional rather than expressive."[151] The *Mitel* decision squarely addressed and rejected the protectability of interface specifications.

---

147. Response of the United States to Microsoft's Motion for Summary Judgment, *U.S. v. Microsoft,* 1998 U.S. Dist. LEXIS 14231 (D.D.C. September 14, 1998) at 77.

148. *Lotus Dev. Corp. v. Borland Int'l Inc.,* 49 F.3d 807 (1st Cir. 1995), *aff'd by an equally divided Court,* 116 S. Ct. 804 (1996); *DSC Communications v. DGI Technologies,* 81 F.3d 597, 601 (5th Cir. 1996); *Mitel v. Iqtel,* 124 F.3d 1366 (10th Cir. 1997); *Mitek Holdings v. Arce Eng'g,* 89 F.3d 1548 (11th Cir. 1996); *Sega Enterprises Ltd. v. Accolade, Inc.,* 977 F.2d 1510 (9th Cir. 1992); *Vault v. Quaid Software,* 847 F.2d 255 (5th Cir. 1988).

149. *Stewart v. Abend,* 495 U.S. 207 (1990); *Twentieth Century Music Corp. v. Aiken,* 422 U.S. 151 (1975).

150. U.S. Response at 79.

151. Id. *Mitel* is discussed in greater detail above in subsection 2.1.2.4.

2.3.1.3 The Doctrine of Copyright Misuse

The Government then argued that copyright does not provide Microsoft with the unfettered right to license its intellectual property as it sees fit. The Government argued that the doctrine of copyright misuse imposes significant restrictions on the ability of a copyright owner to leverage the copyright into control of adjacent markets, to prevent the development and use of interoperable programs by competitors, or to impose anti-competition restrictions on licensees. The Government found several cases instructive, including *DSC v. DGI*, in which the Fifth Circuit held that it probably was copyright misuse for DSC to use its copyright in the computer program operating a telephone switch to try to prevent a competitor from designing and testing a compatible switch that used DSC's protocol.[152] The response also cited two other appellate decisions, *Lasercomb America v. Reynolds* and *PMI v. AMA*,[153] both of which found copyright misuse where a copyright owner entered into license agreements that restricted its licensees from competing with it.

2.3.1.4 Copyright Confers No Antitrust Immunity

Finally, the Government rebutted Microsoft's claim that licensing of copyrighted materials is exempted from antitrust scrutiny. Noting that a copyright does not give its owner immunity from antitrust laws and other laws of general applicability, the Government stated that a copyright owner may not use licensing agreements to impose anti-competition restrictions on its licensees. Furthermore, the Government quoted Justice Scalia's dissent in *Eastman Kodak v. Image Technical Services*, in which he asserted that power gained through a legal advantage in copyright "can give rise to liability if a seller exploits his dominant position in one market to expand his empire into the next."[154]

2.3.2 The Federal Trade Commission

A few months after the Second Circuit's issuance of *Computer Associates v. Altai*, the Ninth Circuit handed down an equally momentous decision: *Sega v. Accolade*.[155] In *Sega*, the court held that the copying incidental to the reverse engineering of software for the purpose of achieving interoperability

152. 81 F.3d at 601. *DSC* is discussed in greater detail above in subsection 2.2.2.
153. *Lasercomb America v. Reynolds*, 911 F.2d 970 (4th Cir. 1990); *Practice Management Info. Corp. v. American Med. Ass'n*, 121 F.3d 516 (1997), *cert. denied*, 524 U.S. 952.
154. 504 U.S. 451, 498 (1992) (Scalia, J., dissenting).
155. 977 F.2d 1510 (9th Cir. 1992).

was permitted under copyright's fair-use doctrine. Although the U.S. government never questioned the case domestically, in foreign contexts both the Patent and Trademark Office and the Office of the U.S. Trade Representative suggested that *Sega* was a minority view.[156] They did this in an effort to dissuade foreign governments from adopting exceptions to their copyright laws permitting the reverse engineering of software.

However, on October 30, 1998, staff members of the Federal Trade Commission's Policy Planning Office and Bureaus of Consumer Protection and Competition sent a letter[157] to the drafters of article 2B of the Uniform Commercial Code in which they publicly voiced concerns over several of the draft's provisions.[158] In particular, the FTC staff stated that article 2B's provisions could limit the reverse engineering permitted under *Sega* and thereby dampen competition in the software industry. Thus, the FTC staff agreed with the *Sega* court's reasoning and underlying pro-competition policy.

In a section titled "Balance of Innovation and Competition Incentives in Article 2B," the FTC staff explained that article 2B was inconsistent with existing intellectual-property and antitrust laws and policies:

Some provisions in Article 2B implicitly endorse a contracting/licensing structure that allows software and other information to be distributed with significant restrictions on users' rights to compete. Those restrictions could be contract/license terms that explicitly forbid competition with the seller/licensor of the good or terms that restrict in some manner 'reverse engineering,' i.e., the detailed analysis by one firm of another firm's product in order to produce a related good.[159]

The FTC staff summarized the testimony the FTC had received during its 1995 hearings on Competition Policy in the New High-Tech, Global Market. It discussed expert testimony that "next-generation innovations

156. See, e.g., Band and Katoh, *Interfaces on Trial* at 297–316. Also see sections 5.1 and 5.3 of the present volume.
157. The first footnote in the letter notes: "This comment represents the views of the Bureaus of Consumer Protection and Competition and of the Policy Planning office and does not necessarily represent the views of the FTC or any individual Commissioner. The FTC, however, has authorized the staff to submit this comment."
158. Proposed article 2B of the Uniform Commercial Code ultimately became the Uniform Computer Information Transactions Act (UCITA). The interoperability debate in the context of article 2B/UCITA is discussed below in subsection 4.2.2.
159. Letter from the staff of the Federal Trade Commission Policy Planning Office and Bureaus of Consumer Protection and Competition to the drafters of article 2B of the Uniform Commercial Code (October 30, 1998) at 5, available at www.ftc.gov.

. . . are often built on the basis of access to information regarding prior-generation products."[160] Accordingly, contractual restrictions on access to such information may inhibit the quantity, the quality, and the rate of future innovation.

The FTC staff then surveyed relevant principles of intellectual-property law and quoted the Supreme Court's statement in *Feist v. Rural Telephone*[161] that copyright "assures authors the right to their original expression, but encourages others to build freely upon the ideas and information conveyed in a work." The FTC staff noted that "several courts of appeal have held that the Copyright Act's protection for 'fair use' of a copyrighted product precludes a software vendor's attempt to enjoin a purchaser's reverse engineering."[162] The staff proceeded to quote passages from the Ninth Circuit's decision in *Sega v. Accolade*:

The Ninth Circuit . . . found that if it were to hold that reverse engineering "is *per se* an unfair use, the owner of the copyright [would gain] a de facto monopoly over the functional aspects of his work—aspects that were expressly denied copyright protection by Congress." The court said that such "an attempt to monopolize the market by making it impossible for others to compete runs counter to the [Copyright Act's] statutory purpose of promoting creative expression and cannot constitute a strong equitable basis for resisting the invocation of the fair use doctrine."[163]

The FTC staff turned to copyright-misuse and antitrust cases in which copyright owners had attempted to use licensing to expand their copyright protection. Citing *PMI* and *Lasercomb*, the staff observed that restrictions that run afoul of the copyright laws include: a provision requiring the licensee to use the licensor's product exclusively; and a provision suppressing any attempt by the licensee to independently implement the idea expressed by the licensor's product.

After this survey of applicable legal principles, the FTC staff addressed article 2B. It objected to article 2B's broad scope of "contractual use restriction" on the ground that it could inhibit innovation and competition in the markets for computer software and other products containing information. Under article 2B, the reverse engineering necessary to develop a product could be prohibited by a license term. Although such a term may well be unenforceable under the copyright laws or the antitrust laws, article 2B declares that the restrictive term "would in most circumstances be

160. Id. at 6.
161. 499 U.S. 340, 350 (1991).
162. FTC staff letter at 7.
163. Id. (citations omitted).

enforceable."[164] In the FTC staff's view, this statement of presumptive validity could discourage licensees from asserting rights under federal and state
intellectual-property and antitrust laws.

2.4 Congress's Endorsement of Copyright Case Law

Not to be left out of the act, Congress expressed its support for software
reverse engineering and interoperability. Section 1201 of the Digital Millennium Copyright Act, passed by Congress in October of 1998, implements
the provisions of the World Intellectual Property Organization Internet
Treaties relating to technological protection measures.[165] Specifically, section 1201 prohibits the development, distribution, and use of technologies that circumvent other technologies that protect an author's copyright.
Developers of interoperable software explained to Congress that this prohibition could prevent reverse engineering necessary for achieving interoperability. If a software vendor placed a software "lock" on a program that
prevented the reverse engineering of the program, the circumvention of
that software lock would violate section 1201. Thus, section 1201 could
prevent the interoperable software developer from exercising the fair-use
privilege recognized in *Sega*. Accordingly, Congress created an exception
explicitly directed at reverse engineering. Section 1201(f) allows software
developers to circumvent technological protection measures in a lawfully
obtained computer program in order to identify the elements necessary
to achieve interoperability of an independently created computer program
with other programs. Section 1201 also permits a person to develop and
employ technological means to circumvent for the purpose of achieving
interoperability.[166] This exception represents the first Congressional recognition of the legitimacy of software reverse engineering.

164. The proposal recognized only *enforceable* "contractual use restrictions." See §
2B-102 Reporter's Note 11: "The adjective 'enforceable' clarifies that the definition
does not include terms invalidated under this Article or other law, including federal
intellectual-property law and state laws which limit enforcement of some restrictions
on use of information."
165. 17 U.S.C. § 1201. We discuss the DMCA's impact on interoperability in chapter 3.
166. Thus, section 1201(f) provides an exception to all the prohibitions of section
1201: section 1201(a)(1)'s prohibition on the circumvention of access controls, section 1201(a)(2)'s prohibition on the manufacture and distribution of devices which
circumvent access controls, and section 1201(b)'s prohibition on the manufacture
and distribution of devices which circumvent copy controls.

To be sure, Congress *did not* say that all software reverse engineering was permissible, or that all copying incidental to reverse engineering would always be a fair use. Rather, Congress simply indicated that it would permit circumvention when the underlying reverse engineering was not an infringement. But permitting circumvention when this condition was met indicated that Congress believed that the condition could be met—that is, that the copying incidental to reverse engineering could be a fair use. This signals Congress's basic agreement with the judicial rulings in *Sega v. Accolade* and its progeny.

The Senate Judiciary Committee's report could not have been clearer on the committee's agreement with *Sega*. The report stated that this exception was "intended to allow legitimate software developers to continue engaging in certain activities for the purpose of achieving interoperability to the extent permitted by law prior to the enactment of this chapter."[167] The committee evidently understood that if a dominant vendor placed on its program a technological measure that prevented reverse engineering, a legal prohibition on circumventing that technological protection could preclude other companies from obtaining the interface information necessary to operate in the dominant vendor's computing environment. Citing *Sega*, the committee stated that "[t]he objective is to ensure that the effect of current case law interpreting the Copyright Act is not changed by enactment of this legislation for certain acts of identification and analysis done in respect of computer programs."[168] The committee concluded by noting that "[t]he purpose of this section is to foster competition and innovation in the computer and software industry."[169]

In this passage, the Senate Judiciary Committee asserted that *Sega v. Accolade* is good law. Although this is an obvious proposition to serious students of software copyright law, the Patent and Trademark Office and the Office of the United States Trade Representative, as well as some software industry representatives, argued that *Sega* was a minority view and not entitled to much deference.[170] This passage significantly undermined that argument. Further, in this passage the Senate Judiciary Committee recognized not only that *Sega* is good law, but also that it is good policy: Reverse engineering "foster[s] competition and innovation in the computer and software industry."[171]

167. S. Rep. No. 105–190, at 32 (1998).
168. Id.
169. Id.
170. See chapter 5 below.
171. S. Rep. No. 105–190, at 32 (1998).

The FTC letter and section 1201 of the Digital Millennium Copyright Act indicate that it is the policy of the U.S. government to encourage competition in the software industry by eliminating barriers on reverse engineering. Likewise, the Government's brief in the *Microsoft* case proclaims that copyright law cannot be abused to prevent legitimate competition. The executive and legislative branches have caught up with the judicial branch, and the pro-competition position of the U.S. government is unambiguous.

3   Interoperability under the DMCA

Section 1201 of the Digital Millennium Copyright Act (DMCA), passed by Congress in October of 1998, implements the provisions of the World Intellectual Property Organization Internet Treaties relating to technological protection measures. Specifically, section 1201 prohibits the development, distribution, and use of technologies that circumvent other technologies that protect an author's copyright. Developers of interoperable software explained to Congress that this prohibition could prevent reverse engineering that was necessary for achieving interoperability. If a software vendor placed on a program a software "lock" that prevented reverse engineering of the program, the circumvention of that software lock would violate section 1201. Thus, section 1201 could prevent a developer of interoperable software from exercising the fair-use privilege recognized in *Sega v. Accolade*.

Fortunately Congress, in response to advocacy by developers of interoperable software, included in the DMCA an exception explicitly directed at software reverse engineering and interoperability. And the courts generally have refused to apply the DMCA in a manner that prevents interoperability.

3.1   The Long Road to the DMCA

3.1.1   The Green Paper
In July of 1994, the Clinton administration's Working Group on Intellectual Property (chaired by Bruce Lehman, the Commissioner of the Patent and Trademark Office) issued a Green Paper that proposed a prohibition on the production and distribution of devices that circumvent anticopying technology.[1] The copyright community, including the Motion Picture

---

1. This subsection is based on Jonathan Band, "Throwing Out the Baby with the Bathwater, or Can Congress Prohibit Anticopy Circumvention Devices without Preventing Legitimate Copying?" *Computer Law Reporter*, March 1996, at 7. For a detailed discussion of the DMCA and its history, see Jessica Litmann, *Digital Copyright* (Prometheus, 2001).

Association of America, the Recording Industry Association of America, and the Business Software Alliance, lobbied vigorously for such a prohibition as an essential weapon in their battle against infringement in the digital age. But the policy rationale for the prohibition was based on a series of assumptions that contained a fundamental logical flaw. The proponents of a circumvention ban assumed that the ease of infringement that digital networks made possible would encourage widespread disregard of the copyright laws. The proponents further assumed that technological protection measures could prevent this infringement. The proponents, however, recognized that the technological protection measures could be circumvented. Accordingly, the proponents supported legal remedies against the circumvention of technological protection measures. The logical flaw in this argument is as follows: If people would disregard a legal prohibition on reproduction and dissemination of copyrighted works, why would they respect a legal prohibition on circumvention of technological protection measures? In particular, why would they respect a legal prohibition on circumvention when they could readily access the circumvention tools using the Internet? The copyright community certainly had legitimate concerns that the Internet could erode the legal protection afforded by copyright. Nonetheless, the Working Group on Intellectual Property should have recognized that in the digital environment a circumvention law would be no more effective than a copyright law.

In the four years between the issuance of the Green Paper (1994) and the adoption of the DMCA (1998), there was extensive discussion of the need for and the likely effectiveness of a ban on circumvention. Within this broad discussion, there was a narrower debate on the effect of a circumvention prohibition on interoperability. Although the circumvention provision first proposed by the Green Paper was intended to prevent wholesale misappropriation of copyrighted works flowing through the information infrastructure, it arguably might have restricted certain forms of software reverse engineering. If, for example, a software developer included in her program some code that prevented the disassembly of the program,[2] disabling the anti-disassembly code for the purpose of performing otherwise lawful reverse engineering might have been unlawful under the terms of the proposed provision.

The European Union's Software Directive requires the member states to prohibit the distribution or a possession of devices for circumventing anticopying technology, but it explicitly states that this prohibition shall

2. Disassembly involves translation of machine-readable object code into a higher-level, human-readable form.

not prejudice reverse-engineering rights under articles 5 and 6.[3] Conversely, the Green Paper's proposed language did not contain a reverse-engineering exemption. Instead, it broadly provided that "[n]o person shall import, manufacture or distribute any device . . . the primary purpose or effect of which is to avoid . . . , without authority of the copyright owner or the law, any process . . . which prevents. . . the violation of any of the exclusive rights under section 106."[4] In the comment period after this proposal, several trade associations noted that this language might prevent the manufacture of anticopying-circumvention devices that are used to enable the making of lawful copies—e.g., back-up copies under 17 U.S.C. §117 or fair-use copies created during the course of reverse engineering.[5] Working Group officials responded that the phrase "without the authority of . . . the law" restricted the provision to circumvention of anticopy devices for unlawful purposes. The trade associations pointed out that the provision's "primary purpose or effect" test undermined this restriction. The American Committee for Interoperable Systems (ACIS) explained:

[C]onsider a software vendor who has incorporated an anticopy device in its business software applications. Another vendor develops a mechanism that can circumvent the anticopy device. A year after this mechanism is placed on the market, it is determined that 55% of the copies made using the mechanism are unlawful copies, while 45% of the copies are lawful section 117 archival copies. Under such circumstances, what would be the "primary purpose or effect" of the mechanism? It seems clear that such a mechanism would be illegal under the proposed section. . . . It seems equally clear that this result would be inconsistent with the purposes and policies underlying the Copyright Act. To be sure, the makers of the unlawful copies are infringers and should be liable for damages, and, where appropriate, criminal penalties. At the same time, the vendors of the circumvention mechanism should be free from liability.[6]

ACIS also distinguished the other anticopying-circumvention provisions cited by the Green Paper as analogies. In particular, ACIS noted that the Serial Copyright Management System provision in the Audio Home

3. Council Directive 91/250/EEC, art. 7(1)(c), 1991 O.J. (L 122). The 1999 amendments to the Australian copyright law contain a similar provision. See subsection 5.1.3.2 of the present volume.

4. Information Infrastructure Task Force, *Intellectual Property and the National Information Infrastructure* 128 (July 1994).

5. Two associations that raised concerns were the American Committee for Interoperable Systems and the Computer & Communications Industry Association.

6. ACIS Comments on Intellectual Property Issues Involved in the National Information Infrastructure Initiative 5, n. 5 (December 10, 1993).

Recording Act permitted the end user to make at least one digital copy and unlimited analog copies of a digital original.

At the request of the U.S. government, expansive anticopying-circumvention language appeared in an October 5, 1994 draft of the proposed Protocol to the Berne Convention.[7] This too elicited the concern of developers of interoperable programs. In a letter to PTO Commissioner Lehman concerning the Berne Protocol proposal, ACIS acknowledged that devices that defeat anticopy technologies could threaten the exclusive rights of authors, but argued as follows:

U.S. law clearly permits the making of reproductions without the author's permission under certain circumstances. . . . Accordingly, any provision intended to regulate anti-copy circumvention devices must be carefully drafted so as to accommodate the making of lawful reproductions. . . . One possible approach would be to focus on the products resulting from the use of anti-copy circumvention devices, rather than on the devices themselves.[8]

3.1.2 The White Paper

Notwithstanding the aforementioned critique, the Working Group's final report—the so-called White Paper, issued on September 5, 1995—retained the anticopying-circumvention language. The White Paper did, however, reply to the concerns raised by ACIS and others. The White Paper first argued that "[t]he fair use doctrine does not require a copyright owner to allow or to facilitate unauthorized access or use of a work" and that "[o]therwise . . . museums could not require entry fees or prohibit the taking of photographs."[9] Accordingly, the fact that the provision might chill fair-use rights was not seen as a legitimate ground for amending or eliminating the provision. Second, the White Paper repeated the Working Group's earlier assertion that a circumvention device "primarily intended and used for legal purposes, such as fair use"[10] would not violate the provision. Nevertheless, the White Paper acknowledged that manufacturers "may inadvertently find themselves liable for devices which they intended for legal purposes, but which have the incidental effect of circumventing copyright protection systems."[11] Accordingly, the White Paper proposed the adoption

---

7. Memorandum of WIPO International Bureau, ¶ 98(a)(i) (October 5, 1994).

8. Letter from Peter Choy, ACIS Chairman, to Bruce Lehman, Commissioner, U.S. Patent and Trademark Office (November 23, 1994).

9. Information Infrastructure Task Force, *Intellectual Property and the National Information Infrastructure*, at 231.

10. Id.

11. Id. at 233, n. 569.

of an innocent-infringer provision whereby a court could reduce damages if the violator proves that it "was not aware and had no reason to believe that its actions constituted a violation."[12]

On September 28, 1995, the White Paper's legislative proposals, including the anticopying-circumvention language that was included as a new section (1201) in the Copyright Act, were introduced in both the House of Representatives (as H.R. 2441) and the Senate (as S. 1284). On November 15, 1995, in a joint Senate Judiciary Committee–House Intellectual Property Subcommittee hearing on the legislation, Register of Copyrights Marybeth Peters specifically addressed the proposed section 1201, noting that "the Copyright Office supports the concept of outlawing devices or services that defeat copyright protection systems."[13] Nonetheless, Peters expressed concerns about the "breadth of the language of Section 120[1] as drafted."[14] With respect to the "primary purpose" test, Register Peters observed that "'purpose' is often difficult to prove, and which of several potential purposes is 'primary' may not be evident."[15] Similarly, with respect to the "primary effect" test, she said "it is possible that a device intended for entirely legitimate purposes may be put to use primarily to defeat copyright protection technology, or that some unrelated function of a device may unintentionally interfere with such technology."[16] Although she acknowledged the "innocent violation" defense, Peters preferred "to define the offense so as not to potentially sweep within its scope legitimate business behavior."[17]

Despite her concern that section 1201 as drafted could restrict legitimate business behavior, Register Peters agreed with the White Paper in its rejection of the argument that section 1201 was flawed because it could restrict legitimate copying such as disassembly: "It has always been a fundamental principle of copyright law that the copyright owner has no obligation to make his work available to the public."[18] Peters's and the White Paper's analysis on this point, however, appears misdirected, as an examination of their examples reveals. The White Paper noted that a museum

12. Id.
13. Joint Hearing on H.R. 2441 and S. 1284 Before the House Subcomm. on Courts, Intellectual Property, and the Administration of Justice of the House Comm. on the Judiciary, and the Senate Judiciary Committee, 104th Cong. 24 (1995) (statement of Marybeth Peters, Register of Copyrights).
14. Id. at 25.
15. Id.
16. Id.
17. Id.
18. Id. at 26.

may require an entry fee and may prohibit the taking of photographs of a displayed painting. The White Paper neglected to mention, however, that the museum owns the painting itself but does not own the copyright in the painting. The museum's ability to charge an entry fee and prohibit photography is not a function of federal copyright law, but a function of state property and contract law. The White Paper did not explain why the Copyright Act should be amended to improve enforcement of rights under state property and contract law.

Register Peters's example involved an author who chose to keep his work locked in his office. To be sure, it would be unlawful for a would-be fair user to break into the office to gain access to the work; the violation, however, would not be of the federal Copyright Act, but of the state penal code (which criminalizes breaking and entering) and of state property law (which prohibits trespassing). In short, although copyright law tradition- ally does not require access, it does not prevent access either. Rather, access is prevented by state law.

3.1.3   The WIPO Diplomatic Conference

As has been noted above, the Clinton administration was advancing the anticopying-circumvention provision in the World Intellectual Property Organization as well as in Congress. On November 15, 1995, in the joint hearing, Senator Orrin Hatch made it clear that he did not want the Berne Protocol process to preempt Congress's consideration of the pending leg- islation in any way. Further, in his statement introducing S. 1284, Senator Hatch emphasized that the bill in its present form was just the "starting point" of an in-depth deliberative process. Nonetheless, PTO Commis- sioner Lehman aggressively pushed the circumvention issue at the WIPO Diplomatic Conference in Geneva in December of 1996. At the Diplomatic Conference, WIPO adopted a Copyright Treaty and a Performances and Phonograms Treaty. Both treaties contained provisions requiring contract- ing parties to provide legal remedies against the circumvention of techno- logical measures that protect authors' copyrights.[19] In short, Commissioner Lehman did precisely what Senator Hatch had instructed him not to do.

---

19. Article II of the WIPO Copyright Treaty states: "Contracting Parties shall provide adequate legal protection and effective legal remedies against circumvention of effective technological measures that are used by authors in connection with the exer- cise of their rights under this treaty or the Berne Convention and that restrict acts, in respect of their works, which are not authorized by the authors concerned or permitted by law." Article 18 of the WIPO Performances and Phonograms Treaty contains similar language. (See the final section of the Statutory Appendix to the present volume.)

He did an end-run around Congress by convincing WIPO to include in
two treaties a prohibition on circumvention of technological protection
measures.

3.1.4 The Administration's Proposal for Implementation of the WIPO Treaties

After the 1996 WIPO Diplomatic Conference, the U.S. Patent and Trademark Office began formulating the Clinton administration's proposal for
implementing the WIPO treaties.[20] The PTO's proposal was modified by
the Office of the General Counsel of the Department of Commerce, which
submitted it to Congress in July of 1997. The Administration's proposal was
promptly introduced in both chambers.[21] Although the final law enacted
by Congress is more balanced than the Clinton administration's proposal,
the basic framework of the administration's section 1201 endured in the
legislation enacted by Congress.

Section 1201(a)(1) prohibits gaining unauthorized access to a work
by circumventing a technological protection measure (e.g., encryption)
put in place by the copyright owner to control access to the copyrighted
work.[22] To facilitate enforcement of the copyright owner's ability to control access to his copyrighted work, section 1201(a)(2) prohibits manufacturing or making available technologies, products, and services that can
be used to defeat technological measures controlling access.[23] Similarly,
section 1201(b) prohibits the manufacture and distribution of the means
of circumventing technological measures protecting the rights of a copyright owner (e.g., measures that prevent reproduction). Thus, section 1201
prohibits two categories of circumvention devices: those that circumvent
access-control technologies (section 1201(a)(2)) and those that circumvent

---

20. This subsection is based on Jonathan Band and Taro Isshiki, "The New Anti-
Circumvention Provisions in the Copyright Act: A Flawed First Step," *Cyberspace
Lawyer*, February 1999, at 2.

21. H.R. 2281, 105th Cong. (1997); S. 1121, 105th Cong. (1997).

22. 17 U.S.C. § 1201(a)(1). To "circumvent a technological measure" means to
"descramble a scrambled work, to decrypt an encrypted work, or otherwise avoid,
bypass, remove, deactivate, or impair a technological protection measure." A technological measure effectively controls access to a work "if the measure, in the ordinary
course of its operation, requires the application of information, or process or treatment, with the authority of the copyright owner, to gain access to the work." 17
U.S.C. § 1201(a)(3). The full text of section 1201 appears in the Statutory Appendix
to the present volume.

23. 17 U.S.C. §§ 1201(a)(2), (b).

copy-control technologies (section 1201(b)).[24] Violation of section 1201 leads to civil and criminal liability. A repeat offender can be imprisoned for 10 years and fined $1 million.

While the Clinton administration was still formulating its proposal, manufacturers of personal computers noted that a PC could be programmed to function as a circumvention device. To ensure that legitimate multi-purpose devices could continue to be made and sold, the administration limited the prohibition to devices primarily designed or produced for the purpose of circumventing, devices that have only a limited commercially significant purpose or use other than to circumvent, and devices marketed for use in circumventing. Even with this modification, the provision still had fundamental defects: it prohibited the circumvention of access controls for lawful purposes, and it prohibited the manufacture and distribution of technologies that enabled circumvention for lawful purposes. To be sure, the administration inserted a savings clause (now section 1201(c)) stating that section 1201 did not affect rights, remedies, limitations, or defenses to copyright infringement. A defense to copyright infringement, however, is *not* a defense to the independent prohibition on circumvention and circumvention devices established in the new chapter 12 of Title 17. The Clinton administration made another modification that gave the appearance of addressing this issue. Section 1201(b) originally contained a provision parallel to section 1201(a)(1)—a prohibition on the act of circumventing a copy control. The administration eliminated this provision in response to the library and education communities' concerns about the impact of the legislation on fair use. The administration suggested that if the prohibition on the circumvention of copy controls were to be eliminated, a library engaged in such circumvention for purposes of replacement copying (permitted under 17 U.S.C. § 108) would incur no liability. Though this is technically correct, the administration failed to note that so long as section 1201(b) prohibited the manufacture of devices that could circumvent copy controls, the library had no way of engaging in the circumvention necessary to exercise its section 108 privilege.

Thus, the section 1201 proposed by the Clinton administration would have allowed the copyright owner to "circumvent" the panoply of exceptions and limitations on copyright owners' exclusive rights established by Congress and the courts over the course of 200 years. A copyright owner

---

24. Section 1201(b) also prohibits the manufacture of devices that circumvent technologies which protect the copyright owner's other rights under the Copyright Act, including the distribution and performance rights.

could surround his or her work with a technological protection, and could thereby prevent purchasers from making fair-use copies because the necessary devices would not be available. Moreover, under the regime established by section 1201, a copyright owner could, as a practical matter, extend the term in the work indefinitely, because the uncircumventable technological protection would prevent reproduction once the term expired.

3.1.5 Introduction of Alternatives

Recognizing the basic defect just noted, Senator John Ashcroft (R-MO) and Representatives Rick Boucher (D-VA) and Tom Campbell (R-CA) introduced alternative legislation implementing the WIPO treaties.[25] The Ashcroft-Boucher-Campbell (ABC) approach read as follows:

No person, *for the purpose of facilitating or engaging in an act of infringement*, shall engage in conduct so as knowingly to remove, deactivate or otherwise circumvent the application or operation of any effective technological measure used by a copyright owner to preclude or limit reproduction of a work or a portion thereof.[26]

Unlike the Clinton administration's proposal, the ABC formulation focused only on the act of circumvention, not on circumvention devices. Moreover, the ABC formulation did not target all acts of circumvention, only acts of circumvention that facilitated infringement. This would have permitted circumvention for non-infringing purposes.

The copyright community rejected the ABC formulation as too difficult to enforce; it feared that if circumvention devices were available to consumers, consumers would engage in circumvention that would lead to infringement. Accordingly, the copyright community urged Congress to proceed with the administration's proposal to ban circumvention devices.

Notwithstanding the absence of any evidence supporting the copyright community's concerns of rampant circumvention, Congress decided to follow the Clinton administration's proposal. However, it soon became aware that the administration's proposal, because of its breadth, prohibited many legitimate activities. Thus, as the bill advanced through Congress, numerous exceptions were grafted onto section 1201. These exceptions have different thresholds for qualification, and apply to different subsections of section 1201. The result is a confusing patchwork of prohibitions and exceptions that encourages litigation and impedes innovation. By being responsive to the copyright community's concerns, Congress adopted an

25. S. 1146, 105th Cong. (1997); H.R. 3048, 105th Cong. (1997).
26. S. 1146, § 1201 (emphasis added).

approach that restricts access to information and threatens technological development.

In Congress's defense, another dynamic was in operation with respect to section 1201 in addition to responsiveness to the copyright community: the grand compromise of the Digital Millennium Copyright Act. Title I of the DMCA, which implemented the WIPO treaties, benefited the copyright community. Congress offset this benefit with a provision the copyright community did not want: title II of the DMCA, which limited the copyright-infringement liability of online service providers. In other words, Congress did not consider section 1201 in isolation, as we are doing here. Rather, it considered section 1201 in the context of a much broader piece of legislation, and it concluded that this broader legislation, taken as a whole, achieved a relatively balanced result.

3.1.6 Exceptions and Limitations to Section 1201

Only the reverse-engineering exception in section 1201(f) relates to interoperability. However, the other exceptions are worth considering.

3.1.6.1 Interoperability

Section 1201(f) allows software developers to circumvent technological protection measures in a lawfully obtained computer program in order to identify the elements necessary to make an independently created computer program interoperable other programs. A person may engage in this circumvention only if the elements necessary to achieve interoperability are not readily available and the reverse engineering is otherwise permitted under the copyright law.[27] A person may develop the tools necessary for such circumvention, whether for his own use or for use by other reverse engineers. Furthermore, a person may develop and employ technological means to circumvent, and may make such means available to others, for the purpose of achieving interoperability. In other words, section 1201(f) provides an interoperability exception to all the prohibitions of section 1201: section 1201(a)(1)'s prohibition on the circumvention of access controls, section 1201(a)(2)'s prohibition on the manufacture and distribution of devices that circumvent access controls, and section 1201(b)'s prohibition on the manufacture and distribution of devices that circumvent copy controls. This exception is notable in several respects.

First, section 1201(f), although it is titled "Reverse engineering," goes far beyond circumvention for reverse engineering. It expressly permits the

---

27. 17 U.S.C. § 1201(f).

Table 3.1
Exceptions to section 1201 of the DMCA.

	1201(a)—Access Controls		1201(b)—Copy Controls
	Circumvention	Devices	Devices
Interoperability	x	x	x
Encryption research	x	x	
Security testing	x	x	
Law enforcement	x	x	x
Monitoring children		x	
Privacy	x		
Libraries	x		
Rulemaking	x		

development and use of technological means of circumventing a technological measure for the purpose of enabling interoperability. In other words, a user may circumvent the lock on a platform every time he wishes to run an application on that platform. Moreover, a developer may provide the user with the lock-pick. Thus, section 1201(f)(2) provides an exemption from DMCA liability for circumvention of persistent access controls that prevent interoperability.[28] However, the exemption evaporates if the circumvention infringes copyright or violates another provision of law, such as the Computer Fraud and Abuse Act (18 U.S.C. § 1030).

Second, the definition of "interoperability," and the language describing the acts of reverse engineering that justify circumvention, come directly from article 6 of the EU Software Directive. This may well be the first time language from an EU directive has been incorporated verbatim into the U.S. Code. Incorporation of article 6 language was no accident. Competing factions of the computer industry have long fought over the permissibility of software reverse engineering. The language of the Software Directive, adopted in 1991, resulted from a compromise between these factions. Accordingly, it was only logical to include this language, which both factions could accept, in the U.S. statute.[29]

28. Although section 1201(f) does go beyond reverse engineering, permitting circumvention for reverse engineering is obviously one of its major objectives. On the Senate Judiciary Committee's endorsement of *Sega v. Accolade* in its report on the DMCA, see section 2.4 of the present volume.
29. For a more detailed discussion of the history and meaning of the European Software Directive, see Band and Katoh, *Interfaces on Trial* at 227–262.

Third, although Congress crafted a useful exception with respect to software reverse engineering for purposes of interoperability, circumvention (and circumvention devices) enabling reverse engineering for other purposes remains unlawful. Thus, it appears that a programmer is prohibited from circumventing when he is engaged in error correction or determining whether the target of the reverse engineering infringes his copyright. Representative John Dingell, then the ranking Democrat on the House Energy and Commerce Committee, expressed concern that this exception was too narrow: "That provision is drafted narrowly to protect reverse engineering that is undertaken solely for the purpose of developing 'interoperable' products. While building 'interoperable' products may be a valuable exercise for software developers and producers of electronic games, many U.S. manufacturers use reverse-engineering techniques to build a *better* mousetrap." But Representative Dingell did not succeed in broadening the exception.[30]

3.1.6.2 Encryption Research

Congress provided an exception for encryption research. The exception was intended to advance the state of knowledge in the field of encryption technology and to assist in the development of encryption products.[31] Congress recognized that "[t]he development of encryption science requires ongoing research and testing by scientists of existing encryption methods in order to build on those advances, thus promoting encryption technology generally."[32] Such testing often involves "ethical hacking" in which efforts are made to circumvent the encryption.

Circumvention in the course of good-faith encryption research may be allowed if the following conditions are met: the researcher lawfully obtained the copyrighted work; circumvention is necessary for the encryption research; the researcher made a good-faith effort to obtain authorization from the copyright owner before the circumvention; and circumvention is otherwise permissible under the applicable laws.[33] In addition to these conditions, section 1201(g) directs the court to consider three other factors: whether the information derived from the research was disseminated to advance the knowledge or development of encryption technology or to

30. Statement of the Honorable John D. Dingell regarding the markup of H.R. 2281 (June 17, 1998).
31. 17 U.S.C. § 1201(g).
32. Comm. on the Judiciary, 105th Cong., Section-By-Section Analysis of H.R. 2281 as Passed by the United States House of Representatives on August 4, 1998, at 16 (1998).
33. 17 U.S.C. § 1201(g)(2).

facilitate infringement; whether the researcher is engaged in a legitimate course of study, is employed, or is appropriately trained or experienced in the field of encryption technology; and whether the researcher timely notifies the copyright owner with the findings and documentation of the research.[34]

Furthermore, a person may develop and employ or provide to his collaborator technological means to circumvent for the sole purpose of performing acts of good-faith encryption research. Unlike the reverse-engineering exception, which applies to both access controls and copy controls (sections 1201(a) and (b)), the encryption-research exception applies only to access controls (section 1201(a)).

3.1.6.3   Security Testing

In addition to the exception for encryption research, section 1201 provides another exception for information-security activities. The exception for security testing was added during the last days of the 105th Congress to resolve concerns related to how the anti-circumvention provision might affect efforts to test "the security value and effectiveness of the technological measures" employed to protect "the integrity and security of computers, computer systems, or computer networks." Sometimes the only way for a company to test the security software that it has purchased to protect its computer network is to try to circumvent that software. The conference report analogizes this to a consumer's "installing [a] lock on the front door and seeing if it can be picked."[35] Because the company does not own the copyright in the security software, this circumvention could run afoul of section 1201. The conference report explains that "the conferees were concerned that section 1201(g)'s exclusive focus on encryption-related research does not encompass the entire range of legitimate information security activities" and that "not every technological means that is used to provide security relies on encryption technology, or does so to the exclusion of other methods."[36]

The security-testing exception permits circumvention of access controls conducted in the course of security testing if the circumvention is otherwise legal under applicable law.[37] Security testing is defined as obtaining access to a computer system, with the authorization of the owner or operator of

34. 17 U.S.C. § 1201(g)(3).
35. H.R. Rep. No. 105-796, at 67 (1998) (Conf. Rep.).
36. Id. at 66.
37. 17 U.S.C. § 1201(j).

the computer system, for the sole purpose of testing, investigating, or correcting a potential or actual security flaw or vulnerability.[38] Section 1201(j)(3) requires a court, in determining whether this exception is applicable, to consider whether the information derived from the security testing was used solely to promote the security measures and whether it was used or maintained so as not to facilitate infringement.[39] The conference report makes clear that the circumvention for purposes of security testing can be performed either by the operator of a computer system or by a firm retained to perform such testing.[40] Section 1201(j)(4) also permits development, production, or distribution of technological means for the sole purpose of performing permitted acts of security testing.[41] Like the encryption-research exception, the security-testing exception applies only to section 1201(a) (access controls), and not to section 1201(b) (copy controls).

3.1.6.4 Law-Enforcement and Intelligence Activities
Section 1201(e) permits circumvention and the development of circumvention devices for any lawfully authorized investigative, protective, or intelligence activity by a federal, state, or local government employee, or by a person under contract to the federal government, to a state government, or to a local government.[42] Expanding the exception to contractors is particularly important because it allows the private sector to develop circumvention devices for use by government in law-enforcement activities.

3.1.6.5 Protection of Minors
As the Digital Millennium Copyright Act moved through Congress, concerns were raised that section 1201 might prevent parents from effectively monitoring their children's use of the Internet. Section 1201(h) was added to allow the development of circumvention components that would permit a parent to access a restricted site visited by his or her child. Section 1201(h) is drafted so narrowly, however, that few product developers are likely to take advantage of it. Rather than giving a clear exception for such a component, section 1201(h) merely permits a court to consider whether the component has this beneficial purpose. It does not tell a court what to do once it determines that this is the component's purpose. Moreover,

38. 17 U.S.C. § 1201(j)(1).
39. 17 U.S.C. § 1201(j)(3).
40. H.R. Rep. No. 105-796, at 66–67 (1998) (Conf. Rep.).
41. 17 U.S.C. § 1201(j)(4).
42. 17 U.S.C. § 1201(e).

it applies only if the component is included in a product that does not itself violate the provisions of section 1201.[43] In other words, a stand-alone device intended to perform this function is not permitted. Finally, even if a company develops a component that meets section 1201(h)'s requirements, section 1201(h) arguably does not permit a consumer to use the component. This absurd result flows from the ambiguous manner in which the provision was drafted.

3.1.6.6   Protection of Personally Identifying Information

Section 1201(i) addresses concerns about personal privacy by permitting circumvention for the limited purpose of identifying and disabling technological means of collecting or disseminating personally identifying information reflecting users' online activities, such as "cookies."[44] This exception applies only if: the user is not given adequate notice that information is being collected; the user is not given the capability to prevent or restrict such collection or dissemination; and the circumvention has no other effect on the ability of any person to gain access to any work.

This provision has serious flaws. First, a user may not circumvent to protect his privacy if a website notifies him that it has implanted a cookie. Thus, once the user receives the notice, he must choose whether to sacrifice his privacy or to refrain from proceeding further with his online activity. Second, although this provision permits acts of circumvention to protect privacy, it does not specifically permit the development and distribution of the means of effectuating that circumvention; it creates an exception to section 1201(a)(1), but not an exception to section 1201(a)(2). It is not clear how users are expected to effectuate circumvention if developers are not permitted to manufacture and distribute circumvention devices.

3.1.6.7   Nonprofit Libraries, Archives, and Educational Institutions

Section 1201(d) provides an exemption for nonprofit libraries, archives, and educational institutions to gain access to a commercially exploited copyrighted work solely to make a good-faith determination of whether to acquire such work.[45] A qualifying institution may gain access only when it cannot obtain a copy of an identical work by other means, and the access may not last longer than is necessary. The institution is not allowed to use this exemption for commercial advantage or financial gain.

43. 17 U.S.C. § 1201(h).
44. 17 U.S.C. § 1201(i).
45. 17 U.S.C. § 1201(d).

The provision does not specifically permit the development and distribution of the devices necessary to effectuate the permitted circumvention. Even if permission to develop the devices is implied, the exception is of little practical use. It is highly unlikely that a content provider will not make a work available to potential customers, particularly large institutional customers such as libraries and schools. The library and educational associations did not request this exception; rather, it was "given" to them by the House Subcommittee on Courts and Intellectual Property so that the Subcommittee could claim to have responded to their concerns.

3.1.6.8 "No Mandate"

Section 1201 contains a "no mandate" provision which specifies that manufacturers of consumer electronics, telecommunications, and computing products are not required to design their products to respond to any particular technological protection measure.[46] The consumer electronics and computer industries had feared that section 1201 otherwise might require videocassette recorders and personal computers to respond to inconsistent types of technological protection. The "no mandate" provision also makes clear that manufacturers will not have to retrofit VCRs and PCs already on the market to accommodate new forms of protection that may be incorporated in copyrighted material in the future.

This section contains a highly technical provision that specifically addresses the protection of analog television programming and pre-recorded movies in relation to recording capabilities of ordinary consumer analog VCRs. Section 1201 requires analog VCRs to conform to the two forms of copy-control technology that were in wide use in the market in 1998: automatic gain control and colorstripe copy control.[47] This provision prohibits rendering these analog copy-control technologies ineffective by redesigning VCRs or by using "black boxes" or "software hacks."

Congress included specific encoding rules to preserve long-standing home taping practices. Copyright owners may use these technologies to prevent the making of a viewable copy of a pay-per-view program or a pre-recorded tape, for example, but may not limit the copying of traditional over-the-air broadcasts or of programming provided through cable or other wireline or satellite systems or through future over-the-air systems. In addition, copyright owners may utilize these technologies only to prevent the making of a "second generation" copy of an original transmission provided

---

46. 17 U.S.C. § 1201(c)(3).
47. 17 U.S.C. § 1201(k).

through a pay-television service. Professional devices and Beta and 8-millimeter VCRs are exempt from this provision's requirements.

3.1.7 Rulemaking

Congress understood that, aside from the exceptions mentioned above, there may be other legitimate reasons for circumventing technological protections. Accordingly, Congress suspended application of the prohibition on circumvention of access controls for two years, until the Librarian of Congress could conduct a rulemaking proceeding to determine whether additional exceptions were needed. The DMCA further requires the Librarian of Congress to conduct a similar rulemaking every three years thereafter.[48] The Librarian's principal question is whether the prohibition on circumvention will adversely affect the ability of users of copyrighted works to make non-infringing use of them.[49]

Under the rulemaking process, the Librarian of Congress is authorized only to create additional exceptions to section 1201(a)(1)—the prohibition on circumvention of access controls. On the face of the statute, however, the Librarian does not appear to be authorized to create additional exceptions to the device prohibitions of sections 1201(a)(2) and (b). Read literally, the statute allows the Librarian to permit acts of circumvention in additional situations, but not the devices necessary to perform acts of circumvention.

At the time of the DMCA's adoption, questions were raised about the constitutionality of empowering the Librarian of Congress to issue regulations. If the Library of Congress is part of the legislative branch, it may not have the constitutional authority to issue regulations. The constitutional structure of checks and balances would be frustrated if Congress could delegate rulemaking authority to its own entity. The Department of

48. Under section 1201(a)(1)(C), the Librarian of Congress grants exemptions upon the recommendation of the Register of Copyrights, who is required to consult with the Assistant Secretary for Communications and Information of the Department of Commerce (who heads the National Telecommunications and Information Administration).

49. The Librarian is directed to examine "(i) the availability for use of copyrighted works; (ii) the availability for use of works for nonprofit archival, preservation, and educational purposes; (iii) the impact that the prohibition on the circumvention of technological measures applied to copyrighted works has on criticism, comment, news reporting, teaching, scholarship, or research; (iv) the effect of circumvention of technological measures on the market for or value of copyrighted works; and (v) such other factors as the Librarian considers appropriate." 17 U.S.C. § 1201(a)(1)(C).

Justice reportedly raised concerns about this issue, which President Clinton attempted to cure in his statement upon signing the DMCA. The president asserted that the Library of Congress is, for constitutional purposes, an executive-branch entity. Thus, in his view, the Librarian could issue regulations.[50]

It remains to be seen whether President Clinton's statement really fixes the separation-of-powers problem. If it does not, the question then becomes whether this constitutional flaw can be separated from the rest of section 1201, or whether it poisons the entire provision.

This problem arose because of a jurisdictional squabble between the Commerce and Judiciary Committees in each chamber. Logical entities for a rulemaking of this sort would be the Patent and Trademark Office or the National Telecommunications and Information Administration. Those agencies, however, reside in the Department of Commerce, and the Judiciary Committees in the House and the Senate feared that granting the rulemaking authority to the Department of Commerce would lessen the Judiciary Committees' claim to primary jurisdiction over this issue. As a compromise to resolve this "turf battle," the committees granted the ultimate rulemaking authority to the Librarian of Congress, but required the librarian to consult with the NTIA.

In November of 2006, after the third rulemaking, the Librarian of Congress adopted the following six exemptions, which remained in effect at the beginning of 2010:

• Audiovisual works included in the educational library of a college or university's film or media studies department, when circumvention is accomplished for the purpose of making compilations of portions of those works for educational use in the classroom by media studies or film professors.
• Computer programs and video games distributed in formats that have become obsolete and that require the original media or hardware as a condition of access, when circumvention is accomplished for the purpose of preservation or archival reproduction of published digital works by a library or archive. A format shall be considered obsolete if the machine or system necessary to render perceptible a work stored in that format is no longer manufactured or is no longer reasonably available in the commercial marketplace.

50. In *Live365 v. Copyright Royalty Bd.*, 2010 WL 621718 (D.D.C. February 23, 2010), the District Court for the District of Columbia found that the Library of Congress was an executive department, at least for purposes of the Appointments Clause of the U.S. Constitution.

• Computer programs protected by dongles that prevent access due to mal-function or damage and which are obsolete. A dongle shall be considered obsolete if it is no longer manufactured or if a replacement or repair is no longer reasonably available in the commercial marketplace.

• Literary works distributed in ebook format when all existing ebook edi-tions of the work (including digital text editions made available by autho-rized entities) contain access controls that prevent the enabling either of the book's read-aloud function or of screen readers that render the text into a specialized format.

• Computer programs in the form of firmware that enable wireless tele-phone handsets to connect to a wireless telephone communication net-work, when circumvention is accomplished for the sole purpose of lawfully connecting to a wireless telephone communication network.

• Sound recordings, and audiovisual works associated with those sound recordings, distributed in compact disc format and protected by techno-logical protection measures that control access to lawfully purchased works and create or exploit security flaws or vulnerabilities that compromise the security of personal computers, when circumvention is accomplished solely for the purpose of good faith testing, investigating, or correcting such secu-rity flaws or vulnerabilities.[51]

As was noted above, these exemptions technically apply only to the act of circumvention under section 1201(a)(1), and not to the trafficking in cir-cumvention devices under section 1201(a)(2). However, no plaintiff has yet initiated legal action against a provider of a device manufactured and sold to carry out circumvention permitted by an exemption.

---

51. 71 *Fed. Reg.* 68472 (November 27, 2006). In the fourth rulemaking cycle, which began at the end of 2008, the Electronic Frontier Foundation sought a new exemp-tion for the circumvention of technological protection measures that prevent unau-thorized applications from running on cell phone handsets. The EFF specifically sought to permit the "jailbreaking" of the Apple iPhone so that iPhone owners can install applications from sources other than the iTunes Music Store. Apple filed a detailed opposition to the EFF's request. Apple's central legal argument was that "jail-breaking" invariably involved the infringement of the iPhone operating system. In order to run unauthorized applications on an iPhone, a user had to install a copy of the operating system that did not include the module that locked out unauthenti-cated applications. The user unlocked his handset by replacing the operating system with an abridged version of the operating system, i.e., a derivative work. Accordingly, the supplier of the replacement operating system provided not only a key but also an infringing copy. On this basis, Apple argued that the EFF's request should be denied.

3.1.8 An Assessment of Section 1201 as Enacted

Without question, the exceptions and the "no mandate" provision address many of the most serious deficiencies of the prohibitions proposed by the Clinton administration and first introduced in Congress. Nonetheless, the provision continues to prohibit some legitimate, socially useful activities, such as circumvention for error correction. And although the Librarian of Congress has approved some exemptions, the rulemaking process is burdensome and the Librarian has rejected far more exemptions than he has approved. Also, as will be discussed below, the DMCA has been used by aggressive plaintiffs to prevent competition and interoperability.

Section 1201 may have another unintended consequence. Both section 1201(a)(2) and section 1201(b) prohibit trafficking in circumvention devices. Will an Internet service provider that hosts a site that makes circumvention devices available be liable for trafficking in the devices, even if it had no knowledge of the presence of the devices on the site? The ISP probably would not face criminal liability if it had no knowledge; but it might well assume civil liability, because section 1201 does not contain a scienter requirement. Because Title II of the DMCA provides safe harbors from copyright liability to ISPs, it would be ironic if Title I of the DMCA imposed additional liability on the ISPs. (The safe harbors of Title II provide shelter only from copyright liability, not section 1201 circumvention liability.)

Congress chose the approach of adopting an extremely broad prohibition, then granting an exception to any group powerful enough to lobby effectively for one. The breadth of the exception also turned on lobbying power; the security-testing exception is more comprehensive than the privacy exception because the banks and accounting firms that pushed for the security-testing exception had more political clout than the public-interest groups concerned about privacy.

The critical mistake Congress made that resulted in this complex, inconsistent provision was its acceptance of the Clinton administration's overly broad prohibition. The administration's proposal was too broad in three different ways:

• It regulated both devices and conduct, rather than just conduct. Because it regulated devices, Congress had to fashion exceptions for devices used in legitimate ways. Virtually any technology can be used for good or evil; the user determines the role the technology plays. Section 1201's approach ran directly contrary to the Clinton administration's stated philosophy with respect to the Internet; it relied on heavy regulation rather than on market-driven solutions.

• It regulated circumvention, regardless of whether the circumvention actually facilitated infringement. By divorcing the act of circumvention from the act of infringement, Congress had to create exceptions for acts of circumvention that did not lead to infringement.

• It addressed the circumvention of access-control technologies *and* copy-control technologies, rather than just the circumvention of copy-control technologies. Because access control is far removed from copyright protection, the prohibition implicated many legitimate activities. Had Congress dealt only with copy controls, the majority of the exceptions—those for encryption research, security testing, protecting personal privacy, library purchasing, and monitoring children's use of the Internet—would not have been needed.

Significantly, the WIPO treaties require none of these overly broad features. The treaties simply require that "[c]ontracting Parties shall provide adequate legal protection and effective legal remedies against the circumvention of effective technological measures that are used by authors in connection with the exercise of their rights under this Treaty or the Berne Convention and that restrict acts, in respect of their works, which are not authorized by the authors concerned or permitted by law."[52]

The WIPO treaties say nothing about devices; they speak only of circumvention. The content community argued that a ban on devices is necessary to afford them "adequate legal protection" and "effective legal remedies," but this interpretation has no basis in the negotiating history of the treaties.

The WIPO treaties also say nothing about prohibiting circumvention in the absence of infringement. Indeed, the treaties could be read as prohibiting only circumvention that does in fact lead to infringement.

Finally, the WIPO treaties say nothing about controlling access to a work. Rather, the treaties speak of the exercise of their rights under the treaties or the Berne Convention, which do not include an exclusive right over access to the work.

Thus, section 1201's problematic nature flows directly from the Clinton administration and Congress going far beyond the requirements of the WIPO treaties. Conversely, the approach sponsored by Ashcroft, Boucher, and Campbell went only as far as was required by the treaties, and thereby avoided the DMCA's inadvertent restriction on legitimate activities.

52. World Intellectual Property Organization Copyright Treaty (1996), Art. 11; World Intellectual Property Organization Performances and Phonograms Treaty (1996), Art. 18.

3.2   Efforts to Amend the DMCA

3.2.1   The Boucher-Doolittle Bill

On October 3, 2002, Representatives Boucher and Doolittle (R-CA) introduced the Digital Media Consumers' Rights Act of 2002 (H.R. 5544).[53] One
of the bill's provisions would have amended section 1201.[54] As was discussed above, section 1201(a)(1) prohibits the circumvention of access controls, even if done for a non-infringing purpose, unless the circumvention
is specifically permitted by one of the exceptions specified in section 1201.
Likewise, sections 1201(a)(2) and 1201(b) prohibit the manufacture and
distribution of circumvention devices, even if they are intended to be used
for non-infringing purposes, unless the devices fall within section 1201's
specific exceptions. In other words, section 1201 prohibits circumvention
activity and devices regardless of whether the circumvention results in
infringement.

In introducing their bill, Representatives Boucher and Doolittle recognized that section 1201, by divorcing circumvention from infringement,
had the effect of prohibiting lawful uses of copyrighted works. Thus,
although section 1201(c)(1) provided that section 1201 did not affect
defenses to copyright infringement, including fair use, fair use was not a
defense to a circumvention offense.[55] Accordingly, Representatives Boucher
and Doolittle proposed amendments that would have made non-infringe-
ment a defense to circumvention liability. Specifically, their bill would have
amended section 1201(c)(1) to provide that "it is not a violation of this section to circumvent a technological measure in connection with access to, or
the use of, a work if such circumvention does not result in an infringement
of the copyright in the work."

---

53. H.R. 5544, 107th Cong. (2002). This subsection is based on Masanobu Katoh and
Jonathan Band, "Backlash: Legislative Responses to Entertainment Industry Initia-
tives in the 107th Congress," *Journal of Internet Law*, March 2003, at 8.

54. The bill also would have required record companies to label CDs that were copy
protected or that would not play on certain devices, such as the CD drives of personal
computers. In 2002, record companies began to use various forms of copy protection
on their CDs without notifying consumers. When the consumers found that they
couldn't play the CDs on their computers or burn copies of them, they assumed that
either the CDs or the computers were malfunctioning. The labeling requirement in
the Boucher-Doolittle bill was intended to prevent this form of customer confusion.

55. See *Universal City Studios, Inc., v. Corley*, 273 F.3d 429 (2d Cir. 2001). For a critical
discussion of the application of section 1201 since enactment, see "Unintended Consequences: Ten Years under the DMCA" at www.eff.org.

Further, the Boucher-Doolittle bill would have created an exception to the prohibition on the manufacture and distribution of circumvention devices when "the person is acting solely in furtherance of scientific research into technological protection measures." This provision would have codified an argument made by the U.S. Department of Justice during the declaratory judgment action brought by Edward Felten (a professor at Princeton University) against the Recording Industry Association of America.[56] Felten sought a judicial declaration that his research on encryption was lawful. The RIAA responded that the case was moot because the RIAA had withdrawn its objections to his research. The Department of Justice filed a brief in support of the RIAA that argued, among other things, that Felten's research was plainly permitted by the DMCA. In particular, the Department of Justice argued that, insofar as Felten had developed his software tools for research purposes, he obviously had not developed them "for the purpose of circumventing a technological measure that effectively controls access to a work"—a purpose that triggers liability under section 1201(a)(2)(A). In other words, even though Felten's tool circumvented a technological measure, the tool's real purpose was research, not circumvention.

Shortly after the introduction of the Boucher-Doolittle bill, Intel, Philips, Sun Microsystems, Verizon, and Gateway announced their support, as did the American Library Association, Consumers Union, and the Electronic Frontier Foundation. The content providers condemned the bill, asserting that the new exceptions would swallow the circumvention prohibition.[57]

Soon after the introduction of the Boucher-Doolittle bill, Richard Clarke, then the head of the White House Office of Cyber Security, asserted that the DMCA should be amended to permit the research of security flaws in software. Characterizing threats against academic researchers as a misuse of the law, Clarke said "I think a lot of people didn't realize that it would have this potential chilling effect on vulnerability research."[58]

No action was taken on the Boucher-Doolittle bill before Congress adjourned for the 2002 elections. However, at the beginning of the 108th Congress, in early January of 2003, Representatives Boucher and Doolittle reintroduced their bill.[59] The bill (now designated H.R. 107—an intentional

56. *Felten v. Recording Industry Ass'n of America, Inc.*, Case No. 01-CV-2669, Defendant John Ashcroft's Memorandum in Support of Motion to Dismiss at 15–18, filed September 25, 2001 (D.N.J.), available at www.eff.org.
57. "Capitol Hill," *Washington Internet Daily*, November 19, 2002.
58. Hiawatha Bray, "Cyber Chief Speaks on Data Network Security," *Boston Globe*, October 17, 2002.
59. H.R. 107, 108th Cong. (2003). They were joined as co-sponsors by Representatives Patrick Kennedy (D-RI) and Spencer Bachus (R-AL).

allusion to section 107 of the Copyright Act, which codifies the fair-use doctrine) was referred to the House Energy and Commerce Committee. While Representative Billy Tauzin (R-LA) remained chairman, the committee took no action on the bill. But H.R. 107's prospects improved after Tauzin resigned in February of 2004, and Representative Joe Barton (R-TX) assumed the chairmanship. Barton, who had signed on as a co-sponsor of H.R. 107 shortly after its introduction, reiterated his strong support after becoming chairman.

On May 12, 2004, the House Energy and Commerce Subcommittee on Commerce, Trade, and Consumer Protection held a hearing on H.R. 107. The subcommittee heard from fourteen witnesses, including Jack Valenti of the Motion Picture Association of America, Cary Sherman of the RIAA, Robert Holleyman of the Business Software Alliance, Gary Shapiro of the Consumer Electronics Association, Miriam Nisbet of the American Library Association, and two law professors: Peter Jaszi (for the Digital Future Coalition) and Lawrence Lessig.

Valenti, Sherman, and Holleyman all testified that the legislation would facilitate piracy of content. But many of the other witnesses spoke strongly in favor of the bill, and Chairman Barton indicated his intention to report it out of the committee in the 108th Congress. However, strong lobbying by the copyright industries prevented progress of H.R. 107 in the 108th Congress and of H.R. 1201 (a similar bill introduced by Representative Boucher in the 109th Congress).[60]

3.2.2 The Lofgren Bill

On October 2, 2002, Representative Zoe Lofgren (D-CA) also introduced a bill directed at section 1201 of the DMCA: the Digital Choice and Freedom Act of 2002, H.R. 5522.[61] The Lofgren bill, however, took a somewhat narrower approach than the Boucher-Doolittle bill. Under the Lofgren approach, a person could circumvent an access control if the circumvention was "necessary to make a non-infringing use of the work" and "the copyright owner fails to make publicly available the necessary means to make such noninfringing use without additional cost or burden to such person." Similarly, a person could manufacture and distribute the means to circumvent an access control if the "means are necessary to make a noninfringing use," the means are "designed, produced, and marketed to make a noninfringing use," and "the copyright owner fails to make available the

60. H.R.1201, 109th Cong. (2005).
61. H.R. 5522, 107th Cong. (2002).

necessary means." The Lofgren bill did not detail how the extra step of the copyright owner's failing to make available the means of circumventing would operate.

The Lofgren bill contained several other provisions not related to circumvention. The general purpose of these provisions was to preserve in the digital environment exceptions that existed in the analog environment. Thus, the bill would have created a new section 123 to the Copyright Act that would have permitted a person who lawfully obtained a copy of a digital work to "reproduce, store, adapt, or access the digital work . . . for archival purposes . . . and . . . in order to perform or display the work, or an adaptation of the work, on a digital media device, if such performance or display is not public." This provision would have codified the practice of "time-shifting" and "space-shifting" practiced by many consumers.

Additionally, the new section 123 would have provided that "[w]hen a digital work is distributed to the public subject to nonnegotiable license terms, such terms shall not be enforceable . . . to the extent that they restrict or limit any of the limitations on exclusive rights." This provision was intended to invalidate "shrinkwrap" or "click-on" license terms that restrict fair use and other privileges Congress has granted to consumers. Significantly, section 123 would not apply to software, which was excluded from the definition of "digital works."

The provision mentioned in the preceding paragraph was Representative Lofgren's response to the Uniform Computer Information Transactions Act (UCITA), which would have rendered shrinkwrap and click-on licenses enforceable under state contract law. Opponents of UCITA argued that under it the private law of contract would supersede the public law of copyright. Accordingly, UCITA's opponents sought, with limited success, provisions within UCITA that would preclude the enforceability of contract terms inconsistent with fair use and other copyright exceptions and limitations.[62] This provision of the Lofgren bill addressed this issue at the federal level.

Finally, the Lofgren bill would have updated the first-sale doctrine for the digital age, allowing a person to transmit a work to another person provided that he deleted his copy of the work.

3.2.3   H.R. 1201 in the 110th Congress

On February 27, 2007, Representative Boucher introduced another bill to reform the DMCA. Although once again designated H.R. 1201, this bill was

---

62. We discuss this issue in great detail in subsection 4.2.2.

narrower than H.R. 1201 in the 109th Congress or H.R. 107 in the 108th Congress.[63] Instead of amending section 1201 to require a nexus between circumvention and infringement, the new H.R. 1201 codified the exemptions approved by the Librarian of Congress in the 2006 rulemaking.[64] Additionally, H.R. 1201 established other exceptions critical to preserving fair use in the digital age.[65]

3.3   DMCA Cases Relating to Interoperability

Since their enactment in 1998, the DMCA's anti-circumvention provisions have generated strong reactions from various stakeholders.[66] The motion picture industry credits the DMCA with the enormous success of the DVD.[67] The DMCA has permitted the studios and their business partners in the consumer electronics industry to prevent the distribution of DeCSS software, which enables circumvention of the encryption system that protects movies distributed on DVDs.

Technologists, however, argued that the DMCA could chill legitimate research into computer security and the development of innovative

63. H.R. 1201, 110th Cong. (2007).

64. See section 3.1.7 above.

65. H.R. 1201 would exempt the following from liability under section 1201(a)(1) (A):

(i) an act of circumvention that is carried out solely for the purpose of making a compilation of portions of audiovisual works in the collection of a library or archives for educational use in a classroom by an instructor;

(ii) an act of circumvention that is carried out solely for the purpose of enabling a person to skip past or to avoid commercial or personally objectionable content in an audiovisual work;

(iii) an act of circumvention that is carried out solely for the purpose of enabling a person to transmit a work over a home or personal network, except that this exemption does not apply to the circumvention of a technological measure to the extent that it prevents uploading of the work to the Internet for mass, indiscriminate redistribution;

(iv) an act of circumvention that is carried out solely for the purpose of gaining access to one or more works in the public domain that are included in a compilation consisting primarily of works in the public domain;

(v) an act of circumvention that is carried out to gain access to a work of substantial public interest solely for purposes of criticism, comment, news reporting, scholarship, or research; or

(vi) an act of circumvention that is carried out solely for the purpose of enabling a library or archives meeting the requirements of section 108(a)(2), with respect to works included in its collection, to preserve or secure a copy or to replace a copy that is damaged, deteriorating, lost, or stolen.

66. This section is based on Jonathan Band, "A New Day for the DMCA: The Chamberlain and Lexmark Decisions," 9 *Electronic Commerce & Law Report* 987 (November 2004).

67. DVD sales in the U.S. exceeded $12 billion in 2003. Source: Chris Jones, "Power to the People," *Chicago Tribune*, February 1, 2004.

products. Libraries and universities contended that the DMCA could prevent copying that was lawful under copyright's fair-use doctrine or under its library exceptions.

DMCA critics' worst fears about the anti-competitive effect of the statute seemed to be validated when two dominant companies attempted to use the DMCA to threaten competitors in aftermarkets. The *Chamberlain* case involved universal transmitters for garage door openers; the *Lexmark* case involved toner cartridges for printers. Fortunately, the judges in these cases interpreted the DMCA in a manner that prevented its use to restrict legitimate competition in interoperable components.

Section 1201(a)(1) of 17 U.S.C. prohibits the circumvention of access controls, regardless of the purpose of the circumvention, unless the circumvention is specifically permitted by one of the exceptions contained in section 1201. Likewise, sections 1201(a)(2) and 1201(b) prohibit the manufacture and distribution of circumvention devices, even if they are intended to be used for non-infringing purposes, unless the devices fall within section 1201's specific exceptions. Although section 1201(c)(1) provides that section 1201 does not affect defenses to copyright infringement, including fair use, courts had ruled that fair use was not a defense to a circumvention offense.[68] In sum, before the *Chamberlain* and *Lexmark* decisions section 1201 was understood to prohibit circumvention activity and devices, regardless of whether the circumvention results in infringement.

3.3.1   *Universal v. Reimerdes* (2000)

The first circuit court interpretation of section 1201 of the DMCA, *Universal City Studios, Inc. v. Corley,*[69] involved the distribution of DeCSS, a small computer program capable of decrypting the Content Scrambling System (CSS) used to protect digital versatile discs (DVDs). The defendants' primary statutory defense before the district court and the Second Circuit was that the savings clause in section 1201(c)(1) permitted circumventions that enabled fair uses.[70]

The defendants also raised an interoperability defense before the district court. They claimed that DeCSS was necessary to achieve interoperability between computers running the Linux operating system and DVDs, and

68. See *Universal City Studios, Inc. v. Corley,* 273 F.3d 429 (2d Cir. 2001).
69. Id.
70. As will be discussed later in this chapter, the Second Circuit rejected this defense. The Federal Circuit in *Chamberlain* attempted to minimize any apparent inconsistency between its holding that section 1201 liability required a nexus between circumvention and language in the *Corley* decision suggesting that section 1201(a) imposes liability even if the access cannot facilitate infringement.

thus section 1201(f) permitted their circumvention activities. In granting the plaintiffs' motion for a preliminary injunction, the district court
rejected this contention:

[T]he legislative history makes it abundantly clear that Section 1201(f) permits reverse engineering of copyrighted computer programs only and does not authorize
circumvention of technological systems that control access to other copyrighted
works, such as movies. In consequence, the reverse engineering exception does not
apply.[71]

In other words, section 1201(f) applies to achieving interoperability between
two computer programs, but not to achieving interoperability between
a computer program and other entertainment products. But what if the
entertainment product is a computer program, such as a computer game?
As will be discussed below with respect to *Davidson v. Jung*, the interoperability exception should apply in such a situation.[72]

Interestingly, when the district court issued its decision on the merits
after trial, it omitted the aforementioned basis for rejecting the defendants'
section 1201(f) defense. Instead, the district court found as a factual matter that DeCSS was developed and run on Windows. Thus, the developers "knew that DeCSS could be used to decrypt and play DVD movies on
Windows as well as Linux machines. They knew also that the decrypted
files could be copied like any other unprotected computer file. . . . Hence,
the Court finds that Mr. Johansen and the others who actually did develop
DeCSS did not do so solely for the purpose of making a Linux DVD player if,
indeed, developing a Linux-based DVD player was among their purposes."[73]
The district court did not explain this change in rationale, and the defendants did not appeal the issue to the Second Circuit.

3.3.2 *Chamberlain v. Skylink* (2004)
As was noted above, after the Second Circuit's *Corley* decision, section 1201
was understood to prohibit circumvention activity and circumvention
devices regardless of whether the circumvention in question resulted in

71. *Universal City Studios v. Reimerdes*, 82 F. Supp. 2d 211, 218 (S.D.N.Y. 2000).
72. See subsection 3.3.6. The district court considered the section 1201(f) interoperability defense in granting a motion for temporary injunction in *Sony Computer Entertainment America Inc., v. Gamemasters*, 87 F. Supp. 2d 976 (N.D. Cal. 1999). In that
case the court enjoined the distribution of the Game Enhancer, a device that allowed
U.S. users to play Sony video games purchased outside the U.S. on Sony PlayStations
by circumventing the territorial codes on the foreign versions of Sony video games.
73. *Universal City Studios v. Reimerdes*, 111 F. Supp. 2d 294, 320 (S.D.N.Y. 2000), *aff'd*,
273 F.3d 429 (2d Cir. 2001).

infringement. The decision of the U.S. Court of Appeals for the Federal Circuit in *Chamberlain Group, Inc. v. Skylink Techs., Inc.*[74] changed this understanding. Skylink had developed a universal transmitter that could activate Chamberlain garage door openers (GDOs). To do so, software in the Skylink transmitter circumvented a lockout code in a computer program embedded in the Chamberlain GDO that controlled the operation of the GDO's motor. Chamberlain sued Skylink, alleging that the Skylink transmitters violated the DMCA because they circumvented a technological protection measure to obtain unauthorized access to the software embedded in the GDO.

The district court granted summary judgment to Skylink on the ground that Chamberlain had given implicit authorization to its customers to circumvent the access controls in the GDOs they had purchased. On appeal, Chamberlain argued that it had not given such authorization. Skylink defended the district court's holding. The Computer & Communications Industry Association filed an *amicus* brief advancing the alternative argument that the circumvention was permitted under the interoperability exception, 17 U.S.C. § 1201(f).

The Federal Circuit agreed with the district court that the customers' circumvention was authorized, but devoted most of its opinion to a rationale completely different from that advanced by Skylink or its *amici*. It interpreted section 1201(a) to prohibit circumvention only if it enables access that infringes or facilitates infringement.

The starting point of the Federal Circuit's analysis was its perception that the DMCA did not create a new property right but, rather, provided property owners with new ways to secure their property. After reviewing the legislative history of the DMCA, the court concluded that Congress's objective had not been to change the balance of interests in the copyright law but instead to preserve them in the new digital environment.

Specifically, the Federal Circuit noted that in the DMCA "Congress attempted to balance the legitimate interests of copyright owners with those of consumers of copyrighted products. . . .Were we to interpret Congress' words in a way that eliminated all balance and granted copyright owners carte blanche authority to preclude all use, Congressional intent would remain unrealized."[75] The court interpreted section 1201(a) as "prohibit[ing] only forms of access that bear a reasonable relationship to the protections that the Copyright Act otherwise affords copyright

74. *Chamberlain Group, Inc. v. Skylink Techs., Inc.*, 381 F.3d 1178 (Fed. Cir. 2004).
75. Id. at 1203.

owners"[76] and ruled that this was the "only meaningful reading of the statute."[77] Thus, the Federal Circuit held that trafficking in a circumvention device violates section 1201(a)(2) only if the circumvention enables access that "infringes or facilitates infringing a right protected by the Copyright Act."[78] Here, Chamberlain failed to show "the critical nexus between access and protection."[79] It "neither alleged copyright infringement nor explained how the access provided by the [Skylink] transmitter facilitates the infringement of any right the Copyright Act protects."[80]

The Federal Circuit took great pains to minimize any apparent inconsistency between its holding and that of *Universal City Studios, Inc. v. Corley*,[81] in which the Second Circuit held that section 1201(c)(1) did not provide a fair-use defense to a circumvention violation. In *Corley*, the plaintiffs provided evidence that the circumvention program at issue, DeCSS, allowed a user to circumvent the CSS protection system and to view or copy a motion picture without authorization. In contrast, Skylink's product permitted *only* lawful uses of the software embedded in the Chamberlain garage door opener. The Federal Circuit acknowledged that some of the language in the *Corley* decision could be understood as suggesting that section 1201(a) imposes liability even if the access cannot facilitate infringement. The Federal Circuit argued, however, that "[i]t is unlikely . . . that the Second Circuit meant to imply anything as drastic as wresting the concept of 'access' from its context within the meaning of the Copyright Act."[82]

3.3.3 *Lexmark v. Static Control Components* (2004)

Less than two months after the Federal Circuit issued its decision in *Chamberlain*, the U.S. Court of Appeals for the Sixth Circuit issued its decision in *Lexmark v. Static Control Components*.[83] The Sixth Circuit's decision is far more complex than that of the Federal Circuit because it contains three opinions and addresses more issues. Although the panel opinion does not go as far as *Chamberlain*, the concurring opinion by Judge Merritt goes even farther.

Lexmark had designed the software embedded in its printer—the printer engine program (PEP)—to permit the printer to operate only if it recognized

76. Id. at 1202.
77. Id. at 1203.
78. Id.
79. Id. at 1204.
80. Id.
81. 273 F.3d 429 (2d Cir. 2001).
82. *Chamberlain*, 381 F.3d at 1199.
83. *Lexmark Int'l, Inc. v. Static Control Components, Inc.*, 387 F.3d 522 (6th Cir. 2004).

an authentication sequence from the toner loading program (TLP) embedded in the toner cartridge. Lexmark had done this to prevent the use of other manufacturers' less expensive toner cartridges in its printers. Static Control Components (SCC) manufactured the Smartek chip, which it sold to manufacturers of replacement toner cartridges. The Smartek chip contained a copy of the Lexmark TLP that enabled the replacement toner cartridges to operate in Lexmark printers. Lexmark sued SCC for infringing the copyright in the TLP and for violating the DMCA by circumventing the technological measures that protected access to the TLP and the PEP. The district court found that Lexmark was likely to prevail on the merits of both claims and entered a preliminary injunction in its favor.

The Sixth Circuit reversed with respect to both the copyright claim and the DMCA claim. The majority and dissenting opinions focus largely on the copyrightability of the TLP. The details of this discussion are significant with respect to the scope of copyright protection for program elements necessary for interoperability, but do not affect the core DMCA analysis relating to the PEP.[84]

3.3.3.1 Access to the PEP

Lexmark argued that the SCC Smartek chip was a device marketed to circumvent the technological measure that controlled access to the PEP. The district court agreed, finding that Lexmark's authentication sequence effectively controlled access to the Printer Engine Program because it controlled the consumer's ability to make use of the program. The Sixth Circuit, however, found that there were other ways for the user to gain access to the PEP:

Anyone who buys a Lexmark printer may read the literal code of the [PEP] directly from the printer memory, with or without the benefit of the authentication sequence, and data from the program may be translated into readable source code after which copies may be freely distributed. No security device, in other words, protects access to the [PEP] and no security device accordingly must be circumvented to obtain access to that program code.[85]

Therefore,

Lexmark did not block another relevant form of "access"—the "ability to obtain" a copy of the work or to "make use of" the literal elements of the program (its code). Because the statute refers to "control[ling] access to a work protected under this title," it does not naturally apply when the "work protected under this title" is oth-

84. We discuss the scope of protection issues in subsection 2.1.2.6.
85. 387 F.3d at 546–547.

erwise accessible. Just as one would not say that a lock on the back door of a house "controls access" to a house whose front door does not contain a lock and just as one would not say that a lock on any door of a house "controls access" to the house after its purchaser receives the key to the lock, it does not make sense to say that this provision of the DMCA applies to otherwise-readily-accessible copyrighted works.[86]

Lexmark argued that in other DMCA cases courts had interpreted "access" as meaning "make use of." The Sixth Circuit distinguished those cases. The Sixth Circuit explained that in cases such as *321 Studios v. MGM Studios*[87] or *Corley* copyright protection exists on two planes: in the literal code of the work and the audio or visual manifestation generated by the code's execution. In these cases, restricting the use of the code had the effect of preventing consumers from gaining access to the audio or visual manifestation of the work. In this case, by contrast, the PEP operated only on one plane: the literal elements of the program. Unlike the code underlying a video game or a DVD, the execution of the PEP did not create protectable expression—just functional output. Hence, restricting use of the PEP code did not prevent access to any protectable expression.

3.3.3.2 The Interoperability Exception

The Sixth Circuit then addressed the DMCA's interoperability exception, section 1201(f). The district court had found that the exception was available for achieving interoperability between an independently created program and other programs. Because SCC had copied the TLP, it had not been created independently, and thus SCC could not avail itself of the section 1201(f) defense. However, the Sixth Circuit found that there was evidence that the Smartek chip contained programs "independently created" by SCC in addition to a copy of the TLP. Circumvention of the technological protection was necessary to allow these other programs to interoperate with the PEP.

Lexmark argued that these independently created programs had to exist before the reverse engineering of the TLP. The Sixth Circuit rejected this contention, holding that "nothing in the statute precludes simultaneous creation of an interoperability device and another program; it just must be 'independently' created."[88] Lexmark also argued that "the technological means must be necessary or absolutely needed" to enable interoperability. The court responded that "the statute is silent about the degree to which the 'technological means' means must be necessary, if indeed they

---

86. Id. at 547 (citations omitted).
87. 307 F. Supp. 2d 1085 (N.D. Cal. 2004).
88. 387 F.3d at 551.

are necessary at all, for interoperability."[89] In any event, the court found that SCC did in fact need to copy the TLP to achieve interoperability with the PEP.

The Sixth Circuit's suggestion that the statute is silent about whether the technological means must be "necessary at all" to achieve interoperability is curious in view of the plain language of section 1201(f). Section 1201(f)(1) authorizes circumvention "for the sole purpose of identifying and analyzing those elements of the program that are *necessary to achieve interoperability*." Similarly, section 1201(f)(2) permits the development of technological means to circumvent, "if such means are *necessary to achieve . . . interoperability*."

Interestingly, the Sixth Circuit didn't mention the Copyright Office's opinion concerning the section 1201(f) defense. After the district court ruled in this case, SCC asked the Copyright Office for an exemption from section 1201(a) pursuant to the DMCA rulemaking procedure. The Copyright Office concluded that an exemption was unnecessary because of section 1201(f). Since the Sixth Circuit's view of section 1201(f) coincides with that of the Copyright Office, it is surprising that the Sixth Circuit didn't cite the Copyright Office opinion.

Judge Feikens, in an opinion that dissented in part and concurred in part, developed a different rationale concerning the PEP DMCA claim. "By buying a Lexmark printer," he said, "the consumer acquires an implied license to use the [PEP] for the life of that printer."[90] Because of this implied license, the consumer was authorized to circumvent the technological protection measures to gain access to the PEP. This argument is similar to the district court's rationale in *Chamberlain*.[91]

3.3.3.3 Judge Merritt's Concurrence
Judge Merritt wrote a concurring opinion that attempted to broaden the majority's DMCA holding. "We should make clear," he wrote, "that in the

89. Id.
90. Id. at 564.
91. Lexmark also asserted that SCC violated the DMCA by accessing the TLP. However, the Sixth Circuit found that the Smartek chip doesn't provide access to the TLP; it replaces the TLP. Moreover, as was noted above, the court found that the TLP was not copyrightable in the first place. Thus, the court held that it was not protected by the DMCA at all. Judge Feikens had dissented from the finding that the TLP was not copyrightable; accordingly, he could not agree with the majority that the DMCA did not apply to the TLP. Instead, Judge Feikens stated that the Smartek chip was not primarily designed or produced for the purpose of circumventing the protection of the TLP; its primary purpose was to access the PEP.

future companies like Lexmark cannot use the DMCA in conjunction with copyright law to create monopolies of manufactured goods for themselves just by tweaking the facts of this case: by, for example, creating a [TLP] that is more complex and 'creative' than the one here, or by cutting off other access to the [PEP]. . . .The key question is the 'purpose' of the circumvention technology."[92]

Judge Merritt rejected Lexmark's interpretation of the DMCA, which would have imposed liability for any circumvention of a technological measure regardless of the purpose of the circumvention. If the court were to adopt Lexmark's reading of the statute, he noted, "manufacturers could potentially create monopolies for replacement parts simply by using similar, more creative, lock-out codes. Automobile manufacturers, for example, could control the entire market for replacement parts for their vehicles by including lock-out chips."[93] According to Judge Merritt, this reading "ignores . . . the main point of the DMCA—to prohibit the pirating of copyright protected works such as movies, music, and computer programs."[94] Judge Merritt concluded that unless a plaintiff can show that a defendant "circumvented protective measures 'for the purpose' of pirating works protected by the copyright statute,"[95] its claim should not be allowed to go forward. This interpretation of the DMCA is similar to the Federal Circuit's in *Chamberlain*. Judge Merritt, however, did not cite *Chamberlain*, even though the Federal Circuit decided it two months before he wrote his opinion.

Judge Merritt also opined that Lexmark's interpretation ran contrary to the objective of the intellectual-property clause of the Constitution—promoting the progress of science and useful arts:

[Lexmark's reading] would allow authors exclusive rights not only over their own expression, but also over whatever functional use they can make of that expression in manufactured goods. Giving authors monopolies over manufactured goods as well as their own creative expression will clearly not "promote the Progress of Science and the useful Arts," but rather would stifle progress by stamping out competition from manufacturers who may be able to design better or less expensive replacement parts like toner cartridges.[96]

92. 387 F.3d at 551–552 (Merritt, J., concurring).
93. Id. at 552.
94. Id.
95. Id.
96. Id. at 553.

3.3.4 The Significance of the *Chamberlain* and *Lexmark* Decisions

The *Chamberlain* decision was a major development in DMCA jurisprudence. By requiring a nexus between the circumvention of access controls and infringement, the Federal Circuit prevented the DMCA from being employed to prevent legitimate competition in aftermarkets. The circuit court's reasoning should also apply in other circumstances far removed from the facilitation of infringement.[97]

The panel decision in *Lexmark* is far narrower. To be sure, its holding that circumvention of one form of access control does not violate the DMCA so long as other unprotected means of access exist is significant. But in the future, product developers will be able to avoid this problem simply by eliminating other means of access. For example, Lexmark could encrypt the PEP in its next generation of printers.

However, both concurring opinions in *Lexmark* support a more far-reaching interpretation of the DMCA—an interpretation similar to *Chamberlain*'s. As was noted above, Judge Merritt expressed concern that the panel's decision was too narrow and could be avoided "just by tweaking the facts of this case."[98] Thus, Judge Merritt stated that "a better reading of the statute is that it requires plaintiffs as part of their burden of pleading and persuasion to show a purpose to pirate on the part of defendants."[99] Judge Feikens appeared to reach a similar conclusion. He described the DMCA's legislative history as demonstrating that "Congress did not intend this provision to apply to devices that merely facilitated legitimate access."[100] Judge Feikens reasoned that "[b]ecause Defendant's chip can only make non-infringing uses of the Lexmark [PEP], it is clear that Congress did not intend to apply the DMCA to this situation."[101]

These two concurring opinions may not be binding precedent in the Sixth Circuit, but other courts certainly should find it persuasive that two of the three judges on the *Lexmark* panel agreed with the *Chamberlain* panel that DMCA liability should attach only to circumvention that facilitates infringement. In sum, these decisions accomplish precisely what Ashcroft, Boucher, and Campbell sought in their alternative to the Clinton administration's WIPO-implementation bill and what Representative Boucher attempted to achieve in his amendments to section 1201.

97. See discussion of *Storage Technology v. Custom Hardware* in subsection 3.3.5.
98. 387 F.3d at 551 (Merritt, J., concurring).
99. Id. at 552.
100. Id. at 564 (Feikens, J., concurring in part).
101. Id.

Although the *Chamberlain* panel and the *Lexmark* "majority" agreed that there must be a nexus between circumvention and infringement, they seem to have disagreed on the extent of the nexus. *Chamberlain* dealt only with a situation in which circumvention was incapable of facilitating infringement; it did not consider a situation in which circumvention facilitated both infringing and non-infringing uses. In a footnote, the Federal Circuit "[left] open the question as to when § 107 [the fair-use doctrine] might serve as an affirmative defense to a *prima facie* violation of § 1201."[102]

In contrast, Judge Merritt seemed willing to permit circumvention so long as infringement was not intended, even if it was possible. Congress, he averred, "only sought to reach those who circumvented protective measures 'for the purpose' of pirating works protected by the copyright statute."[103] Later he stated that the DMCA, properly read, imposed on the plaintiff the burden of proving "a purpose to pirate on the part of the defendant."[104] Judge Merritt's interpretation of the DMCA would appear to allow circumvention for the purpose of making a fair use.[105]

The *Chamberlain* court's caution seems to suggest a desire to avoid a conflict with earlier DMCA decisions—particularly *Corley*, in which the Second Circuit explicitly held that fair use was not a defense to circumvention. The *Chamberlain* court explained that in earlier DMCA decisions "the access alleged . . . was intertwined with a protected right."[106] By restricting its holding to situations where the circumvention could not enable infringement, the *Chamberlain* court steered clear of those other cases. Perhaps because he was merely writing a policy-oriented concurring opinion, Judge Merritt did not appear to be constrained by these earlier decisions. He did not address the apparent inconsistency between his view and other DMCA decisions. Indeed, Judge Merritt did not cite any decisions whatsoever. He referenced only the Constitution's intellectual-property clause, the DMCA, and Lawrence Lessig's book *Free Culture*.

The *Chamberlain* court also left open the question of the effect of a contractual restriction on circumvention on DMCA liability: "It is not clear whether a consumer who circumvents a technological measure controlling access to a copyrighted work in a manner that enables uses permitted under the Copyright Act but prohibited by contract can be subject to liability

102. *Chamberlain*, 381 F.3d at 1200 n.14.
103. *Lexmark*, 387 F.3d at 552.
104. Id.
105. Judge Feikens did not address this issue in his opinion.
106. *Chamberlain*, 381 F.3d at 1199.

under the DMCA."[107] The Federal Circuit declined to address this question because Chamberlain had not attempted to limit its customers' use by contract before it had sued Skylink. However, the question is far from academic; after the district court handed down its opinion that Chamberlain had implicitly authorized its users to employ universal transmitters, Chamberlain began to sell its garage door openers subject to a license that prohibited use of competitors' transmitters.

The Federal Circuit's *dicta* certainly suggest that it would have preferred not to impose DMCA liability under such circumstances. In rejecting Chamberlain's argument that it was entitled to prohibit legitimate purchasers of embedded software from using it in a certain manner, the Federal Circuit stated that this entitlement would "allow any copyright owner, through a combination of contractual terms and technological measures, to repeal the fair use doctrine with respect to an individual copyrighted work."[108] The Federal Circuit stated that this implication contradicted the section 1201(c)(1) savings clause directly. But even if circumvention in defiance of a contractual term was not a DMCA violation, the Federal Circuit's decision in *Bowers v. Baystate*[109] suggested that such circumvention could be a breach of contract. In *Bowers*, the Federal Circuit enforced a contractual restriction on software reverse engineering permitted by the Copyright Act.[110]

A remaining question is why both courts engaged in complex analysis of the DMCA and its legislative history when they could have decided the cases on simpler, narrower grounds. In *Chamberlain* the Federal Circuit could merely have affirmed the district court's finding that Chamberlain had authorized the circumvention, or it could have found the circumvention permitted under the interoperability exception (section 1201(f)).[111] Similarly, since the *Lexmark* panel found that section 1201(f) could apply,

107. Id. at 1202 n.17.
108. Id. at 1202.
109. *Bowers v. Baystate Technologies, Inc.*, 320 F.3d 1317 (Fed. Cir.), *cert. denied*, 539 U.S. 928 (2003). We discuss enforceability of contractual restrictions on reverse engineering in chapter 4.
110. Judge Dyk's dissent in *Bowers*, however, could form the basis for a panel's declining to enforce a contractual restriction on circumvention. See subsection 4.1.2.2 below.
111. The Federal Circuit did not reach the interoperability exception: "Because § 1201(f) is an affirmative defense, it becomes relevant only if Chamberlain can prove a *prima facie* case and shift the burden of proof to Skylink." *Chamberlain*, 381 F.3d at 1201 n.15.

it had no need to rule that a circumvention did not violate the DMCA if other means of access existed.

Clearly, both panels objected to the DMCA's being used "offensively" to prevent competition in aftermarkets. But, as the *Lexmark* panel recognized, "Congress added the interoperability provision in part to ensure that the DMCA would not diminish the benefits to consumers of interoperable devices in the consumer electronics environment."[112] Since Congress included section 1201(f) precisely to address these kinds of cases, why did the courts look beyond that section? Judge Merritt provided one explanation of the reluctance to rely on the interoperability exception:

> [W]e should be wary of shifting the burden to a rival manufacturer to demonstrate that its conduct falls under such an exception in cases where there is no indication that it has any intention of pirating a protected work. A monopolist could enforce its will against a smaller rival simply because the potential cost of extended litigation and discovery where the burden of proof shifts to the defendant is itself a deterrent to innovation and competition. Misreading the statute to shift the burden in this way could allow powerful manufacturers in practice to create monopolies where they are not in principle supported by law.[113]

By placing the initial burden of proving intent to infringe on the plaintiff, Judge Merritt (and perhaps the *Chamberlain* panel too) hoped to prevent abusive litigation by companies with market power.

The *Chamberlain* and *Lexmark* decisions reflect the practical wisdom of the federal appellate courts. Both panels were confronted by conduct that appeared to constitute *prima facie* violations of the DMCA, even though Congress clearly did not intend to target such conduct. Cognizant that in the future dominant companies might bring similar DMCA actions to prevent competition from smaller firms, judges on both panels adopted broad rationales that not only would dictate the correct outcome in these cases but also would influence the course of the litigation. By placing on plaintiffs the burden of proving intent to infringe, the judges permitted smaller defendants to "short-circuit" the litigation through dispositive motions in cases where infringement is nowhere to be seen.

3.3.5 *Storage Technology Corp. v. Custom Hardware* (2005)

In 2005, the U.S. Court of Appeals for the Federal Circuit reaffirmed its *Chamberlain* holding in *Storage Technology Corporation v. Custom Hardware.*[114]

---

112. *Lexmark*, 387 F.3d at 549 (citations omitted).
113. Id. at 552 (Merritt, J., concurring).
114. 421 F.3d 1307 (Fed. Cir. 2005).

This second Federal Circuit ruling solidified the requirement of a nexus between circumvention and infringement. The case involved the actions of Custom Hardware, an independent service organization (ISO) that had circumvented the technological protection in diagnostic software included in storage systems offered by Storage Technology Corporation (StorageTek). The district court found that StorageTek was likely to prevail on its copyright claim that the ISO had infringed the copyright in the diagnostic software when the ISO had booted up the customer's computer. The district court further found that StorageTek was likely to prevail on its claim that the ISO had violated section 1201 of the DMCA by overriding a password protection system to gain access to error messages generated by the diagnostic software.

The Federal Circuit reversed on both grounds. The court found that Custom Hardware was not liable for making a copy of the program in the computer's random-access memory when it booted up the customer's computer; the court held that the RAM copy exception for ISOs provided by 17 U.S.C. § 117(c) permitted the RAM copies the ISO had made. (In response to the Ninth Circuit's decision in *MAI v. Peak*, Congress included Title III of the DMCA to expand section 117 to protect hardware maintenance by ISOs.)

With respect to the DMCA claim, the Federal Circuit followed its ruling in *Chamberlain* and reversed the lower court. The Federal Circuit ruled that "[t]o the extent that [the ISO's] activities do not constitute copyright infringement or facilitate copyright infringement, StorageTek is foreclosed from maintaining an action under the DMCA."[115] Similarly, because "StorageTek's rights under the copyright law are not at risk, the DMCA does not create a new source of liability."[116] "A court," the Federal Circuit explained, "must look at the threat that the unauthorized circumvention potentially poses in each case to determine if there is a connection between the circumvention and a right protected by the Copyright Act."[117] Here, there was no nexus between circumvention and infringement, for two reasons. First, as was noted above, section 117(c) permitted the RAM copies made by the ISO. Second, the RAM copying occurred automatically whenever the program rebooted, regardless of whether the ISO circumvented the technological protection. Thus, the circumvention did not facilitate infringement.[118]

115. 421 F.3d at 1318.
116. Id.
117. Id. at 1319.
118. In *Nordstrom Consulting, Inc. v. M&S Technologies, Inc.*, 2008 U.S. Dist. LEXIS 17259 (N.D. Ill. March 4, 2008), the court relied on *Chamberlain* and *Storage Technology* to find that an ISO that bypassed a password system to service a program did not

3.3.6   *Davidson v. Jung* (2005)

In contrast to the sophisticated analysis of the DMCA by the Federal Circuit in *Chamberlain* and by the Sixth Circuit in *Lexmark*, the U.S. Court of Appeals for the Eighth Circuit's incorrect interpretation of the interoperability exception in *Davidson & Associates v. Jung*[119] reveals obvious misunderstandings of fact and law.[120] Thus, other courts should not accord it much weight.

3.3.6.1   Facts

Blizzard Entertainment, a subsidiary of Vivendi Universal Games, offers a service, called Battle.net, that allows owners of Blizzard games to play against one another online. Some dissatisfied users of Battle.net developed an open-source alternative that they named bnetd. They designed the bnetd software to emulate much of the functionality of Battle.net. In particular, owners of Blizzard games could log onto the bnetd server and play against other Blizzard gamers who had logged onto that server.

To develop the bnetd software, the gamers reverse engineered the Blizzard game and its communications with the Battle.net software after they had accepted end-user license agreements (EULAs) in both the games and the Battle.net website that prohibited reverse engineering. Additionally, the bnetd software did not contain an authentication feature that was present in Battle.net. Blizzard assigned a unique identifier to each copy of its games. Battle.net would not allow a gamer to log on if another gamer with the same number was already logged on. This made it difficult for possessors of infringing copies to log on to Battle.net, for the infringing copies had the same identifier as the original from which they were copied. Because bnetd did not contain this authentication feature, bnetd interoperated freely with infringing copies of Blizzard games.

3.3.6.2   The District Court's Decision

Blizzard alleged that the developers of bnetd had breached the EULAs prohibiting reverse engineering. Following the Federal Circuit's decision in

---

violate section 1201: "Plaintiffs have failed to show that Defendants' circumvention of the password protection to gain access to [Plaintiffs'] software infringed or facilitated infringing on Plaintiffs' rights under the Copyright Act. It is undisputed that [Defendant] accessed [Plaintiffs'] software in order to repair or replace the software of a client of [Defendant] and a valid licensee of [Plaintiffs'] software."

119. 422 F.3d 630 (8th Cir. 2005).

120. This subsection is based on Jonathan Band, "Caught in a Blizzard," *Journal of Internet Law*, November 2005.

Bowers v. Baystate,[121] the district court found that the EULAs were not pre-empted by section 301(a) of the Copyright Act and that the bnetd developers had breached them.

Blizzard also claimed that the developers of bnetd had enabled the circumvention of a technological protection measure in violation of section 1201 of the DMCA. Specifically, bnetd allowed owners of Blizzard games to circumvent a technological protection in the game so that the gamers could play their games in the Battle.net mode on a bnetd server rather than on the Battle.net server. After finding that bnetd enabled circumvention of the technological protection, the district court considered, and rejected, the interoperability defense contained in section 1201(f) of the DMCA.

Section 1201(f)(2) permits software developers to provide consumers with means of circumventing technological protection measures for the purpose of achieving interoperability between two computer programs. The district court dismissed the interoperability defense on the grounds that the bnetd developers' actions "constituted more than enabling interoperability" and "extended into the realm of copyright infringement."[122] The district court, however, did not clearly explain how the defendants' actions "extended into the realm of copyright infringement."

The developers of bnetd appealed the district court's ruling concerning preemption and the DMCA's interoperability exception.

3.3.6.3   The Eighth Circuit's DMCA Holding[123]

The Eighth Circuit correctly acknowledged that the DMCA "contains several exceptions, including one for individuals using circumvention technology 'for the sole purpose' of trying to achieve 'interoperability' of computer programs through reverse engineering."[124] The court then accurately listed the requirements of the exception, including that "the alleged circumvention did not constitute infringement."

The Eighth Circuit next stated that "Appellants' circumvention in this case constitutes infringement." It proceeded to describe the bnetd developers' actions, none of which constituted infringement by the developers. "The bnetd.org emulator," the court observed, "enabled users of Blizzard games to access Battle.net mode features without a valid or unique CD Key to enter Battle.net. The bnetd.org emulator did not determine whether the

---

121. 320 F.3d 1317 (Fed. Cir. 2003). We discuss this case in greater detail in subsection 4.1.1.

122. *Davidson & Associates v. Internet Gateway*, 334 F. Supp. 2d 1164 (E.D. Mo. 2004), *aff'd*, 422 F.3d 630 (8th Cir. 2005).

123. We discuss the Eighth Circuit's preemption holding in subsection 4.1.2.

CD Key was valid or currently in use by another player. As a result, unauthorized copies of the Blizzard games were freely played on the bnetd.org servers."[125]

The Eighth Circuit failed to recognize that the developers of bnetd had not made the copies of the Blizzard games; the gamers had. Moreover, the bnetd developers had not contributed to this infringement; at most, they had provided a venue for the infringing copies to be used *after* the infringement had occurred.

But even if the developers of bnetd had infringed or induced the infringement of the copyright in Blizzard games under *MGM Studios v. Grokster,*[126] that would not have affected the availability of the section 1201(f) defense with respect to bnetd. Under sections 1201(f)(2) and (3), a person may develop, employ, and make available to others a technological means of circumventing a protection for purposes of achieving interoperability so long as the development, employment, or distribution of the technology does not constitute infringement. Thus, the relevant question was whether the bnetd program itself infringed any Blizzard copyright.

Interestingly, the developers entered into a consent decree under which they admitted that they had copied Blizzard code, files, and images in bnetd. In their brief on appeal, the developers argued that these were "a few small, unrelated icon files" that were included in bnetd "to help players recognize others when they 'chatted' on the system."[127] They claimed that this "de minimus" copying had nothing to do with accessing the Battle.net mode or with any circumvention. Blizzard, in its brief to the Eighth Circuit, emphasized this copying: "Appellants copied into their final product original works of Blizzard—its images and code were unnecessary for an independent work and unnecessary to achieve interoperability—solely because Appellants wanted to recreate Battle.net Mode as faithfully as possible."[128]

It is hard to understand why the Eighth Circuit ignored the admitted copying by the developers of bnetd and instead based its rejection of the 1201(f) defense on infringements by unknown third parties. It is conceivable that the Eighth Circuit did not fully comprehend the complex

124. *Jung,* 422 F.3d at 641.
125. Id. at 642.
126. 545 U.S. 913.
127. Opening Brief of Defendants-Appellants, *Davidson v. Jung,* 422 F.3d 630 (8th Cir. 2005) (No. 04-3654), 2005 WL 1467962, at 45.
128. Opposition Brief of Plaintiffs-Appellees, *Davidson v. Jung,* 422 F.3d 630 (8th Cir. 2005) (No. 04-3654), 2005 WL 1521191.

technical facts before it, or that it misread the statute. Surely the Eighth Circuit did not intend to deprive software developers of the 1201(f) safe harbor on account of infringements by unaffiliated third parties.

Consider the following example: Company X develops accounting software which users can install in their computers to maintain their household finances. When taxes are due, a user can log onto Company X's website, where a program calculates the amount of taxes the user owes. The website and the accounting software have an authentication protocol—a "secret handshake"—which ensures that only authorized owners of the accounting software can log onto the website and use the tax calculator. Although the accounting software is well designed, the tax calculator makes serious errors. Accordingly, Company Y designs its own tax calculator, which users of X software can access. In order to interoperate with the users' X software, the Y calculator emulates the X calculator's handshake. However, because the Y calculator's handshake is somewhat simpler than the X calculator's, it allows users of infringing copies of X accounting software to gain access to the Y calculator.

From a policy perspective, it makes no sense to deny the 1201(f) safe harbor to Y just because some users have made unauthorized copies of X's accounting software. Legitimate users of X accounting software should not be denied the use of a superior tax calculator just because infringers of the accounting software can also use the superior tax calculator. The plain language of 1201(f) does not require such an absurd result.

In any event, given the confusing facts in this case, subsequent courts are likely to focus on the Eighth Circuit's statement that "Appellants' circumvention in this case constitutes infringement," and not to worry about the details. Future defendants will be able to distinguish this case if they are able to convince courts that their acts of circumvention did not constitute infringement. And if a court looks into how the circumvention in this case constituted infringement, the record indicates that bnetd copied original Blizzard material.

3.3.7   The *TracFone* Cases (2007, 2008)

Two district courts in Florida have issued problematic decisions that are inconsistent not only with *Chamberlain* and *Lexmark* but also with a specific exemption to section 1201(a) granted by the Librarian of Congress.

A mobile telephone handset contains a computer program, in a firmware format, that enables the handset to connect to the network of a mobile communications provider. The program in the handset can be reprogrammed to enable a user to connect to another provider's network.

To prevent this reprogramming, and thereby lock a user into a particular network, the provider typically employs a technological measure that prevents access to the program.

TracFone adopted a business model of making handsets available below cost while generating profit by selling prepaid airtime cards. Several competitors purchased the inexpensive TracFone handsets in bulk, circumvented the technological protection measure on the handsets' programs, reprogrammed the handsets so that they could connect to another network, and sold the reprogrammed handsets to consumers. TracFone sued the competitors for violating the DMCA, and the competitors applied for an exemption in the 2006 rulemaking cycle.

In her recommendation to the Librarian of Congress to grant an exemption, the Register of Copyrights found that a user who unlocks a phone to connect to another network is not "engaging in copyright infringement or in an activity that in any way implicates copyright infringement or the interests of the copyright holder."[129] Once the program was unlocked, it was reprogrammed, not copied. The reprogramming of a particular piece of firmware could be seen as making an adaptation of a copyrighted work, but 17 U.S.C. 117(a)(1) specifically permits the owner of a copy of a program to adapt that copy "as an essential step in the utilization of the computer program in conjunction with a machine." Accordingly, the Librarian of Congress approved the following exemption: "Computer programs in the form of firmware that enable wireless telephone handsets to connect to a wireless telephone communication network, when circumvention is accomplished for the sole purpose of lawfully connecting to a wireless telephone communication network."[130]

Notwithstanding the exemption, TracFone has continued to sue its competitors for violating section 1201(a) of the DMCA. Two federal district courts in Florida have ruled, for the flimsiest of reasons, that the exemption does not apply. The exemption permits circumvention when it is "accomplished for the sole purpose of lawfully connecting to a wireless telephone communication network." However, according to the courts in *TracFone v. GSM Group*[131] and *TracFone v. Dixon*,[132] the competitors circumvented for the purpose of reselling handsets for a profit, not for the purpose of connecting to a communications network. In other words, the exemption

129. Recommendation of the Register of Copyrights 50 (November 17, 2006).
130. 71 *Fed. Reg.* 68472 (November 27, 2006).
131. 555 F.Supp. 2d 1331 (S.D. Fla. 2008).
132. 475 F.Supp. 2d 1236 (M.D. Fla. 2007).

was available only to the user who would actually connect to the communications network, and not to the firm with the expertise to reprogram the handset for the user. This limitation of the exemption to end users effectively renders the exemption nugatory—a result the Librarian of Congress could not have intended when he granted the exemption. The courts' flawed reasoning could also be applied to the other exemptions granted by the Librarian, rendering them ineffective as well.

In the rulemaking cycle beginning in December of 2008, TracFone's competitors requested a modification of the exemption to clarify its application to the providers of reprogrammed handsets in addition to end users. The competitors could not rely on the interoperability exception in section 1201(f), because the objective of the circumvention is not achieving interoperability between two computer programs; rather, the objective is receiving a wireless frequency. On the other hand, under the *Chamberlain* court's interpretation of section 1201(a), the TracFone competitors had not violated the DMCA, because there is no nexus between their circumvention and copyright infringement.

3.3.8 *MDY Industries v. Blizzard Entertainment* (2009)

In early 2009, a federal district court in Arizona issued a problematic DMCA decision concerning the computer game World of Warcraft (WoW). MDY had developed Glider, a computer program that continued playing WoW while the user was away from the computer. Blizzard, owner of the copyright in WoW, had implemented technological measures to defeat programs such as Glider. For example, Blizzard used a program called Warden, which scanned a user's hard drive for unauthorized programs before allowing the user to log onto the game server. Another component of Warden periodically scanned the user's memory while the user was playing WoW, again looking for unauthorized software such as Glider. MDY had redesigned Glider several times to avoid detection by Warden.

Blizzard sued MDY, claiming (among other things) that it was trafficking in a circumvention technology in violation of 17 U.S.C. 1201(a)(2). The district court found that Blizzard had succeeded in showing all the elements of a circumvention violation.[133] The court held that Glider's efforts to avoid detection by Warden constituted circumvention of a technological protection measure. The court further found that Warden prevented access to "dynamic nonliteral elements" of WoW controlled by the server

---

133. *MDY Indus., LLC v. Blizzard Entm't, Inc.*, 2009 U.S. Dist. LEXIS 9898 (D. Az. January 28, 2009).

software. These dynamic elements were "the real-time experience of travel-ing through different worlds, hearing their sounds, viewing their structures, encountering their inhabitants and monsters, and encountering other players." MDY argued that these elements were not sufficiently fixed to constitute protectable works. Although the court's reasoning on this point is weak, some of the nonliteral elements probably are sufficiently fixed to constitute protectable works.

The court acknowledged that under the Federal Circuit's decision in *Chamberlain v. Skylink* the circumvention had to infringe or facilitate infringement. The court found that because Glider enabled a user to access the dynamic nonliteral elements by circumventing Warden, the *Chamberlain* "nexus to infringement" requirement was met. However, any user without Glider could also access the dynamic nonliteral elements and record them. Glider did not provide a user with any special access that facil-itated infringement. This aspect of the decision appears erroneous. Also, the interoperability exception in section 1201(f) could have been used to excuse MDY's circumvention. Glider avoided detection by Warden for the purpose of achieving interoperability with the WoW server software. How-ever, the court did not address section 1201(f) in its opinion.

3.4 Free-Trade Agreements

Pursuant to the Trade Promotion Authority Act of 2002, the United States has negotiated a series of free-trade agreements (FTAs) with its trading part-ners. Each of these agreements contains an intellectual-property chapter that, among other things, requires parties to take measures to "provide adequate legal protection and effective legal remedies against the circum-vention of effective technological measures"[134] used by authors to restrict unauthorized uses of their works. The agreements then specify that the par-ties shall provide legal remedies against any person who "circumvents with-out authority any effective technological measure that controls access to a protected work."[135] Further, the parties must impose liability on any person who manufactures, offers to the public, or otherwise traffics in devices or components that are primarily designed for the purpose of enabling or facil-itating the circumvention of an effective technological measure. In other words, through the free-trade agreements, the United States is exporting section 1201 to its trading partners. Like section 1201, the circumvention

134. See, e.g., Korea-U.S. Free Trade Agreement, Art. 18.4.7(a), June 30, 2007.
135. Id. at (a)(i).

provisions of the FTAs grossly exceed the requirements of the circumvention articles of the WIPO Internet treaties.

The FTAs include exceptions modeled on the exceptions to section 1201. With respect to interoperability, each party may permit "[n]oninfringing reverse engineering activities with regard to a lawfully obtained copy of a computer program, carried out in good faith with respect to particular elements of that computer program that have not been readily available to the person engaged in those activities, for the sole purpose of achieving interoperability of an independently created computer program with other programs."[136]

The FTAs mandate that parties confine limitations and exceptions to those enumerated in the agreement or subsequently approved through "a legislative or administrative proceeding by substantial evidence." The FTAs thus do not permit parties to restrict the prohibition on circumvention activities only to situations where there is a nexus between circumvention and infringement. Thus, the *Chamberlain* and *Lexmark* decisions arguably render the United States non-compliant with its obligations under the FTAs.

The FTAs' high degree of specificity with respect to circumvention constrain the ability of U.S. law to evolve in response to new technologies and other changed circumstances. Senator Patrick Leahy (D-VT), chairman of the Senate Judiciary Committee, criticized this characteristic of the FTAs in 2007, when the Senate was considering the U.S.-Peru Trade Promotion Agreement. Senator Leahy observed that in the Trade Promotion Act, Congress instructed the Clinton administration to negotiate agreements with other nations that reflect a standard of intellectual-property protection "similar to that found in the United States." Although the Peru agreement met that goal in many respects, Leahy voiced concern. "Some aspects of the intellectual property chapter," said Leahy,

136. Id. at (d)(i). The United States has proposed that the Anti-Counterfeiting Trade Agreement (ACTA) now being negotiated include a provision based on section 1201. Under the U.S. proposal, each party "shall provide adequate legal protection and effective legal remedies against the circumvention of effective technological measures that are used by authors ...in connection with the exercise of their rights and that restrict unauthorized acts in respect of their works...." The U.S. proposal, however, does not specifically require adoption of an interoperability exception. Instead, the proposal simply provides that each country "*may* adopt exceptions and limitations to measures implementing subparagraph (4) so long as they do not significantly impair the adequacy of legal protection of those measures or the effectiveness of legal remedies for violations of those measures." (Emphasis added.) Thus, the U.S. proposal makes the circumvention prohibition mandatory, but exceptions only permissive. In this manner, the U.S. proposal lacks the balance found in section 1201.

prescribe rules for protection so specifically that Congress will be hampered from making constructive policy changes in the future. The art of drafting the chapter is in raising intellectual property protections to a standard similar to ours, without limiting Congress's ability to make appropriate refinements to the intellectual property law in the future. The flexibility necessary for the proper balance is found in many provisions of the intellectual property chapter, for which I commend the U.S. Trade Representative. Other provisions, however, are too fixed and rigid, and may have the perverse effect of restricting the Congress's ability to make legitimate changes in United States law, while keeping our international commitments.[137]

There is a positive aspect to the export of the DMCA via the FTAs: Trading partners now have interoperability exceptions to their laws prohibiting circumvention.[138] Many of these countries have not yet addressed the permissibility of software reverse engineering in their copyright laws. The presence of a statutory interoperability exception relating to circumvention implies legislative support for the lawfulness of the underlying reverse-engineering activity.

Two events during the summer of 2010 demonstrated the ongoing relevance of the DMCA to interoperability. First, the Fifth Circuit, in *MGE UPS Systems Inc. v. GE Consumer and Industrial Inc.*, 2010 WL 2820006, at *3 (5th Cir. July 20, 2010), agreed with the Federal Circuit in Chamberlain that DMCA liability cannot result from "accessing a work simply to view it or to use it within the purview of 'fair use' permitted under the Copyright Act." Rather, "the DMCA prohibits only forms of access that violate or impinge on the protections the Copyright Act otherwise affords copyright owners." Second, the Librarian of Congress granted an exemption under section 1201(a)(1)(C) for the "jailbreaking" of cell phone handsets, discussed in footnote 51 above. The prohibition on circumvention will not apply to "computer programs that enable wireless telephone handsets to execute software applications, where circumvention is accomplished for the sole purpose of enabling interoperability of such applications . . . with computer programs on the telephone handset" (75 *Fed. Reg.* 43825, July 27, 2010). However, the Librarian narrowed the exemption for unlocking a handset to connect to another provider's network to used handsets.

137. Congressional Record S14720, December 4, 2007 (Statement of Senator Leahy).
138. See, e.g., subsection 5.1.4 below.

4 Contractual Limitations on Reverse Engineering

Most software is distributed subject to a license of some sort, and many of these licenses prohibit reverse engineering for any reason. The EU Software Directive fashioned a simple rule that contractual restrictions on reverse engineering permitted under that directive were null and void. But the situation in the United States is far more complex and unsettled. There seems little doubt that a reverse-engineering restriction contained in a negotiated agreement between parties of equal bargaining strength would be enforceable. Moreover, in *Bowers v. Baystate Techs., Inc.*[1] the Federal Circuit ruled that a shrinkwrap restriction on reverse engineering is also enforceable.[2] However, the dissent in *Bowers* raises serious questions concerning the majority's opinion, highlighting its divergence from the Fifth Circuit's decision in *Vault Corp. v. Quaid Software Ltd.*[3] In *Bowers* the Federal Circuit also assumed, perhaps erroneously, that the shrinkwrap license was an enforceable contract under state law. In sum, whether shrinkwrap restrictions on reverse engineering are enforceable in the United States is far from resolved.

4.1 Preemption

4.1.1 *Bowers v. Baystate Technologies* (2003)

4.1.1.1 Facts
Harold L. Bowers (doing business as HLB Technology) and Baystate Technologies, Inc. both produced software tools for CADKEY, a tool used in computer-aided design. At one point, Bowers suggested to Baystate that

1. 320 F.3d 1317 (Fed. Cir.), *cert. denied*, 539 U.S. 928 (2003).
2. A shrinkwrap license is printed on or within the plastic wrapping enclosing a software product. According to most shrinkwrap licenses, the licensee agrees to its terms by tearing the plastic shrinkwrap, which the licensee must do to use the product.
3. 847 F.2d 255 (5th Cir. 1988).

they bundle their software together; Baystate declined, saying it could develop those functions internally. Instead, Baystate obtained Bowers' software, reverse engineered it in disregard of the shrinkwrap license, and incorporated many elements of Bowers' software in its own product. Baystate subsequently purchased Cadkey, Inc. and Bowers went out of business. Bowers sued for copyright infringement, patent infringement, and breach of contract. The jury found for Bowers on all three counts. Baystate appealed. In its first decision, the U.S. Court of Appeals for the Federal Circuit, applying what it understood to be the law of the First Circuit, reversed the finding of patent infringement, but upheld the holding that Baystate had breached the license by reverse engineering Bowers' software. Baystate petitioned for rehearing, arguing primarily that the shrinkwrap prohibition on reverse engineering was preempted by the Intellectual Property Clause of the Constitution. The Computer & Communications Industry Association and other groups filed an *amicus* brief in support of Baystate's arguments. The panel issued a new decision in late January of 2003.[4] Two of the judges generally restated their earlier opinion, with some additional discussion of the points raised by Baystate in its petition for rehearing. Judge Dyk, however, filed a sharp dissent, in essence adopting the arguments of Baystate and its *amici*. We now wade into the abstruse dispute between the majority and the dissent.

4.1.1.2 Section 301(a) Preemption

There are two theories of preemption: statutory preemption under section 301(a) of the Copyright Act, and constitutional preemption under the Intellectual Property Clause. Section 301(a) preempts state laws creating "rights that are equivalent to any of the exclusive rights within the general scope of copyright." Courts have interpreted section 301(a) as not preempting a state cause of action that requires proof of "extra elements" not present in a copyright claim. The Seventh Circuit ruled in *ProCD, Inc. v. Zeidenberg*[5] that section 301(a) did not preempt enforcement of a contract prohibiting the copying of telephone listings, because the contract claim required proof of an extra element: the existence of an enforceable contract.

On the other hand, the copyright treatise *Nimmer on Copyright* has rejected the *ProCD* analysis:

[A]t times a breach of contract cause of action can serve as a subterfuge to control nothing other than the reproduction, adaptation, public distribution, etc. of works

4. 320 F.3d 1317 (Fed. Cir. 2003).
5. 86 F.3d 1447 (7th Cir. 1996).

within the subject matter of copyright. That situation typically unfolds when the "contract" at issue consists of a "shrinkwrap license" to which the copyright owner demands adhesion as a condition to licensing its materials. To the extent that such a contract is determined to be binding under state law, then that law may be attempting to vindicate rights indistinguishable from those accorded by the Copyright Act. Under that scenario, the subject contract cause of action should be deemed pre-empted. . . . Although the vast majority of contract claims will presumably survive scrutiny . . . nonetheless pre-emption should strike down claims that, although denominated "contract," nonetheless complain directly about the reproduction of expressive materials.[6]

The district court in *Selby v. New Line Cinema*[7] relied on the preceding passage in *Nimmer on Copyright* when it declined to enforce an implied-in-fact contract prohibiting the use of an idea without attribution. Similarly, in *Symantec Corp. v. McAfee Assocs., Inc.*,[8] the district court rejected a state law unfair-competition claim based on an alleged breach of a contractual restriction on reverse engineering. The court found that the mere existence of the agreement was not sufficient to transform "what essentially is a copyright infringement claim" into "something more."[9]

6. Melville B. Nimmer and David Nimmer, *Nimmer on Copyright*, § 1.01[B][1][a] at 1–19 and 1–22 (2001) (citations omitted).
7. 96 F. Supp. 2d 1053 (C.D. Cal. 2000).
8. 1998 WL 740798 (N.D. Cal. June 9, 1998).
9. Id. at *5. See *Kabehie et al. v. Zoland, et al.*, 125 Cal. Rptr. 721 (Cal. Ct. App. 2002): The cases that have decided the issue of federal copyright preemption of state breach of contract causes of action can be roughly divided into two groups: (1) a minority of the cases hold state breach of contract causes of action are never preempted by federal copyright law; and (2) a majority of the cases hold state breach of contract actions are not preempted by federal copyright law when they seek to enforce rights that are qualitatively different from the exclusive rights of copyright. . . . We adopt the majority view. . . . The promise alleged to have been breached in a breach of contract action does not always make the contract action qualitatively different from a copyright infringement action. If the promise was simply to refrain from copying the material or infringing the rights protected by copyright, then the promisor has promised nothing more than that which was already required under federal copyright law. The promise not to infringe adds nothing to a breach of contract action for copyright infringement. A breach of contract action based on this type of promise must be preempted in order to prevent parties from circumventing federal copyright law and nullifying the preemption provided for in section 301.
    See also *Health Grades Inc. v. Robert Wood Johnson University Hospital, Inc.*, 2009 WL 1763327 (D. Colo. June 19, 2009); *Ritchie v. Williams*, 395 F.3d 283, 287 n. 3 (6th Cir. 2005); *Wrench LLC v. Taco Bell Corp.*, 256 F.3d 446, 457 (6th Cir. 2001);

The *Bowers* majority cited First Circuit authority that seemed to agree with the analysis in *Nimmer on Copyright*. In *Data Gen. Corp. v. Grumman Sys. Support Corp.*,[10] the First Circuit noted that not every extra element will establish a qualitative variance between rights under copyright and those protected by state law. Thus, if the extra elements are "illusory . . . mere labels attached to the same odious business conduct,"[11] preemption will occur. Nonetheless, the *Bowers* majority agreed with *ProCD* and found that the shrinkwrap license constituted an extra element.

Rather than challenge *ProCD* directly, Judge Dyk distinguished it. He said that in *ProCD* the shrinkwrap enabled price discrimination between commercial and non-commercial users. Non-commercial users received fewer rights under the shrinkwrap in exchange for a lower price. Thus, the shrinkwrap in *ProCD* really was an extra element, and not just a prohibition on copying permitted under the Copyright Act. In this case, by contrast, the shrinkwrap was simply intended to limit fair use.

4.1.1.3 Constitutional Preemption

Both the majority and the dissenting opinions in *Bowers* also discussed constitutional preemption—an issue not addressed by the *ProCD* court. In 1988, the U.S. Court of Appeals for the Fifth Circuit set aside a contractual restriction on reverse engineering in *Vault Corp. v. Quaid Software Ltd.*[12] The Fifth Circuit cited *Sears, Roebuck & Co. v. Stiffel Co.*,[13] in which the Supreme Court relied on the U.S. Constitution's Supremacy Clause to conclude that "[w]hen state law touches upon an area of [the copyright statutes], it is 'familiar' doctrine' that the federal policy 'may not be set at naught, or its benefits denied' by state law."[14] The Fifth Circuit held that a reverse-engineering prohibition in a shrinkwrap license "conflicts with the rights of computer program owners under section 117 and clearly 'touches upon an area' of federal copyright law."[15] Likewise, the Supreme Court in *Bonito Boats v. Thunder Craft Boats* relied on the Supremacy Clause to preempt a

---

Tavormina v. Evening Star Prods., Inc., 10 F. Supp. 2d 729, 734 (S.D. Tex. 1998); *Am. Movie Classics Co. v. Turner Entm't Co.*, 922 F. Supp. 926, 931 (S.D. N.Y. 1996).

10. 36 F.3d 1147 (1st Cir. 1994).
11. Id. at 1165.
12. 847 F.2d 255 (5th Cir. 1988).
13. 376 U.S. 225 (1964).
14. *Sears*, 376 U.S. at 229 (citations omitted).
15. *Vault*, 847 F.2d at 270.

Florida "anti-plug-molding" statute it found inconsistent with the federal intellectual-property system.[16]

Judge Dyk, in his dissent in *Bowers*, followed the reasoning of *Vault* and *Bonito Boats* to argue for constitutional preemption. The majority responded with a line of First Circuit cases upholding the waiver of privileges by contract. Judge Dyk countered by saying that a waiver might be valid in the context of a negotiated agreement, but not a shrinkwrap license. He emphasized that the majority's position would allow publishers to eliminate fair use and other copyright limitations by printing words to that effect on a copyrighted work.[17]

In sum, the *Bowers* majority found that all contracts always provide an extra element and thus are never preempted. The *Bowers* dissent stated that a negotiated contract provided an extra element, but a shrinkwrap license did not. *New Line Cinema, Symantec,* and *Kabehie* could be understood as holding that a contract never provides the extra element, unless it imposes an obligation not related to the exclusive rights under the Copyright Act. *Vault v. Quaid* reaches the same conclusion under the Constitution rather than section 301(a).

4.1.2   *Davidson v. Jung* (2005)

Davidson & Assocs. v. Jung[18] concerned gamers who had developed an alternative platform on which they could play a popular computer video game.[19] The game's developer sued, claiming that the gamers had violated the Digital Millennium Copyright Act by circumventing a lockout system on the platform and had breached the end user license agreement's prohibition on reverse engineering. The DMCA issues were discussed above in chapter 3.[20] Here, we will examine the Eighth Circuit's flawed adherence to *Bowers*.

4.1.2.1   Facts

Blizzard Entertainment provides the Battle.net service, which allows owners of Blizzard games to play against one another online. Some users of Battle.net developed an open-source alternative, bnetd, to emulate much of the functionality of Battle.net. Owners of Blizzard games could log onto

16. *Bonito Boats, Inc. v. Thunder Craft Boats, Inc.*, 489 U.S. 141 (1989).
17. We discuss Judge Dyk's dissent in greater detail in subsection 4.1.2.
18. 422 F.3d 630 (8th Cir. 2005).
19. This subsection is based on Jonathan Band, "Caught in a Blizzard," *Journal of Internet Law*, November 2005.
20. See subsection 3.3.6.

the bnetd server and play against other Blizzard gamers also logged onto the bnetd server.

To develop the bnetd software, the gamers reverse engineered the Blizzard game and its communications with the Battle.net software after accepting end-user license agreements (EULAs) in both the games and the Battle.net website that prohibited reverse engineering. Blizzard alleged that the developers of bnetd had breached the EULAs prohibiting reverse engineering. The district court found that the EULAs were not preempted by section 301(a) of the Copyright Act and that the bnetd developers had breached them. The bnetd developers appealed the district court's ruling concerning preemption.

4.1.2.2 The Eighth Circuit's Preemption Holding

The U.S. Court of Appeals for the Eighth Circuit correctly recognized that two forms of preemption come into play when considering contractual restrictions on a privilege granted under the Copyright Act: express preemption under section 301(a) of the Copyright Act, and conflict preemption (which arises when state law stands as an obstacle to the accomplishment and execution of the full purposes and objectives of Congress). As was discussed above, courts have interpreted section 301(a) as not preempting a state cause of action that requires proof of "extra elements" not present in a copyright claim. Several courts have held that contract claims survive section 301(a) challenge because they require proof of an extra element: the existence of an enforceable contract.[21]

This leaves constitutional preemption, which was the focus of the bnetd developers' preemption argument. A split on this issue exists between the Fifth Circuit and the Federal Circuit (interpreting the law in the First Circuit). The Fifth Circuit, in *Vault v. Quaid*,[22] considered a Louisiana statute which provided that shrinkwrap licenses prohibiting reverse engineering were enforceable. The court found that a reverse-engineering prohibition in a shrinkwrap license conflicts with the rights of computer program owners under 17 U.S.C. § 117 and clearly "touches upon an area" of federal copyright law.[23] Accordingly, the Fifth Circuit refused to enforce the Louisiana statute and the shrinkwrap prohibition.

In contrast, the Federal Circuit, in *Bowers v. Baystate*, found that the First Circuit permits the waiver of statutory privileges by contract. The Eighth Circuit agreed with the Federal Circuit, quoting its statement that "private

21. See, e.g., *ProCD v. Zeidenberg*, 86 F.3d 1447 (7th Cir. 1996).
22. 847 F.2d 255 (5th Cir. 1988).
23. Id. at 270.

parties are free to contractually forgo the limited ability to reverse engineer a software product under the exemptions of the Copyright Act."[24]

But the Eighth Circuit did not explain why it preferred the Federal Circuit's rule over the Fifth Circuit's. Rather, it simply asserted that "[u]nlike in *Vault*, the state law issue here neither conflicts with the interoperability exception under 17 U.S.C. § 1201(f) nor restricts rights given under federal law."[25] This makes no sense. Numerous courts have interpreted section 107 as excusing the making of reproductions in the course of reverse engineering, and section 1201(f)(1) specifically permits circumvention to effectuate reverse engineering for purposes of achieving interoperability. Thus, enforcing the EULA here creates a direct conflict with the Copyright Act.[26]

Perhaps the Eighth Circuit was attempting to distinguish *Vault* on the ground that *Vault* concerned a state statute rather than a contract. But it was a statute dealing with the enforcement of contracts. There is no difference between refusing to enforce a contractual term and refusing to enforce a statute that provides that a contractual term is enforceable. As Judge Dyk wrote in his dissent in *Bowers*, "[f]rom a preemption standpoint, there is no distinction between a state law that explicitly validates a contract that restricts reverse engineering (*Vault*) and general common law that permits such a restriction (as here)."[27]

Moreover, the Eighth Circuit cited a statement in Judge Dyk's dissent as support for its position. It evidently did not understand that Judge Dyk's statement undercut its position. The Eighth Circuit quoted Judge Dyk as saying that "a state can permit parties to contract away a fair-use defense or to agree not to engage in uses of copyrighted material that are permitted by the copyright law if the contract is freely negotiated."[28] The last clause—"if the contract is freely negotiated"—is Judge Dyk's critical point. Judge Dyk was suggesting a way of reconciling *Vault* with the First Circuit precedent on which the *Bowers* majority relied. In Judge Dyk's view, a person could waive his privileges under the Copyright Act by contract, provided that the

24. *Bowers*, 320 F.3d at 1325–1326.

25. *Jung*, 422 F.3d at 639.

26. See *DVD Copy Control v. Bunner*, 31 Cal. 4th 864, 901 n.5 (Sup. Ct. Cal. 2003) (Moreno, J., concurring) ("[I]f trade secret law did allow alleged trade secret holders to redefine 'improper means' to include reverse engineering, it would likely be preempted by federal patent law, which alone grants universal protection for a limited time against the right to reverse engineer. See *Bonito Boats, Inc. v. Thunder Craft Boats, Inc.*, 489 U.S. 141, 155 (1989).")

27. *Bowers*, 320 F.3d at 1337 (Dyk, J., dissenting).

28. *Jung*, 422 F.3d at 639.

contract was freely negotiated. But a software firm could not eliminate such privileges simply "by printing a few words on the outside of its product."[29] Such an approach "permits state law to eviscerate an important federal copyright policy reflected in the fair use defense."[30]

The Eighth Circuit did not grasp Judge Dyk's proposed reconciliation of the First and Fifth Circuits. It incorrectly concluded that Judge Dyk agreed that contract overrides copyright in all cases. Thus, it enforced the prohibition on reverse engineering in the Blizzard EULAs, although they were not the product of negotiations between the parties. Rather, the EULAs were adhesion contracts imposed by Blizzard; the bnetd developers had to agree to the EULAs' terms before they could use the Blizzard games and the Battle.net server. Had the Eighth Circuit understood Judge Dyk's differentiation between negotiated and non-negotiated contracts, it might have reached a different result.[31]

As the case law continues to evolve, courts may adopt yet another position, somewhere between the *Bowers* majority and the dissent. Courts may conclude that shrinkwrap licenses for mass-market products are "illusory" extra elements, but that shrinkwrap licenses in limited distribution contexts are "real" extra elements. As the distribution is more limited, the relationship between licensor and licensee becomes an increasingly confidential one. This is particularly the case when the licensor provides services such as maintenance in addition to the actual product. *Bowers* involved a specialized product distributed to a specialized market; the court's conclusion may have been different had the case involved a mass-market product, such as the one at issue in *Jung*.

4.2   The Enforceability of Shrinkwrap Licenses

4.2.1   Divergent Case Law

Both the majority and the dissent in *Bowers* assumed that the shrinkwrap license formed an enforceable contract under state contract law, and focused

29. *Bowers*, 320 F.3d at 1337 (Dyk, J., dissenting).

30. Id. at 1335.

31. Judge Dyk also drew a distinction between commercial and non-commercial contracts: "The Copyright Act does not confer a right to pay the same amount for commercial and personal use. It does, however, confer a right to fair use. . . ." (*Bowers*, 320 F.3d at 1338 (Dyk, J., dissenting)) Thus, Judge Dyk might conclude that a prohibition on reverse engineering in a non-commercial license is not preempted, provided that reverse engineering was permitted under a more expensive commercial license.

their attention on whether a particular term of the license was preempted. But the enforceability of shrinkwrap, click-on, or browse-wrap licenses[32] is not a foregone conclusion. Because a user cannot use a program without "agreeing" to the terms of such a license (either by opening the package or by clicking on the "I agree" icon), the user may not have manifested assent to the license's terms. And without a manifestation of assent, there is no binding contract. Courts around the country have just begun to consider the enforceability of shrinkwrap and click-on licenses, and a consensus has not yet emerged.[33] Moreover, numerous commentators have questioned the enforceability of such contracts.[34] If the contracts are not enforceable, then obviously their terms prohibiting reverse engineering have no effect.

To the extent any pattern can be discerned in these cases, courts seem more willing to enforce click-on licenses than to enforce browse-wrap or shrinkwrap licenses, largely because it is difficult for a licensee to argue that he did not manifest assent when he clicked on an "I agree" icon. In

32. A click-on license appears when a user is installing a program on his computer. The user must click on an "I agree" icon in order to complete the installation sequence. A "browse-wrap" license, which typically appears in a website's terms of service, provides that by using the website the user agrees to the terms of service.

33. *Compare Novell, Inc. v. Network Trade Ctr., Inc.*, 25 F. Supp. 2d 1218, 1230 (D. Utah 1997); *Morgan Labs., Inc. v. Micro Data Base Sys., Inc.*, 41 U.S.P.Q.2d 1850 (N.D. Cal. 1997); *Arizona Retail Sys., Inc. v. The Software Link, Inc.*, 831 F. Supp. 759, 764–766 (D. Ariz. 1993); *Step-Saver Data Sys. v. Wyse Tech.*, 939 F.2d 91, 98–100 (3d Cir. 1991); *Foresight Resources Corp. v. Pfortmiller*, 719 F. Supp. 1006, 1010 (D. Kan. 1989); *Ticketmaster Corp. v. Tickets.com, Inc.*, 2000 U.S. Dist. LEXIS 12987 (C.D. Cal. August 10, 2000), *aff'd*, 248 F. 3d 1173 (9th Cir. 2001); *Specht v. Netscape Communications Corp.*, 306 F.3d 17 (2d Cir. 2002); *Softman Prods. Co. v. Adobe Systems, Inc.*, 171 F. Supp. 2d 1075 (C.D. Cal. 2001); and *Klocek v. Gateway, Inc.*, 104 F. Supp. 2d 1332, 1338–1339 (D. Kan. 2000); *with ProCD, Inc. v. Zeidenberg*, 86 F.3d 1447, 1449 (7th Cir. 1996), *Register.com, Inc. v. Verio, Inc.*, 356 F.3d 393 (2d Cir. 2004); *cf. Hill v. Gateway 2000, Inc.*, 105 F.3d 1147, 1150 (7th Cir. 1997), *cert. denied*, 522 U.S. 808 (1997).

34. E.g., Michael J. Madison, "'Legal Ware': Contract and Copyright in the Digital Age," 67 *Fordham Law Review* 1025 (December 1998); Robert J. Morrill, "Contract Formation and the Shrink Wrap License: A Case Comment on *ProCD, Inc. v. Zeidenberg*," 32 *New England Law Review* 513, 537–550 (1998); Apik Minassian, "The Death of Copyright: Enforceability of Shrinkwrap Licensing Agreements," 45 *UCLA Law Review* 569 (1997); Christopher L. Pitet, Comment, "The Problem with 'Money Now, Terms Later': *ProCD, Inc. v. Zeidenberg* and the Enforceability of 'Shrinkwrap' Software Licenses," 31 *Loyola of Los Angeles Law Review* 325 (1997); L. Ray Patterson and Stanley W. Lindberg, *The Nature of Copyright: A Law of Users' Rights* 220 (University of Georgia Press, 1991).

addition, courts seem more willing to enforce these licenses against corporate licensees than against consumers, presumably because they feel that corporate licensees are better able to protect their interests. The assumption of enforceability in *Bowers* is consistent with the latter view.

4.2.2 UCITA

The Uniform Computer Information Transactions Act (UCITA) was a project of the National Conference of Commissioners on Uniform State Laws (NCCUSL), which adopted UCITA in 1999 after a lengthy drafting process. A fundamental goal of UCITA was to render shrinkwrap and click-on licenses clearly enforceable as a matter of state contract law. UCITA encountered opposition from state attorneys general, organized groups of licensees, the American Law Institute, the Federal Trade Commission, and the American Bar Association. For this reason, only two states, Maryland and Virginia, have adopted UCITA. Nonetheless, even in states where UCITA has not been adopted, courts might look to it and its lengthy comments as an authoritative statement concerning contract law in the digital age.

Accordingly, UCITA has weakened the argument that shrinkwrap and click-on licenses are unenforceable as a matter of state contract law. For this reason, entities interested in preserving the reverse-engineering privilege attempted to persuade the UCITA drafters to adopt an explicit reverse-engineering exception.

Initially, the UCITA drafters took the position that any conflict between UCITA and the federal Copyright Act was addressed by UCITA's general preemption provision included: "A provision of this Act which is preempted by federal law is unenforceable to the extent of the preemption."[35] In an effort to rebut criticism of UCITA, some UCITA proponents asserted that under this provision a contractual term that attempted to limit a privilege granted under the Copyright Act was *per se* unenforceable. The UCITA reporter's comments, however, noted that "[e]xcept for rules that directly regulate specific contract terms, no general preemption of contracting arises under copyright or patent law."[36] In other words, the Copyright Act as a general matter did *not* preempt contract terms. The comment observed that preemption occurs only when the Copyright Act specifically prohibits a particular term, or in other situations recognized by the evolving case law.

Advocates of user privileges, including reverse engineering, argued that the limited and uncertain scope of preemption acknowledged in the

---

35. Uniform Computer Information Transactions Act (UCITA) § 105(a).
36. UCITA § 105(2), Reporter's Cmt.

reporter's comment rendered preemption a questionable means of preserving user privileges in an era in which the distribution of content subject to shrinkwrap or click-on license was increasingly prevalent. Ten years or more might pass before the Supreme Court rules on whether a shrinkwrap license term limiting a user privilege under the copyright laws impermissibly interferes with the federal intellectual-property system. In the meantime, courts in UCITA jurisdictions would enforce the license terms.

In response to this argument, NCCUSL adopted section 105(b), which permits "public policy invalidation": If a term of a contract violates a fundamental public policy, the court may refuse to enforce the contract, may enforce the remainder of the contract without the impermissible term, or may limit the application of the impermissible term so as to avoid a result contrary to public policy, in each case to the extent that the interest in enforcement is clearly outweighed by a public policy against enforcement of the term.[37] The reporter's comments to this provision explicitly discuss reverse engineering:

This Act does not address . . . issues of national policy, but how they are resolved may be instructive to courts in applying this subsection. A recent national statement of policy on the relationship between reverse engineering, security testing, and copyright in digital information can be found at 17 U.S.C. Section 1201 (1999). It expressly addresses reverse engineering and security testing in connection with circumvention of technological protection measures that limit access to copyrighted works. It recognizes a policy not to prohibit some reverse engineering where it is needed to obtain interoperability of computer programs. . . . It further recognizes a policy to not prohibit security testing where it is needed to protect the integrity and security of computers, computer systems or computer networks. . . .This policy may outweigh a contract term to the contrary.[38]

Without question, section 105(b) and the reporter's comments provided some comfort to developers of interoperable software. This comfort, however, was limited. First, the comment was very cautious; it implied that reverse engineering for purposes of achieving interoperability was a fundamental public policy, but it did not say so explicitly. Second, the reporter's comments had no legal status; a court was not required to give them any weight. Thus, notwithstanding the comments' implications, there was no guarantee that a court would conclude that reverse engineering for purposes of interoperability was a fundamental public policy. Third, even if a court did conclude that reverse engineering was a fundamental public

37. Id. at § 105(3).
38. Id.

policy, it still had to balance that policy against the policy favoring enforcement of contracts. Section 105(b) directed courts to refuse to enforce a term only "to the extent that the interest in enforcement is *clearly outweighed* by a public policy against enforcement of the term."[39] "Clearly outweighed" is a very high standard to meet. The comment suggested that reverse engineering "*may* outweigh a contract term to the contrary," but did it *clearly* outweigh a term to the contrary?

In the face of this uncertainty, supporters of reverse engineering continued to press for an express exemption, even after NCCUSL adopted UCITA in 1999, and after UCITA was enacted in Virginia and Maryland in 2000. In November of 2001, the UCITA Standby Committee held an open meeting to consider possible amendments to the official text of UCITA. Several amendments relating to reverse engineering were proposed and debated at the meeting.

On December 17, 2001, the Standby Committee issued a report that recommended adopting the following new section concerning reverse engineering:

Section 115. Terms on Reverse Engineering

Notwithstanding the terms of a contract under this Act, a licensee that lawfully obtained the right to use a copy of a computer program may identify, analyze, and use those elements of the program which are necessary to achieve interoperability of an independently created computer program with other programs, if:

the elements have not previously been readily available to the licensee;
the identification, analysis, or use is performed solely for the purpose of enabling such interoperability; and
the identification, analysis, or use is not prohibited by other law.

In this section, "interoperability" means the ability of computer programs to exchange information, and of such programs mutually to use the information that has been exchanged.[40]

The report's comment on section 115 explains that it "adopts the position taken in Europe, which permits reverse engineering despite a contrary contract clause if the reverse engineering is needed for interoperability and is permitted under trade secret, copyright and other law."[41] And indeed the language of section 115 is very similar to that of the reverse-engineering exception in section 1201(f) of the DMCA, which in turn is similar to the

---

39. UCITA § 105(b)(emphasis added).
40. Standby Committee Report Recommendation 19 at 25.
41. Id. at 25–26.

language of article 6 of the EU Software Directive. Thus, section 115 harmonizes U.S. law with EU law.

In January of 2002, the NCCUSL Executive Committee adopted the recommendation, along with the other amendments proposed in the December 2001 report. In the summer of 2002, the reverse-engineering provision was adopted by the NCCUSL commissioners, at their annual meeting, as section 118 of UCITA. However, Maryland and Virginia have not amended their enactments of UCITA to reflect this reverse-engineering provision.

In sum, notwithstanding the Federal Circuit's decision in *Bowers*, strong arguments can still be made that both the Constitution and the Copyright Act preempt enforcement of contractual restrictions on reverse engineering. Additionally, such terms in shrinkwrap licenses may not be enforceable under state contract law if users do not manifest their assent to the terms. The new section 118 of UCITA provides a "bright line," but it has not yet been enacted in any jurisdiction.

5 Interoperability Overseas

The Internet has convinced policy makers around the world of the importance of interoperability. In particular, Australian and Asian policy makers have concluded that their domestic firms can participate in the global market for information technology only if those firms' products can interoperate with the products developed by the dominant U.S. firms. As policy makers in the Asia-Pacific region have studied the issue, they have learned that the domestic firms can achieve interoperability only if they can reverse engineer the dominant firms' products.

Because of the nature of computer programs, most forms of software reverse engineering require the making of an interim copy of the program. Making such a copy may infringe the copyrights of the program's developer, unless it is permitted by an exception to the developer's exclusive rights. Two models for such exceptions emerged during the 1990s. First, the European Union adopted a software directive that contains a specific exception for reverse engineering.[1] (All the member states of the European Union have implemented the EU Software Directive, as have several other countries in Eastern Europe.) Second, courts in the United States found the copying incidental to software reverse engineering to be excused under the U.S. Copyright Act's fair-use doctrine.[2]

The Asia-Pacific countries considering the issue of reverse engineering had these two models before them. These countries, however, did not confront reverse engineering in a complete vacuum. First, the British Commonwealth countries had to consider whether their fair-dealing provisions,

1. Council 91/250/EEC 1991 O.J. (L 122). For more detailed discussions of the EU Software Directive, see section 1.2 above and pp. 227–282 of Band and Katoh, *Interfaces on Trial*.
2. We discuss U.S. case law concerning reverse engineering in subsection 1.3.2 and in section 2.2.

which were based on British copyright law, were flexible enough to permit software reverse engineering. The Court of Appeal in Singapore, for example, determined that its fair-dealing provision *did not* permit reverse engineering, which led the Singapore Parliament to amend the copyright law. Second, these countries had to deal with political pressure from dominant U.S. software companies and from the Office of the U.S. Trade Representative (USTR). These U.S. interests generally opposed any amendment permitting reverse engineering. At the same time, these U.S. interests signaled a preference for the U.S. fair-use approach over the EU Software Directive approach if the country decided to proceed with an amendment. Although the United States persuaded Hong Kong to adopt the fair-use approach rather than the Software Directive approach, it did not succeed in convincing it to abandon a reverse-engineering provision altogether, as it had previously convinced Korea and Japan.[3] Australia adopted the Software Directive approach notwithstanding strong U.S. government opposition. The Philippines responded to the U.S. pressure by enacting a hybrid of Software Directive and fair use.

It is not entirely clear why the USTR and the U.S. software firms preferred the fair-use approach to the Software Directive approach. As will be discussed below, the former is more flexible than the latter, and might permit a wider range of reverse-engineering activities. This preference for the fair-use approach might have reflected a belief that *Sega Enters. Ltd, Inc. v. Accolade, Inc.*[4] was an anomalous decision that U.S. courts eventually would reject. However, the opposite occurred; as was discussed in chapter 2, *Sega* has become more firmly entrenched in U.S. jurisprudence.

5.1   Australia

5.1.1   The Report of the Australian Copyright Law Review Committee

On April 12, 1995, the Australian Copyright Law Review Committee (CLRC) concluded a nearly eight-year study of copyright issues having to do with software.[5] The CLRC's 350-page final report culminated an open process of public hearings, several rounds of comments, technical demonstrations,

3. On the U.S. defeat of the Japanese reverse-engineering initiative, see pp. 297–316 of Band and Katoh, *Interfaces on Trial*. We discuss the defeat of the Korean initiative in section 5.5 of the present volume.
4. 977 F.2d 1510 (9th Cir. 1992).
5. This subsection is based on passages in the following publications: Jonathan Band and Masanobu Katoh, "Interoperability Down Under: The Australian Copyright Law

and draft recommendations.[6] For each of the many issues it considered, the final report carefully discussed all perspectives; it then reached the conclusion that a statutory amendment was necessary.

Among the more contentious issues to emerge in the course of the CLRC's deliberations were the protectability of interface specifications and the permissibility of software reverse engineering. As was noted above, these same issues contemporaneously were the subject of debate in the European Union and the United States. The CLRC explained its approach to these issues as follows:

[I]n the creation and protection of any property rights, an attempt must be made to strike the right balance between adequate protection and the need to provide the community with reasonable access to intellectual property and the benefits which it confers. . . . The striking of the balance is something which must be attempted in the public interest. The task has not been an easy one.[7]

In this subsection, we discuss how the CLRC approached its difficult task and ultimately succeeded in striking the right balance.

5.1.1.1 The Copyright Law Review Committee

The Copyright Amendment Act of 1984 brought computer programs under the protection of the Australian copyright law. In October of 1988, the Attorney General asked the CLRC (an officially convened group of jurists, intellectual-property lawyers, and industry representatives) to consider whether Australian copyright law "adequately and appropriately protects computer programs."[8] In February of 1989, the CLRC requested comments from interested parties on this question, and in April of 1990 it released an issues paper based on those comments. The paper recited the arguments for and against a reverse-engineering exception. Although the paper did not specifically address the protectability of interface specifications, it did discuss protection for program structure. Making no recommendations on the issues it raised, the paper invited further comments.

Review Committee's Final Report," *The Computer Lawyer*, July 1995, at 20; Jonathan Band and Taro Isshiki, "Interoperability in the Pacific Rim: Reversal of Fortunes in Singapore and Australia," *Journal of Proprietary Rights*, July 1997, at 2; Jonathan Band, "Software Reverse Engineering Amendments in Singapore and Australia," *Journal of Internet Law*, January 2000, at 17.

6. Copyright Law Review Committee, *Computer Software Protection* (1995) (henceforth cited as CLRC Report).

7. CLRC Report at 4.

8. CLRC Issues Paper 1 (April 1990).

On July 26 and 27, 1990, the CLRC held a public hearing. Alcatel STC testified that reverse engineering was essential to the computer industry, and that copyright law should not be permitted to impede the practice. The U.S. Software Publishers Association, in contrast, testified that most copyright owners are vehemently opposed to permitting the reverse engineering of their products.

In September of 1990, IBM submitted written comments to the CLRC stating that "no special category of 'fair use,' or similar exception, [should] be created which might sanction the incidental copying of computer programs where it is part of the process of decompilation."[9] In October of 1990, Fujitsu Australia submitted detailed comments taking an opposing view. Fujitsu Australia argued that if Australian software vendors "cannot develop products that conform to *de facto* interfacing standards (almost always established *outside* Australia, most typically in the U.S.)," then "programmers in Australia face extremely limited market opportunities (both in Australia and overseas)."[10] Accordingly, "the rules, formats, languages, protocols and similar information underlying a program, including its interfaces, should not themselves be copyrightable."[11]

Fujitsu Australia further argued that "[r]everse analysis is an essential tool in the development of interoperable products. Unless discrete information can be discerned through machine analysis techniques, the development of compatible products can be frustrated; whether intentionally or otherwise. The absence of an ability to engage in reverse analysis would lead to de facto protection for product-to-product interfaces whenever a company failed to document that information."[12] For this reason, Fujitsu Australia urged that reverse engineering "used to analyze or understand the uncopyrightable elements of a computer program" should be "viewed as completely permissible under Australian law."[13]

On November 22, 1990, IBM conducted a demonstration of reverse engineering before the CLRC. IBM sought to show how decompilation facilitated disguised piracy. IBM also submitted a detailed paper on decompilation. IBM stated unambiguously that no reverse-engineering technique short of

9. IBM Submission to the CLRC 25 (September 1990). Decompilation is a technique of software reverse engineering that involves converting machine-readable object code into a higher-level, human-readable form.
10. Fujitsu Australia, Submission to the CLRC 11 (October 5, 1990).
11. Id. at 3.
12. Id. at 18.
13. Id. at 3.

decompilation is "regarded as objectionable or fundamentally inconsistent with the principles of copyright law."[14] Nonetheless, IBM asserted, "there is no justification for legitimizing" decompilation, which "involves a flagrant infraction of the copyright owner's exclusive rights to control reproduction, especially where the intent of such process is to quickly develop a substitute program."[15]

IBM emphasized that decompilation would facilitate undetectable piracy, and that decompilation is unnecessary because "software suppliers publish ample information about their programs" and because less intrusive means of reverse engineering exist.[16] IBM argued that permitting decompilation would reduce a competitor's costs and the first developer's lead time. This, in turn, would reduce the incentives to create new programs. IBM, then the world's largest computer vendor, was particularly solicitous of small developers: "An exception could impose particular hardship on small vendors who may have only a single successful innovative product."[17]

Several developers of interoperable software sought to attend IBM's reverse–engineering demonstration, but IBM insisted that the CLRC exclude them. This galvanized the developers of interoperable software into action. They formed Supporters of Interoperable Systems in Australia (SISA), which conducted its own reverse-engineering demonstration before the CLRC on February 7, 1991.[18] SISA also provided the CLRC with presentations on the users' perspective and the business perspective. The main thrust of SISA's advocacy was that the CLRC should clearly exclude interface specifications from copyright protection and should permit access to interface specifications by reverse engineering so that the Australian information-technology industry could compete effectively in a global market.

5.1.1.2 *Autodesk v. Dyason* (1992)
On February 12, 1992, while the CLRC was considering the submissions of SISA and the proprietary vendors, the High Court of Australia handed down its decision in *Autodesk v. Dyason*.[19] This confused decision underscored the

14. IBM, Submission to the CLRC 6 (November 22, 1990).
15. Id. at 6–7.
16. Id. at 13.
17. Id. at 14.
18. SISA's members included, in addition to several software companies based in Australia, the Australian subsidiaries of Bull, ICL, Unisys, NCR, Sun Microsystems, and Fujitsu.
19. *Autodesk Inc. v. Dyason*, (1992) 173 C.L.R. 330.

importance of the CLRC's work by demonstrating the need for clarification of the proper application of copyright law to computer programs.

Autodesk produced the computer-assisted design program AutoCAD. It sold AutoCAD with a hardwired lock that had to be physically installed on the PC or terminal on which AutoCAD was running. Because only one lock was sold with each AutoCAD program, the lock ensured that only as many copies of AutoCAD as had been purchased were in operation at any time. The AutoCAD program issued a repeating cycle of challenges to the AutoCAD lock. Using a shift register, the lock transmitted a series of responses to the AutoCAD program. The AutoCAD program then used a lookup table to determine whether the responses matched the challenges. If it did not receive a proper response, the AutoCAD program (not the lock) would issue instructions to stop the program.

After reverse engineering the AutoCAD lock, the defendants developed an "Auto Key lock" that responded properly to the challenges issued by AutoCAD. This made it possible to use copies of AutoCAD on PCs without the AutoCAD lock. The Auto Key lock, therefore, allowed a user to circumvent the Autodesk lock and use unauthorized copies of Autodesk.

The *Autodesk* case presented several issues of first impression for Australian courts. First, the trial court had to determine whether the hardwired AutoCAD lock constituted a computer program at all. The AutoCAD lock did not issue instructions; rather, it issued a data stream in response to the AutoCAD program's data stream, which the program then evaluated. Second, the court had to determine whether the defendant had copied any of the plaintiff's protected expression.

The trial court found for Autodesk, ruling that the AutoCAD lock was a computer program and that the Auto Key lock infringed the AutoCAD copyright because it performed the same function. The trial court's decision also implied that the defendant's studying the AutoCAD lock's output using an oscilloscope might be improper under copyright law.

The full Federal Court reversed the trial court, finding that the AutoCAD lock was not a computer program and that similarity in function did not infringe copyright. The High Court then reversed the Federal Court and restored the trial court's finding of infringement, but for reasons different from those articulated by the trial court. The High Court agreed with the Federal Court that the AutoCAD lock was a piece of hardware and not a computer program, and thus was not covered by the Australian copyright law. The High Court nonetheless found infringement because the defendant's Auto Key lock, even though a computer program, reproduced the protected expression of the AutoCAD lookup table, and this lookup table represented a "substantial part" of the AutoCAD program. Further, one of the concurring opinions suggested, as did the trial court, that the defendant's act of reverse engineering also infringed Autodesk's copyright.

In a detailed criticism of the *Autodesk* decision, submitted to the CLRC, SISA stated that "[t]he danger of the High Court's *Autodesk* decision is that it will be portrayed as holding that all interface information by which two separate products interoperate is necessarily protectable 'expression' in Australia."[20] SISA first argued that the High Court had erred in treating the lookup table as protected expression: "[d]ata which serves a purely functional purpose should not be viewed as expressive material." SISA next argued that even if the lookup table contained expressive elements, those elements merged with the "idea" of achieving interoperability with the program:

[I]n order for Auto Key to work in place of the AutoCAD lock, the responses or return codes to signals sent to [the AutoCAD program] had to be identical. There was a very real functional imperative which limited the possible responses to stimuli sent from [the AutoCAD program] . . . . [I]f a discrete amount of data that is passed between computer programs must be identical in order for the programs to work together, that very real absence of choice on the part of the developer creating a new product intended to work with or substitute for an existing product must be considered in determining whether, as to that bit series, "idea" and "expression" have merged.[21]

SISA further contended that *Autodesk* should not be interpreted as prohibiting reverse engineering. Finally, SISA argued that *Autodesk* was an instance of bad facts leading to bad law.

The High Court understandably had little sympathy for the defendant, who had sought to circumvent Autodesk's copy-protection device. Dyason's product was not intended to increase consumer choice, but to facilitate unauthorized copying. SISA concluded that "[i]n light of the High Court's *Autodesk* decision SISA believes more than ever in the importance" of amending Australian copyright law" to exclude interface specifications from protection and to permit reverse engineering.[22]

5.1.1.3 The CLRC's Draft Report
In July of 1993, the CLRC issued a 350-page draft report[23] that contained a lengthy and somewhat confusing discussion of U.S. case law on the scope of protection for non-literal program elements. The draft report recommended

20. SISA's Views on the High Court's *Autodesk* Decision 9–10 (1992).
21. Id. at 16.
22. Id. at 18.
23. CLRC Draft Report on Computer Software Protection (1993).

against any amendment to the Australian Copyright Act specifically dealing with the scope of protection. Thus, it did not support SISA's request for a provision specifically excluding interface specifications from copyright protection.

The draft report also contained a lengthy discussion of reverse engineering. It acknowledged that because programs typically are distributed in an object-code form that is not understandable by humans, certain exceptions to the copyright owner's exclusive rights are required to ensure that the public has access to the unprotected elements of the program. The draft report recommended the adoption of a provision similar to article 6 of the EU Software Directive, permitting decompilation for purposes of achieving interoperability.[24] Indeed, the draft report improved on the language of the Software Directive by eliminating article 6's confusing reference to the Berne Convention.[25] The draft report also endorsed permitting decompilation for error correction. Finally, the draft report recommended that the "fair dealing" provision of the Australian Act govern the permissibility of decompilation "to understand techniques."

Thus, the CLRC proposed decompilation rights somewhat broader than those under the Software Directive. The CLRC envisioned an unambiguous right to decompile for purposes of interoperability and error correction, and a flexible case-by-case fair-use approach to determining the lawfulness of decompilation to understand elements of the target program not related to interoperability. The draft report, however, made no mention of a provision similar to article 5(3) of the Software Directive, which permits black-box reverse engineering.[26]

24. The draft report recommended the following language:

[D]ecompilation of a computer program should be allowed where it is necessary to achieve the interoperability of an independently created computer program with other programs provided:

(a) decompilation is performed by the owner of a lawfully acquired copy of the program or another person having a right to use the copy or on their behalf by a person authorized to do so;
(b) the information necessary to achieve interoperability has not previously been readily available; and
(c) the acts are confined to the parts of the program necessary to achieve interoperability.

The following limitations should apply:

(i) the decompilation should only be used to achieve interoperability; and
(ii) the information obtained should only be given to others when necessary for the interoperability of the independently created program.

25. See Band and Katoh, *Interfaces on Trial* at 254–255.
26. Black-box reverse engineering includes research methods other than decompilation, including line traces and input-output tests.

In detailed comments on the draft report, SISA stated that it believed that the CLRC's draft report struck a fair balance between the interests of copyright holders and the public at large. SISA also believed that the draft report was consistent with and in furtherance of the emerging international consensus of protecting computer programs as literary works while avoiding excess protection by creating express exceptions to the copyright holder's exclusive rights.[27]

SISA did, however, recommend several revisions. First, it renewed its request for a specific exclusion for interface specifications. Second, it advocated the adoption of a black-box reverse-engineering provision similar to article 5(3) of the Software Directive. Third, it recommended several changes to the equivalent of the Software Directive's article 6, most notably broadening it to cover explicitly decompilation for purposes of achieving interoperability between hardware and software.[28]

The U.S. Computer and Business Equipment Manufacturers Association (CBEMA) also filed comments on the draft report on behalf of proprietary vendors.[29] It offered several reasons why Australian copyright law did not need to permit decompilation for purposes of achieving interoperability. First, the policy objective of fostering interoperability "was already being satisfactorily advanced by a combination of market forces and liberal cross licensing policies of software developers," and "there is no evidence at all that a 'crisis' has developed in the industry due to an absence of special rules aimed at fostering interoperability."[30] Second, CBEMA hauled out the disguised-piracy rationale: "the protected expressions obtained through decompilation of computer program, often in an easily disguised form, can be used for a number of illegitimate purposes, which may cause substantial harm to the right holder."[31] Third, citing the reliance of the U.S. Court of Appeals for the Ninth Circuit on the fair-use doctrine to excuse

27. Comments on the Draft Report of the Copyright Law Review Committee on Computer Software Protection submitted by the Supporters of Interoperable Systems in Australia 1 (1993).
28. This had been a contentious, and somewhat unresolved, issue during the legislative battle leading up to the adoption of the EU Software Directive. See Band and Katoh, *Interfaces on Trial* at 248.
29. CBEMA's members included IBM, Apple, and Digital Equipment Corporation. In 2001, the organization changed its name to the Information Technology Industry Council.
30. CBEMA Comments on CLRC Draft Report 6 (October 1993) (hereafter cited as CBEMA Comments).
31. Id. at 7.

decompilation in *Sega v. Accolade*,[32] CBEMA argued that fair dealing (the Australian analogue to fair use) provided the means for "an Australian court to balance interests in the area."[33] Further, "there is little evidence to suggest that Australian courts, as their U.S. counterparts, will have any difficulty in reaching fair results in specific factual situations through the application of the doctrine of fair dealing."[34] The disingenuousness of this argument requires emphasis. In two *amicus* briefs to the Ninth Circuit, CBEMA vigorously opposed excusing decompilation under the fair-use doctrine. Yet in Australia CBEMA employed the Ninth Circuit's fair-use finding as a justification for not adopting a specific decompilation exception.

Perhaps in response to SISA's renewed request for a specific exclusion for interface specifications, CBEMA raised several arguments against the adoption of such an exception. CBEMA first argued that including specific terms of art in statutes "narrows the scope of the law, and, thus reduces its applicability in the full range of factual situations which may arise over time."[35] CBEMA next argued that "the copyrightability of specific elements of a program should be determined by the same rules as the copyrightability of specific elements of any other work."[36] CBEMA finally argued that an express exception for interface specifications for the purpose of promoting standardization and interoperability was unnecessary because over the past decade the software market had become increasingly standardized on its own: "[C]ompatibility (or interoperability) has evolved without specific rules diminishing protection."[37]

The U.S. government also commented on the CLRC draft report. It approved the decompilation provision, noting that it "appear[s] to be generally consistent with the provisions of Article 6 of the EC Software Directive and appear[s] to be directed to achieving the goal of the creation of interoperable programs while protecting the copyright owner against abuse."[38] The U.S. government, however, suggested that the decompilation provision explicitly state, as does Article 6 of the directive, that the "end result of the process must be the creation of a program that is itself

32. 977 F.2d 1510 (9th Cir. 1992).
33. CBEMA Comments at 6.
34. Id.
35. Id. at 3.
36. Id.
37. Id. at 4.
38. United States Government Comments on the Copyright Law Review Committee's Draft Report on Computer Software Protection, United States Government Cable to United States Embassy, Australia (1993).

original."[39] Moreover, the U.S. government expressed concern about permitting decompilation for error correction.

5.1.1.4 The CLRC's Final Report

The CLRC's final report, issued in April of 1995, included several significant changes that favored interoperability.

It adopted the distinction, made by Professor Randall Davis of the Massachusetts Institute of Technology, between computer programs as "text" and computer programs as "behavior."[40] The CLRC concluded that behavior should not receive copyright protection, thereby permitting the development of functionally equivalent programs with different texts.[41]

It did not accept SISA's invitation to specifically exclude interface specifications from copyright protection. It did, however, explicitly endorse the *Computer Associates v. Altai* decision of the U.S. Court of Appeals for the Second Circuit.[42] It described the Second Circuit's three-step test, noting that the unprotectable elements to be removed in the filtration step included "elements dictated by external factors, such as . . . compatibility requirements with other programs." It then stated that the CLRC "regards the test set out by the court in that case as a very practical and useful guide for determining infringement if computer programs and supports the approach it adopted."[43]

The report proceeded to discuss the favorable reception of *Computer Associates* by courts in Canada and the United Kingdom[44] and to reject the district court's decision in *Lotus v. Paperback*.[45] (The appeal in *Lotus v. Borland* was still pending when the final report was drafted.) It also discussed "look and feel," concluding that "the need for standardization and the need for efficient user interfaces to be used and developed outweighs the need to grant authors express copyright protection in the 'look and feel' of their programs' behaviours."[46] "While industrial efficiency may not be a consideration in determining protection of other categories of works," the report stated, "that it is in the case of computer program serves to mark

39. Id.
40. CLRC Report at 102.
41. See id. at 112–113.
42. 982 F.2d 693 (2d Cir. 1992). See subsection 1.3.2 of the present volume.
43. CLRC Report at 109.
44. Id. at 109. See Band and Katoh, *Interfaces on Trial* at 147–149 and 262–269 for a discussion of these cases.
45. 740 F. Supp. 37 (D. Mass. 1990). We discuss this case in subsection 2.1.1.
46. CLRC Report at 114.

them out on account of their functional nature."[47] These statements, taken together, suggest that the CLRC opposed copyright protection for interface specifications.

With respect to reverse engineering, the CLRC adopted SISA's recommendation of a black-box reverse-engineering exception similar to that in article 5(3) of the Software Directive.[48] The CLRC also considered, and rejected, CBEMA's opposition to a decompilation exception. The report concluded that the existing fair-dealing provision in Australian copyright law was narrower than the fair-use doctrine in U.S. copyright law and probably would not permit decompilation in a commercial context.[49]

The CLRC also rejected IBM's contention that decompilation facilitated "disguised piracy." It stated that it found IBM's reverse-engineering demonstration unconvincing: "At that presentation, only a simple form of decompilation was demonstrated, namely the disassembly of a relatively small program. No evidence of generalised decompilation to high level computer languages was provided."[50]

The CLRC noted that "any new program that is produced by reverse engineering an existing program and which is a copy or adaptation of the latter program is no less an infringement."[51] The CLRC thus suggested that the focus of the copyright analysis should be the finished product brought to market, and not the intermediate development steps. The CLRC acknowledged IBM's argument that many operating system interfaces were published, but responded that many other products were not publicly documented. The CLRC further observed that reverse engineering is time consuming, costly, and rarely leads back to a complete version of original source code. For this reason it is likely to be performed only by interoperable-software developers with no alternative means of obtaining the interface information necessary for interoperability.

The CLRC then considered SISA's specific recommendations for amending the decompilation language proposed in the draft report. SISA had opposed the provision limiting decompilation to those parts of the program necessary for interoperability on the ground that it was not possible to know in advance what parts of the program needed to be decompiled. The CLRC agreed and replaced the problematic language. The CLRC also

47. Id. at 113.
48. Id. at 175–176.
49. Id. at 147–149.
50. Id. at 153.
51. Id. at 153.

agreed with SISA's suggestion that decompilation be permitted for purposes of achieving interoperability between hardware and software, as well as between two programs.[52] Further, the CLRC endorsed SISA's suggestion that contractual restrictions on reverse engineering not be enforceable. The CLRC reviewed the criticisms of its provision permitting decompilation for purposes of error correction, particularly those submitted by the U.S. government. The CLRC rejected the criticisms and retained the provision. The CLRC also retained its approval of decompilation to uncover ideas not related to interoperability pursuant to Australia's fair-dealing exception.

Finally, the CLRC considered the status of reverse engineering in other jurisdictions. It correctly concluded that its recommendations were consistent with the Software Directive in the European Union and the *Sega* decision in the United States, and that they complied with the Berne Convention and the World Trade Organization Agreement on the Trade Related Aspects of Intellectual Property Rights (TRIPS).[53]

Because of the parallels between the CLRC's recommendations and the EU Software Directive, the report is particularly useful in interpreting and applying the directive's provisions. Specifically, the report resolves three potential ambiguities in article 6 of the directive: it eliminates the confusing reference to the Berne Convention, it permits decompilation to achieve interoperability between software and hardware, and it removes the technologically infeasible limitation of decompilation to only those parts of

---

52. The final report worded the decompilation exception as follows:

[D]ecompilation of a computer program should be allowed where it is necessary to achieve the interoperability of an independently created computer program or hardware device with other programs or hardware devices provided.. . .

(a) decompilation is performed by the owner of lawfully acquired copy of the program or another person having a right to use the copy or on their behalf by a person authorized to do so; and

(b) the information necessary to achieve interoperability has not previously been readily available; and

(c) the acts are confined to those necessary to achieve interoperability.

The following limitations should apply:

(i) the decompilation should only be used to achieve interoperability; and

(ii) the information obtained should only be given to others when necessary for the interoperability of the independently created computer program or hardware device.

Id. at 10.

53. The final report states that "in Japan the law, if literally interpreted, would prohibit the reproduction and adaptation of computer programs for the purpose of reverse engineering" (CLRC Report at 177). A close examination of Japanese copyright law, however, reveals that it permits reverse engineering. See Band and Katoh, *Interfaces on Trial* at 294–297.

the program that are necessary for interoperability. The CLRC's thoughtful resolution of these potential ambiguities should be followed in Europe.

5.1.2 Case Law after the CLRC Report: *Data Access v. Powerflex* (1996)

After the CLRC issued its final report, an Australian federal court decided a case involving the protectability of functional components of a computer program dictated by compatibility concerns. The court harmed the cause of interoperability by holding that compatibility concerns could not negate the protectability of program elements. What makes this decision particularly interesting is its use and interpretation of United States copyright law, carefully selecting which U.S. decisions it agreed with.

5.1.2.1 Facts

The *Powerflex* case focused on infringement by the end product, not infringement due to copying during the development process. The Data Access Corporation had developed DataFlex, a compilation of programs described by the Australian Federal Court "as an application development system."[54] Specifically, the DataFlex programs were used for not only the creation of databases but also for the development of database application programs, which could in turn be used to create and work with databases. As such, the DataFlex system provided users with a programming language in which they could write their own programs. The DataFlex system also incorporated a "run time" program that allowed a user to operate the applications created through the use of the DataFlex language. The defendants in the copyright infringement suit were David Bennett, his wife, and the company they had incorporated to sell the allegedly infringing product, PFXplus. Bennett, according to the court, "aspired to create an application development system which would be highly compatible with the DataFlex computer language."[55]

As far as issues of interoperability were concerned, the infringement suit focused on two aspects of Bennett's software. First, the PFXplus language used 192 of the 225 instruction words in the DataFlex language. The use of the same words in the source code of either the DataFlex or PFXplus languages caused the computer to perform the same functions. The program code implementing each of these functions, however, was completely different. The second interoperability issue arose in the context of Bennett's intentional reproduction, in identical form, of certain compression tables

---

54. *Data Access Corporation v. Powerflex Services Pty, Ltd.* No. 93-VG473 (Federal Ct. Austl. February 9, 1996) at 2.
55. *Powerflex* at 3.

used in one of the DataFlex programs. These tables, which were elements of the DataFlex "run time" program, merely allowed the software user to save storage space through the compression of the program into smaller data strings. This raised an interoperability issue because of Bennett's assertion in his defense that it was necessary to use the same compression tables in his programs in order to achieve compatibility.

5.1.2.2   The Federal Court's Ruling

Merger of Idea and Expression
Bennett presented a merger defense to the copying of the words of the DataFlex language. His merger defense was based on language in the U.S. Supreme Court decision *Baker v. Selden*,[56] relied upon by the Australian High Court in *Autodesk v. Dyason*,[57] that when an expression of an idea is inseparable from its function, it is part of the idea itself and therefore unprotected by copyright. Specifically, Bennett appealed to the logic of the First Circuit's *Lotus Development Corp. v. Borland International*[58] decision (although not specifically to the "method of operation" argument, since the Australian copyright statute has no companion to section 102(b) of the U.S. Act). It appears that, as in *Borland*, Bennett had to use the same words in order to make PFXplus compatible with DataFlex and desirable to customers who had learned the DataFlex language and did not want to learn a new set of commands.

The Australian court chose to disregard the ruling in *Borland* and instead turned to Judge Keeton's district court decision in *Lotus Development Corp. v. Paperback Software International*,[59] which as a practical matter had been overruled by the First Circuit's *Borland* decision. The Australian court quoted extensively from the *Paperback* decision and seemed to place great importance on Judge Keeton's decision that if the expression of an idea goes beyond the functional elements within that idea and beyond the obvious, *and* if there are numerous other ways of expressing the same idea, that form of expression is copyrightable.[60] The Australian court found that the choice of words here went "beyond the functional elements of the ideas they

56. 101 U.S. 99 (1879).
57. (1992) 173 C.L.R. 330. We discuss this case in subsection 5.1.1.2.
58. 49 F.3d 807 (1st Cir. 1995), *aff'd by an equally divided Court*, 516 U.S. 233 (1996). We discuss this case in detail in subsection 2.1.1.
59. 740 F. Supp. 37 (D. Mass. 1990).
60. See *Powerflex* at 12–13.

express, and beyond the obvious," and that the words were "elements of expression, original and substantial, and therefore copyrightable."[61] Thus, the Australian court rejected *Borland*'s notion that elements of a computer program so "essential to operating something" should be outside the scope of copyright protection.[62]

Elements Dictated by Compatibility

In its findings regarding Bennett's copying of the compression tables, the Australian court demonstrated its position on whether compatibility concerns could affect the protectability of program elements even more starkly. Bennett once again presented a merger defense, arguing that in order for a person using the DataFlex application development system to use a PFX-plus program, the PFXplus compression table must be identical to that of DataFlex. He further contended that this meant there was but one manner in which to express the idea of "function through compatibility," and therefore the idea and the expression merge, making the compression table unprotectable under copyright.[63]

The court rejected this argument, referring once again to Judge Keeton's *Paperback* opinion. The Australian court held that compatibility concerns could not negate the protectability of a program element:

> The function of compression by means of the Hoffman method may be, and has been, performed by any one of very many different expressions in integer code. The expression given in the DataFlex table is but one of the many possible expressions. The conclusion is established that the DataFlex table is copyright [*sic*] before consideration is given to the PFXplus table. *The desire of Dr. Bennett for the compatibility he achieved by reproduction of the DataFlex table, not any inseparability of function and expression of the Hoffman compression method, constrained him to merge function and expression.*[64]

Viewed in this light, the Australian decision was very near the opposite side of the spectrum—in terms of protection offered to interface specifications—from judicial decisions in the United States. Perhaps the contrast can be discerned most clearly by comparing the *Powerflex* decision to the Eleventh Circuit's ruling in *Bateman v. Mnemonics, Inc.*[65] In *Bateman*, the Eleventh Circuit found that, although interface specifications were not *per se* uncopyrightable, compatibility concerns would typically negate the protectability of certain elements of computer programs.

---

61. Id. at 13.
62. *Borland*, 49 F.3d at 816.
63. *Powerflex* at 17.
64. Id. (emphasis added).
65. 79 F.3d 1532 (11th Cir. 1996). We discuss this case in subsection 2.1.2.1.

By distinguishing constraints dictated by compatibility from constraints flowing from the inseparability of function and expression, the Australian court basically decided on a *per se* basis that no elements of computer programs dictated by compatibility concerns could be determined to be unprotected. In light of the state of U.S. law as represented by *Borland* and *Bateman*, the Australian court's reliance on the opinion of Judge Keeton in *Paperback* as an example of U.S. legal authority seems puzzling. Perhaps more mystifying is the Australian court's failure to consider an even more obvious U.S. case relevant to the questions before the court: *Computer Associates International, Inc. v. Altai, Inc.*,[66] which established the abstraction-filtration-comparison test for questions of infringement by non-literal copying of computer programs.

Interestingly, the Australian court made a completely contrary finding with respect to another portion of the facts presented, thereby casting doubt on the above-described holding. Bennett also copied a substantial portion of the error text table contained in the DataFlex programs. When an error occurred during use of the DataFlex software, the program referred to an error table that contained numbered errors corresponding to specific lines of text to be displayed on the computer screen, describing the error to the user. Bennett's error text lines were substantially similar to those provided in the DataFlex table. Nonetheless, in this circumstance, the court found that the "expression of the idea is inseparable from its function and is not copyrightable."[67] The court provided no explanation as to why it so easily applied the merger doctrine to the error text lines, but not to the words of the DataFlex language. However mixed the message of the court may be, it certainly cannot be interpreted as favorable to developers of interoperable software.

Although the court arguably misused U.S. authorities, it did not refer to any of the four recently decided software copyright cases in other Commonwealth countries: two in Canada and two in the United Kingdom.[68]

5.1.3 Australia's Software Reverse Engineering Amendment
In the spring of 1999, four years after the CLRC issued its final report, a set of copyright amendments relating to computer programs, including a

66. 982 F.2d 693 (2d Cir. 1992).

67. *Powerflex* at 15.

68. See Jonathan Band, "*Computer Associates* Crosses the Atlantic and Lake Ontario: *Richardson v. Flanders* and *Delrina v. Triolet*," *International Computer Law*, June 1993, at 2; Band, "*Matrox Electronic Systems v. Gaudreau*," 6 *European Intellectual Property Review* D-138 (1994).

reverse-engineering exception similar to the that of the EU Software Directive, were introduced in the Australian Parliament.[69] The amendments were passed by the Senate on June 29 and by the House of Representatives on August 12. They went into effect on September 30.

5.1.3.1 The Need for a Reverse-Engineering Exception

On August 11, 1999, in the Second Reading Speech, Attorney-General Daryl Williams explained the government's rationale for introducing the legislation. He described the growing importance of computers and computer networks to the economy. With the advent of the Internet, he said, "there is an obvious need for computers and the programs which drive them to communicate, connect, or 'interoperate' with each other."[70] He then explained the need for interface information in order to achieve interoperability, and how, as a technical matter, this information often can be obtained only through reverse engineering. He singled out the reverse-engineering technique known as "decompilation," which involves translating the machine-readable object code into a higher-level, human-readable format.[71]

Williams noted that "the law of the leading software producing country in the world, the United States, allows makers of new programs to use decompilation to find out the interface information of existing programs for achieving interoperability. The countries of the European Union, and other countries, also allow this to be done. However, Australian law does not make such a provision."[72] He contended that an amendment was required to enable the Australian software industry to compete in the world market:

Australia's software producers are recognized as innovative by world standards. Because our industry is not of a scale to compete across the board with such dominant industries as that of the United States, its comparative advantage lies in the ability to cater for niche markets. In order to do this, it must be able to ensure that its successful niche products interoperate with other, existing products, including those produced by big scale producers. . . . If Australian industry is to be allowed to compete on level terms with producers of similar products in the USA and Europe, Australian software copyright laws must be brought more into line with the law in those countries.[73]

69. Copyright Amendment (Computer Programs) Act, 1999.
70. Speech on Copyright Amendment (Computer Programs) Bill 1999, Second Reading at 2.
71. Id. at 2–3.
72. Id. at 3.
73. Id. at 3–4.

At this point, Williams explained the provisions of the amendment: "[A]s an exception to the copyright reproduction right, where interface information about other programs is not readily available to a software producer, the producer will now be able to decompile another program to the extent necessary to get the required interface information for making an interoperable product."[74] He hastened to add that the amendment would "not weaken the existing proscription of software piracy," explaining that pirates do not reverse engineer but rather engage in wholesale copying.[75]

Finally, Williams described two other reverse-engineering exceptions created by the amendment: one for error correction, such as Y2K remediation, where an error-free version is not available at a commercial price, and another for security testing, such as testing a computer's systems protection against hackers or viruses.[76]

5.1.3.2 The Structure of the Reverse-Engineering Exception

In an explanatory memorandum that accompanied the amendment, the government discussed the four alternatives it had considered.[77]

The first alternative was to leave the law unchanged. This was rejected for the reasons outlined in the Speech on Second Reading: the costs to the Australian software industry would be too great.

The second alternative was to expand the fair-dealing provisions of the Copyright Act, presumably to bring it more in line with the fair-use provisions of the U.S. Copyright Act. Although the U.S. government and the Business Software Alliance supported this option, the Australian government did not pursue it, because of the uncertain extent of protection against infringement actions such a provision would provide to software developers. Since fair dealing, like fair use, is determined case by case by courts, the contours of the new fair-dealing provision would emerge only from lengthy and expensive litigation.[78]

The third alternative was to adopt the reverse-engineering provisions of the EU Software Directive. The government found this preferable to simply amending the fair-dealing provision, insofar as a statutory exception provided more certainty to developers of interoperable software. At the same

---

74. Id. at 4.

75. Id.

76. Id. at 5–6.

77. Explanatory Memorandum on Copyright Amendment (Computer Programs) Bill of 1999 at § 4.3.

78. Id.

time, the government concluded that the Software Directive was deficient in two respects. First, it did not permit decompilation for purposes of security testing. Second, the Software Directive could be understood to permit decompilation only for purposes of achieving interoperability between two software products, but not between software and hardware.[79] The Australian government decided that decompilation should clearly be permitted for both software-to-software and software-to-hardware interoperability. Accordingly, the Australian government decided to pursue a fourth alternative: starting with the EU Software Directive and adding provisions concerning security testing and software-hardware interoperability.[80]

The amendment passed by Parliament has five sections concerning reverse engineering.

Black-Box Reverse Engineering

Section 47B(3) parallels article 5(3) of the EU Software Directive and permits the copying done in the course of black-box reverse engineering such as input-output tests. The section permits reproductions "made in the course of running a copy of the program for the purpose of studying the ideas behind the program and the way in which it functions."

Decompilation for Interoperability

Section 47D parallels article 6 of the EU Software Directive and permits making adaptations of a program (e.g., decompiling a program) "for the purpose of obtaining information necessary to enable the owner or licensee to make independently another program (the new program), or an article, to connect to and be used together with, or otherwise to interoperate with, the original program or any other program." The reference to the making of "an article" is the language that permits decompilation for the purpose of achieving software-to-hardware interoperability. The wording of the final clause of the provision—"to connect to and be used together with, or otherwise to interoperate with, the original program or any other program"— makes clear that the exception is directed to the making of both products

---

79. A manufacturer of a peripheral device such as a disk drive or a printer may have to reverse engineer a computer's operating system to ensure that the peripheral device functions properly with the computer. On why the EU Software Directive permits decompilation for software-to-hardware interoperability, see Band and Katoh, *Interfaces on Trial* at 248–249.

80. Explanatory Memorandum on Copyright Amendment (Computer Programs) Bill of 1999 at § 4.3.

that attach to the original program and products that compete with the original program.[81]

The other provisions of section 47D place limits on decompilation. Under subsection (c), the adaptation can be "made only to the extent reasonably necessary to obtain" the interface information. Under subsection (e), decompilation can be performed only when the interface information "is not readily available to the owner or licensee from another source when the . . . adaptation is made." Article 6 of the EU Software Directive contains similar limitations.

Section 47D contains a significant provision not found in the EU Software Directive. Subsection (d) permits decompilation under the following condition: "to the extent that the new program reproduces or adapts the original program, it does so only to the extent necessary to enable the new program to connect to and be used together with, or otherwise to interoperate with, the original program or the other program." This subsection makes it unambiguous that a developer of interoperable software can include in the new program the interface information derived from the original program. Although this concept is implicit in the EU Software Directive (what would be the point of permitting decompilation if one could not use the fruit of that research?), there is no explicit statement allowing the use of the information or declaring such information *per se* unprotected by copyright. The closest the directive gets is in article 1(2), which states that "[i]deas and principles which underlie any element of a computer program, including those which underlie its interfaces, are not protected by copyright."[82] Section 47D(d) eliminates any ambiguity by directly permitting the copying of any element necessary for interoperability.

81. As was discussed in chapter 2, the question of attaching versus competing has long been central in the interoperability debate. Dominant software vendors have argued that reverse engineering should be permitted only for the development of attaching, but not competing, products. However, because these dominant software vendors are typically vertically integrated, the distinction between attaching and competing is artificial. For example, a new word processing product designed to "attach" to Microsoft Windows would also "compete" with Microsoft Word. Moreover, to achieve true backward and forward compatibility—to ensure that the competitive product can interoperate with products on the market as well as those not yet introduced—the competition often must examine both sides of the interface.

82. We discuss this issue in greater detail in subsection 1.3.2. Under U.S. law, the unprotectability of interface information is primarily based on judicial interpretation of 17 U.S.C. 102(b). See *Computer Associates v. Altai*, 982 F.2d 693 (2d Cir. 1992); Band and Katoh, *Interfaces on Trial* at 83–165; subsection 1.3.1 and section 2.1 above.

Error Correction

Section 47E permits reproducing or adapting computer programs to correct an error in the program that prevents it from operating as its author intended or in accordance with specifications or documentation supplied with the original copy. The adaptations can be made only for the owner or licensee of a lawful copy of the original program, only to the extent reasonably necessary to correct the error, and only if an error-free copy is not available within a reasonable time at a commercial price.

The EU Software Directive does not contain a detailed provision dealing exclusively with error correction. However, article 5(1) states that a lawful acquirer of a computer program may engage in any of the acts restricted by articles 4(a) and (b), including reproduction and translation, "where they are necessary for the use of the computer program . . . in accordance with its intended purpose, *including for error correction.*" The Australian amendment, therefore, supplies additional specificity to a concept appearing in the EU Software Directive. This specificity appears to narrow the privileges granted under the directive. Under section 47E the error correction can be performed only if an error-free copy is not available at an ordinary commercial price. Conversely, article 5(1) of the directive contains no such condition.

Security Testing

Section 47F permits the making of a reproduction or adaptation of a program for the purpose of (1) testing the security of the program or a computer system of which the program is a part or (2) investigating or correcting a security flaw or vulnerability in the program or a computer system of which the program is a part. This exception applies only if the information resulting from the reproduction or adaptation is not readily available from another source.

The EU Software Directive does not contain a parallel provision, but the dangers posed by hacking and viruses were better understood in 1999 than in 1991 (when the EU adopted the Software Directive). Moreover, the 1998 U.S. Digital Millennium Copyright Act exempted computer system security testing from its ban on circumvention and circumvention devices.[83]

Limitation on Contractual Terms

Section 47H provides that "[a]n agreement, or a provision of an agreement, that excludes or limits, or has the effect of excluding or limiting, the operation" of the reverse-engineering subsections (i.e., 47B(3), 47D, 47E, and 47F)

---

83. See 17 U.S.C. § 1201(j), discussed above in subsection 3.1.6.3.

"has no effect." This provision prevents a software company from restricting the reverse engineering permitted under the amendment by imposing contract terms prohibiting such reverse engineering. The Australian government recognized that enforcing contractual restrictions on reverse engineering would undermine the pro-competition and pro-interoperability objective of the legislation. The EU Software Directive contains a similar provision in article 9(1).

In enacting a software reverse-engineering amendment, Australia chose to follow the more certain civil-code approach of the EU Software Directive. Because Australia's software industries depend on interoperability, and interoperability often can be achieved only through reverse engineering, the government was impelled to eliminate the legal barriers to software reverse engineering.

5.1.4 Australia's Implementation of the Australia-U.S. Free Trade Agreement

In 2004, Australia and the United States entered into a free-trade agreement that required the parties to "provide adequate legal protection and effective legal remedies against the circumvention of effective technological measures that authors, performers, and producers of phonograms use in connection with the exercise of their rights and that restrict unauthorised acts in respect of their works, performances, and phonograms."[84] The agreement specified that the parties shall provide legal remedies against any person who "knowingly, or having reasonable grounds to know, circumvents without authority any effective technological measure that controls access to a protected work, performance, or phonogram, or other subject matter."[85] The agreement further required the parties to provide remedies against any person who "manufactures, imports, distributes, offers to the public, provides, or otherwise traffics in devices, products, or components, or offers to the public, or provides services..." that circumvent an effective technological measure. The agreement allowed the parties to adopt exceptions to these prohibitions, including one for "non-infringing reverse engineering activities with regard to a lawfully obtained copy of a computer program, carried out in good faith with respect to particular elements of that computer program that have not been readily available to the person engaged in those activities, for the sole purpose of achieving interoperability of an independently created computer program with other programs."[86]

84. Australia-U.S. Free Trade Agreement, Art. 17.4.7(a), May 18, 2004.
85. Id. at (a)(i).
86. Id. at (e)(i).

In 2006, the Australian Parliament amended the Copyright Act of 1968 to implement the changes required by the Australia-U.S. FTA. The amendments included civil and criminal prohibitions on the circumvention of an access-control technological protection measure, on the manufacture or distribution of a device that circumvents a technological protection measure, or on providing a circumvention service. The amendments also provided interoperability exceptions to these prohibitions. Under these exceptions, the prohibitions on circumvention and circumvention devices do not apply when the circumvention:

(i) relates to a copy of a computer program (the original program) that is not an infringing copy and that was lawfully obtained; and

(ii) will not infringe the copyright in the original program; and

(iia) relates to elements of the original program that will not be readily available to the person when the circumvention occurs; and

(iii) will be done for the sole purpose of achieving interoperability of an independently created computer program with the original program or any other program.[87]

Although the FTA refers to "non-infringing reverse engineering activities . . . carried out . . . for the sole purpose of achieving interoperability," these exceptions are not limited to reverse engineering. Rather, they apply to any circumvention activity performed to achieve interoperability between computer programs, including the circumvention of an authentication handshake designed to prevent interoperability with software products developed by other vendors. Thus, the exception in the Australian copyright law has the same breadth as the interoperability exception in section 1201(f) of the Digital Millennium Copyright Act.

5.2 Singapore

Singapore amended its copyright laws to permit software reverse engineering in 1998—the year before Australia adopted its own reverse-engineering

---

87. Copyright (Amendment) Act, 2006 §§ 116AN(3), 116AO(3), 116AP(3), 132APC(3), 132APD(3), and 132APE(3). This exception was anticipated by the CLRC Report's discussion of the modification of "locked" programs. Although the CLRC Report recommended that the "modification of a locked program for the purpose of circumventing the lock should be prohibited" (10.94 at 175), it suggested that circumvention should be permitted for "back-up copying, interoperability, and error correction."

amendment.[88] The two countries employed different legislative processes and statutory approaches, yet ended up in similar places for similar reasons. In each instance, the government made clear that the amendments were necessary to allow the domestic software industry to compete in the global market. As was discussed above, Australians pursued a lengthy and often contentious deliberative process to arrive at an amendment modeled on the EU Software Directive. In contrast, Singapore quietly developed an approach that closely follows the United States' reliance on the fair-use doctrine. Singapore's statutory amendment was necessitated by the 1996 ruling of the Singapore Court of Appeal's decision in *Aztech v. Creative Technologies*—a decision that had the affect of prohibiting software companies from engaging in reverse engineering in Singapore.

5.2.1 Singapore Courts and Interoperability: *Aztech v. Creative Technology* (1997)

In 1995, the High Court in Singapore relied on the U.S. decisions concerning reverse engineering to find the practice permissible under Singapore's copyright law. The following year, the Court of Appeal reversed this decision.

5.2.1.1 Facts

Creative Technology had developed "Sound Blaster" sound cards for use with personal computers. Along with its sound cards, the company packaged some computer software, including a specific program known as TEST-SBC. Somewhat later, Aztech began developing a sound card that would interoperate with applications designed for use with either the Sound Blaster or other standard sound cards in the industry. As part of the process of developing its own sound cards, Aztech copied Creative Technology's TEST-SBC program into the random-access memory of its own computers. This was done to allow Aztech's research-and-development team to run the computer program and to test it by running it along with other programs. Through this process, Aztech's researchers hoped to study the manner in which the Creative Technology program communicated directions to the Sound Blaster sound card. Thus, the reverse engineering involved

88. This section is based on passages in the following publications: Jonathan Band and Taro Isshiki, "Interoperability in the Pacific Rim: Reversal of Fortunes in Singapore and Australia," *Journal of Proprietary Rights*, July 1997, at 2; Jonathan Band, "Software Reverse Engineering Amendments in Singapore and Australia," *Journal of Internet Law*, January 2000, at 17.

only running Creative Technology's program in tests (i.e., black-box reverse engineering), not the decompilation of the program from object code into a higher-level form. The legal issue presented was whether Aztech's copying of the computer program into memory, in order to run the program as part of its hardware development process, qualified as "fair dealing"—the Commonwealth equivalent to the U.S. fair-use doctrine. The court evidently assumed that a transitory RAM copy was a copy within the meaning of Singapore's copyright law.

5.2.1.2 The High Court's Ruling

Fair Dealing
The four enumerated factors applied in determining whether a use should be considered "fair dealing" under the Singapore Copyright Act were remarkably similar to those under section 107 of the U.S. Copyright Act. However, Singapore's statute was more restrictive in that it also required that the use of a literary work be "for the purpose of research or private study."[89] The statute also explicitly excluded from its definition of "research" industrial research or research carried out by companies or other business groups. But even under this restrictive definition of fair dealing the Singapore High Court found the use by Aztech to constitute "private study" within the intended meaning of the statute. "It seems to me," the judge stated, "that a study is *private* if the study and the information and knowledge acquired through it are kept or removed from public knowledge or observation and this is so even if the purpose may be of a commercial nature."[90] This aspect of the decision is important, since a failure to construe "private study" to reach commercially motivated study would necessarily have excluded all forms of reverse analysis of computer software in a commercial context from the fair-dealing defense under Singapore law. It is also notable in that it shows the court's stretching of the traditionally restrictive doctrine to accommodate the analysis practiced by Aztech.

In its evaluation of the four enumerated fair-dealing factors, the court emphasized that Aztech copied the Creative Technology program into the memory of its own computers only in order to run the program. The judge wrote that the program "was copied to the memory of the computer." He continued: "That is the ordinary way of running the program and it was undoubtedly the way Creative intended it to be run. It was not copied in

---

89. *Aztech Systems Pte Ltd v. Creative Technology Ltd* (1996) 1 SLR 683.
90. Id.

any other way nor in any other form. It was not disassembled or printed out. No copies of it in any form were made for distribution or which could be distributed. I think this weighs in favour of fairness."[91] This was important to the first fair-dealing factor—the purpose and character of the dealing—because it indicated that the computer program was copied for the intended purpose of running the program. It was also important to the court's determinations on the second and third factors (the nature of the work and the amount and substantiality of the part copied), since the nature of a computer program requires that it be copied in its entirety into the computer's memory in order for the program to be run efficiently.

A significant distinction emphasized by the court several times during its fair-dealing determination was that Aztech was attempting to develop a competing sound card, not a software program that would compete with Creative Technology's TEST-SBC program: "I think it has to be borne in mind though that the product that was developed and marketed by Aztech was the *sound card*. It was not a *software program* that emulated TEST-SBC or the instructions in it."[92] The court found this to be important in evaluating not only the commercial purpose of the dealing but also the effect upon the potential market or value of the work, since the development of a competing hardware product would not compete directly, or perhaps at all, with the analyzed software.

Finally, the court also considered, as an independent and additional factor in its fair-dealing determination, the public interests advanced by the dealing at issue. Like the Ninth Circuit in *Sega*, the Singapore High Court found that increasing the competitors in the market "to more than just Creative and those licensed by it" would be a benefit "in consonance with the purpose of the Act."[93] The court then concluded that the balance of the considerations required a finding that Aztech's use of Creative Technology's program constituted fair dealing under the act and therefore succeeded as a defense to infringement.

Two Important Caveats

The limited extent of the reverse engineering reviewed in this case must be noted. All the High Court considered was Aztech's copying of the TEST-SBC program into RAM in order to study a specific command of the program. The court specifically observed that Aztech did not decompile Creative

91. Id.
92. Id.
93. Id.

Technology's software. This observation creates the implication that the High Court might have ruled differently in a case involving decompilation of a computer program's object code.

A second potential limitation suggested by the High Court's opinion is that reverse engineering of computer programs for the purpose of developing competing *software* might not be construed as fair dealing. Here, Aztech studied the Creative Technology program in order to develop competing *hardware*. As was stated above, this was a crucial factual distinction in the court's evaluation of two of the four statutory fair-dealing factors. The presence of direct competition might have altered the court's ultimate finding of fair dealing.

Use of Foreign Law

It is interesting that the High Court considered U.S. copyright decisions regarding reverse engineering specifically, and fair use generally, and yet left open the possibility of the limitations discussed above. The court first justified its examination of U.S. decisions because the provisions for fair dealing in Singapore and for fair use in the United States "are in many respects similar."[94] The U.S. decision discussed most extensively by the court was the Ninth Circuit's *Sega* decision. However, *Sega* contains neither of the limitations implicitly imposed by the High Court—the exclusion of decompilation and reverse engineering for the purpose of direct competition. The Singapore High Court instead turned to the *Sega* decision rather warily, embracing only its recognition of the public interest as relevant in fair-use determinations:

While I am conscious of the need to approach the American authorities with caution in view of the development in that jurisdiction of the distinction between *ideas and functional concepts* which are not protected by copyright and the *expression* of those unprotected elements which is protected it is at least comforting to know that the broader public interest is a factor to be taken into consideration albeit in respect of the "purpose and character" of the use although I would prefer to treat it as a separate matter to which regard is to be had.[95]

The court also investigated the applicability of an 1871 patent case, *Betts v. Wilmont*, in which a British court held that a purchaser of goods patented by another party has control of the goods such that, absent a clear and explicit agreement to the contrary, the purchaser may sell or use the articles however he pleases. Aztech argued that under *Betts v. Wilmont* its purchase

94. Id.
95. Id.

of the software from Creative Technology gave it the "right to use it for a *reasonable* purpose."[96] The court agreed:

When a man buys a Sound Blaster sound card and with it comes TEST-SBC he expects to have and to exercise his rights of ownership over it. He can use it. That is one of the rights of ownership. He can run the software in his PC. That is what it is for. To run it the program has to be copied to the PC's memory. He can run the program in as many PCs and as often as he pleases. He can study it to see what it is doing and he can experiment with it. That is exercising his right as an owner to use it. But he cannot make and distribute copies of it. That is not using it. That is not using the software he has bought.[97]

Most importantly, the court located the above-described right in Aztech's ownership of the software, not in the reasonableness of the use for which the software was employed.[98] Thus, even though the court suggested potential limitations on the fair-dealing defense, it provided a fairly broad and independent defense based on the right of ownership as recognized in *Betts v. Wilmont.*

5.2.1.3 Reversal by the Court of Appeal

In 1997, the Court of Appeal reversed the High Court's holding that Aztech's copying of Creative Technology's program during the course of reverse engineering it to develop a compatible product was a fair dealing under the Singapore Copyright Act.[99]

Fair Dealing Defense

Section 35(1) of the act provided that "fair dealing . . . for the purpose of research or private study shall not constitute an infringement of the copyright." Section 35(5) defined "research" as excluding "industrial research, research carried out by bodies corporate . . . or bodies or persons carrying on any business." As was noted above, the High Court had ruled that Aztech's reverse engineering was private study and not research, and therefore was permitted under section 35(1). The Court of Appeal disagreed with the High Court and decided that section 35(1) excludes commercial research as well as private study for commercial purposes. The Court of Appeal said that in order to come within the "private study" exception, the copying must be undertaken by the student. The Court of Appeal was influenced by the

96. Id.
97. Id.
98. See id.
99. *Creative Technology, Ltd v. Aztech Systems Pte Ltd* (1997) 1 SLR 621.

argument that if it were to adopt a broader construction of "private study" to extend to "private study for commercial purposes" it effectively would render meaningless the specific exclusion of commercial research under section 35(5). Since the Court of Appeal concluded that Aztech's admitted copying of TEST-SBC did not qualify as "research or private study," the fair-dealing defense was not available to Aztech.

"Essential Step" Defense

Section 39(3) of SCA, which is derived from section 117 of the U.S. Copyright Act, allows the owner of a computer program to copy or adapt that program as an essential step in the utilization of the program in conjunction with a machine. The Court o f Appeal considered whether the essential steps in using a computer program could include copying it into RAM for the purpose of studying the underlying ideas and concepts of the program. Relying for guidance on interpretations of section 117 of the U.S. Copyright Act, including *Apple Computer, Inc. v. Formula International, Inc.*[100] and *Allen-Myland, Inc. v. IBM Corp.*,[101] the Court of Appeal agreed with Creative Technology that section 39(3) was enacted for the limited purpose of allowing the rightful owner of the program to load and use it in his computer. In the Court of Appeal's view, section 39(3) did not allow copying or adaptation for the purpose of creating of a compatible product. Therefore, Aztech's RAM copy of TEST-SBC could not be deemed an essential step in the utilization of the program. In reaching this conclusion, the Court of Appeal explicitly rejected the Fifth Circuit's decision in *Vault Corp. v. Quaid Software Ltd.*,[102] which held that section 117 permitted RAM copying during the course of reverse engineering.

Implied License

Aztech argued that when it purchased TEST-SBC, it obtained along with its physical ownership the right to use it for a reasonable purpose. Aztech again relied upon the 1871 British patent case, *Betts v. Wilmont,* which held that the purchaser of a patented article has an implied license to sell the article and to use it for any reasonable purpose, absent some clear and explicit agreement to the contrary. Aztech asserted that its use was for a reasonable purpose; the copy of TEST-SBC was made to ascertain functionality

100. 594 F. Supp. 617 (C.D. Cal. 1984), *aff'd*, 725 F.2d 521 (9th Cir. 1984).
101. 746 F. Supp. 520 (E.D. Pa. 1990), *vacated and remanded*, 33 F.3d 194 (3d Cir. 1994), *cert. denied*, 513 U.S. 1066 (1994).
102. 847 F.2d 255 (5th Cir. 1988).

with the object of building a non-infringing compatible product. The trial judge made no finding on whether such use was indeed reasonable, but was persuaded that Aztech merely exercised an inherent right of ownership conferred by the purchase of TEST-SBC.

The Court of Appeal disagreed with the trial judge and held that the proposition in *Betts* is inapplicable in the Singaporean copyright context. The Court of Appeal noted that the exclusive rights granted to the patent owner differ materially from those accorded to the copyright owner and that to uphold such an implied license would run contrary to the provisions of the SCA.

Decompilation of Firmware

At trial and on appeal, Creative Technology alleged that Aztech had decompiled a substantial portion of the firmware embedded in the Sound Blaster microprocessor. The High Court decided as a factual matter that Aztech had not decompiled the firmware.

The Court of Appeal disagreed. After an extensive review of the facts, the Court of Appeal determined that Aztech had the means, the motive, and the opportunity to decompile Creative Technology's firmware. Furthermore, the literal similarities between Aztech's and Creative Technology's firmware raised the "irresistible inference that the chances of independent development on the part of Aztech were low."[103] However, because no more than 4 percent of Aztech's code was identical to Creative Technology's, the Court of Appeal held that Aztech's copying did not amount to a substantial taking.

Although the appellate court found no liability for the decompilation, it nonetheless seemed disturbed by the act of decompilation itself:

This . . . in no way prejudices our finding of [decompilation], which involves a degree of reproduction and adaptation having a greater impact in terms of revealing the ideas and interfaces of a copyright holder's program, insights which would not otherwise have been obtained by independent development or empirical observation within a given time frame.[104]

In other words, the Court of Appeal viewed the decompilation negatively precisely because it revealed features not protected by copyright.

There is a clear contrast between the Court of Appeal's hostile view toward decompilation and the Ninth Circuit's decision in *Sega Enters, Ltd.*

103. *Creative Technology, Ltd v. Aztech Systems Pte Ltd* (1997) 1 SLR 621.
104. Id.

v. Accolade, Inc.[105] In *Sega*, the court decided that decompilation in order to gain access to the unprotectable elements of the program, when no other means of access was available, was a fair use. The *Sega* court did not view decompilation as an independent wrong, but as a legitimate means of studying the ideas of the computer program in order to create a non-infringing product. (Interestingly, the Court of Appeal followed *Sega*'s holding that section 117 did not permit decompilation.)

After the *Aztech* decision, no commercially motivated research or study was entitled to the fair-dealing defense in Singapore. Thus, developers of interoperable software could not use the fair-dealing defense to excuse the interim copies made during decompilation and other forms of reverse engineering, nor could they rely on "essential step" or "implied license" arguments to justify their interim copying.

5.2.2 Responding to *Aztech*: Singapore's Software Reverse-Engineering Amendments

In response to the Court of Appeal's decision in *Aztech*, Singapore's Attorney-General of Law drafted an amendment to the Copyright Act, which was introduced in the Singapore Parliament in February of 1998.[106] The amendment deleted section 35(5), thereby allowing a court to interpret research and private study to include commercial reverse engineering. In introducing the amendment, the Attorney-General of Law stated: "[T]he deletion . . . of section 35(5) of the Act will bring us in line with the United States, the United Kingdom, other European Union countries, Hong Kong, and Australia, which do not bar the use of copyright materials for commercial research."[107]

Professor Chin Tet Yung, in the brief debate of the amendment in Parliament, said:

It is very important to ensure that there is a fair balance in any Copyright Bill between the interests of holders of rights in "cutting edge" software and the interest of competitors who want to design and market non-infringing competing programmes which interface or are inter-operable with the basic programmes.

The Court of Appeal's decision in *Creative Technology v. Aztech* established that currently Singapore's copyright law does not permit most kinds of reverse engineering. Companies cannot decompile programmes to establish how they were put together and armed with that knowledge to develop new inter-operable programmes.

105. 977 F.2d 1510 (9th Cir. 1992).
106. Copyright (Amendment) Bill of 1998.
107. Second Reading of Copyright (Amendment) Bill of 1998 (February 19, 1998). On the interoperability debate in Hong Kong, see section 5.3 of the present chapter.

Whether competitors should be able to reverse engineer and, if so, to what extent, is a very difficult matter to resolve. It seems clear, however, that most countries in the world are trying to draw a line between those two differing computer industry groups so that those who own the copyright in the leading programmes can maintain their strong copyright protection over their software, but that in certain circumstances others may decompile because there is a public interest in doing so.

In the United States, use is made of the "fair use" defence, whereby courts are required to weigh up, on the facts of every case, whether the defendants could justify their activities. In Singapore, with the current amendment to section 35(5), I am pleased to see that the Copyright Bill brings the law of Singapore very close to that of the United States. This is especially welcome and should receive warm support from the industry.[108]

In short, the amendment was clearly intended to overturn the result in *Aztech* and permit software reverse engineering to the extent permitted by the U.S. fair-use doctrine.[109] The government sought to allow Singapore companies to develop interoperable software products.

In 2004, Singapore amended its copyright law to include provisions modeled on the black-box reverse-engineering provision and the decompilation provision of the EU Software Directive. At the same time, it left its amended fair-dealing provision in place. Furthermore, the new provisions (39A and B) specifically stated that they were "without prejudice to the generality of section 35" and "d[id] not limit the operation of that section."[110] Thus, reverse-engineering activities that did not fall directly within the two new provisions could still be permitted by the fair-dealing section.

The 2004 amendments also implemented the Singapore-U.S. Free Trade Agreement, signed by the parties the previous year. Like the Australia-U.S. FTA, the Singapore-U.S. FTA required the parties to provide effective legal remedies against the circumvention of technological protection measures.[111] Similarly, the Singapore-U.S. FTA permitted parties to provide a reverse-engineering exception to the circumvention prohibition. Thus, under section 261D(1)(d) of the Singapore Copyright Act, the prohibitions

---

108. Second Reading of Copyright (Amendment) Bill of 1998 (February 19, 1998).
109. As was discussed above in chapters 1 and 2, the U.S. Court of Appeals for the Ninth Circuit, in *Sega Enter. Ltd. v. Accolade, Inc.*, 977 F.2d 1510, 1527–1528 (9th Cir. 1992), held that "where disassembly is the only way to gain access to the ideas and functional elements embodied in a copyrighted computer program and where there is a legitimate reason for seeking such access, disassembly is a fair use of the copyrighted work, as a matter of law."
110. Copyright Act, Singapore Statutes Chap. 63.
111. See subsection 5.1.4 of the present chapter.

on circumvention and circumvention devices do not apply when the circumvention is done

i. in good faith;

ii. in relation to a copy of a computer program that is not an infringing copy; and

iii. with respect to particular elements of the computer program that are not readily
available to the person doing the act,

for the sole purpose of achieving interoperability of an independently created computer program with another computer program. . . .[112]

5.3   Hong Kong

In the months before the turnover of Hong Kong to China, the Hong Kong
Legislative Council busily worked at revising its copyright laws with the
understanding that the new laws would continue in effect after the departure of the British on July 1, 1997.[113] One of the provisions the Legislative Council considered would have specifically permitted decompilation
for purposes of achieving interoperability. Rather than let the Legislative
Council determine for itself what was in the best interests of Hong Kong,
U.S. software companies represented by the Business Software Alliance[114]
encouraged the U.S. Trade Representative to pressure the Legislative Council into dropping the provision. The Legislative Council ultimately abandoned the decompilation provision, but in its place adopted, with BSA's
blessing, another provision based on the U.S. fair-use doctrine. This fair-use
language arguably permits more reverse engineering than the decompilation provision would have permitted.

5.3.1   The November 1996 Copyright Bill Consulting Paper

In November of 1996, the Department of Intellectual Property of Hong
Kong's Board of Trade and Industry produced a consultation paper on a
new copyright law, which included a proposed text for the bill. Section
57 of the Consultation Paper draft specifically permitted decompilation
of object code for purposes of achieving interoperability. Section 57(1)(a)
defined decompilation as the conversion of a "computer program expressed

112. Copyright Act, Singapore Statutes Chap. 63.

113. This section is based on Jonathan Band, "Gunboat Diplomacy on the Pearl
River: The Tortuous History of the Software Reverse Engineering Provisions of Hong
Kong's New Copyright Bill," *The Computer Lawyer*, February 1998, at 8.

114. The BSA's members included Microsoft, Novell, Autodesk, and Lotus (a subsidiary of IBM).

in a low level language . . . into a version expressed in a higher-level language."[115] The only permitted objective of the decompilation was obtaining "the information necessary to create an independent program which can be operated with the program decompiled or with another program." Section 57(3) prohibited decompilation when the "information necessary to achieve the permitted objective" was "readily available" to the user by other means, when the decompiling was not confined "to such acts as are necessary to achieve the permitted objective," when the information obtained by decompilation was supplied to a person not essential to achievement of the permitted objective, or when the information obtained by decompilation was used "to create a program which is substantially similar in its expression to the program decompiled." Finally, section 57(4) expressly voided contractual restrictions on decompilation otherwise permitted by section 57.

Section 57 of the Consultation Paper closely followed the decompilation provision of the UK copyright statute, section 50B, which closely followed the article 6 of the EU Software Directive. In other words, from a substantive perspective there was nothing controversial about section 57. Nonetheless, section 57 drew a sharp reaction from the U.S. government. In a cable sent in December of 1996, the U.S. government recommended deletion of section 57. The United States specifically objected to the voiding of contractual restrictions on decompilation, noting that this stood "in marked contrast to the EC Software Directive." The cable explained that "a similar restriction on the freedom of contract was proposed and rejected during consideration of the directive." In fact, the opposite was true. Article 9(1) of the directive explicitly provides that "[a]ny contractual provisions contrary to Article 6 [the decompilation provision] . . . shall be null and void." Thus, an official communication between the U.S. government and the Hong Kong Department of Intellectual Property contained an obvious legal error.

The cable suggested that section 57 had a broader permitted objective than article 6 of the EU Software Directive in that section 57 permitted decompilation for the purpose of creating new programs, whereas the EU Software Directive permits decompilation only for the purpose of achieving interoperability of existing programs. However, this interpretation of article 6 of the directive as permitting decompilation only to achieve interoperability between two existing products, and not to develop a new interoperable product, had no basis in the text of the directive or in its legislative history.

---

115. It is this act of conversion or translation that implicates the copyright owner's right to create a derivative work.

The cable also indicated that a decompilation provision would be inappropriate in view of the challenges of enforcing copyrights in Hong Kong. Yet the cable failed to explain how permitting decompilation would weaken enforcement. Good enforcement flows from an effective judicial system, and decompilation, of course, would have no effect on Hong Kong's judiciary. A decompilation provision also would not complicate judicial proceedings; section 57 would not provide a colorable defense to a software "pirate" engaged in wholesale copying.

The cable concluded by suggesting that Hong Kong delete section 57 because several other countries in the Asia-Pacific region, including Australia, New Zealand, Japan, and Korea, had considered and rejected a decompilation provision based on the EU Software Directive. This, too, was a misstatement. The Australian Copyright Law Review Committee in 1995 recommended legislative enactment of a decompilation provision,[116] and, as was discussed above, in 1999 Australia amended its copyright law to include a decompilation exception based on the EU Software Directive. In Japan, a private-sector advisory committee began to consider a reverse-engineering exception at the request of the Cultural Affairs Agency. The CAA's simple act of making the request, however, drew a sharp rebuke from the U.S. government, and the advisory committee concluded that it was premature to consider the issue.[117] Similarly, as will be discussed below, the Korean Ministry of Information and Communications suspended its consideration of a reverse-engineering exception in the face of protests by the U.S. government.[118] In short, neither Japan nor Korea rejected a decompilation provision after considering its merits; rather, they abandoned their efforts in response to U.S. pressure, but left the door open to revisiting the issue in the future.[119]

Although the U.S. government urged the Department of Intellectual Property to discard section 57, the American Committee for Interoperable Systems[120] pressed for amendments to make section 57 even more conducive to interoperability. Specifically, ACIS noted (in comments dated November 27, 1996) that section 57 contained an ambiguity that was

116. See subsection 5.1.1 of the present chapter.

117. See Band and Katoh, *Interfaces on Trial* at 297–316.

118. See section 5.5 of the present chapter.

119. Additionally, most scholars agree that software reverse engineering is currently permitted under Japanese law. See, e.g., Ozaki, "Copyright Protection of Software: The Japanese View," 1990 *Computer Law Reporter* 950 (1990).

120. The members of ACIS included Sun Microsystems, Storage Technology Corporation, 3Com, Fujitsu Systems Business of America, and NCR.

present in article 6 of the EU Software Directive. Both provisions permitted decompilation to achieve interoperability between two software products, but were silent about decompilation to permit interoperability between software and hardware. ACIS observed that the French National Assembly rectified this problem when it implemented the EU Software Directive by explicitly permitting decompilation to achieve software-hardware interoperability. Likewise, the Australian CRLC's decompilation provision applied to software-hardware interoperability. ACIS also urged that section 57 be extended to permit decompilation for purposes of error correction, again citing the Australian CLRC as a precedent.

5.3.2 The First Reading in the Legislative Council

In late February of 1997, the Board of Trade and Industry submitted its Copyright Bill to the Legislative Council, and it had its first reading. The bill retained the decompilation provision, which now appeared as section 60. The new section 60 differed from the original section 57 in one significant respect; whereas original section 57(4) voided contractual restrictions on decompilation, new section 60 expressly stated that the decompilation privilege was "subject to any agreement to the contrary." In other words, the bill on first reading took the completely opposite position on this issue from the Consultation Paper.

On April 11, 1997, ACIS submitted comments to the Legislative Council's Bills Committee applauding the retention of a decompilation exception. ACIS noted the consistency of section 60 with the EU Software Directive, with the case law in the United States treating decompilation as a fair use, and with the Australian CLRC's recommendations.

ACIS proceeded to observe that section 60 differed from its antecedents on the issue of the enforceability of contractual restrictions on reverse engineering. After quoting article 9(1) of the EU Software Directive, which voided contractual restrictions on decompilation, ACIS explained that "[t]he European Community included article 9(1) in the Directive because it correctly understood that without such a provision, software companies with market power would undo the delicate balance reached in the Directive by routinely including in their licenses clauses overriding Article 6." ACIS concluded that "Section 60(4) as a practical matter renders the rest of Section 60 a nullity."

5.3.3 The Bills Committee Hearings

Had the Business Software Alliance simply endorsed section 60 as introduced by the Board of Trade and Industry, it probably would have won the day. Whereas section 60 theoretically permitted decompilation for purposes of achieving interoperability, section 60(4) allowed members of BSA to prohibit decompilation by shrinkwrap license.

BSA, however, continued to lobby for complete elimination of the decompilation privilege. By pitting itself against the Board of Trade and Industry, it set in motion a process that resulted in a legal framework far more liberal than section 60 on first reading, and indeed arguably more liberal than section 57 of the Consultation Paper.

During April and May of 1997, the Bills Committee held a series of public hearings on the Copyright Bill. The Business Software Alliance and the Software Publishers Association testified against section 60; ACIS testified in its favor, provided that section 60(4) was deleted or reversed. (Emery Simon, a former official in the Office of the U.S. Trade Representative, testified for BSA; Peter M. C. Choy, Deputy General Counsel of Sun Microsystems, testified on behalf of ACIS. Transcripts of the hearings are not available.) On April 18, BSA filed a detailed written submission, to which ACIS replied point by point on April 25. BSA made the following arguments:

1. Decompilation reveals the source code of a computer program.
2. Decompilation is cheaper than obtaining a license and easier than developing a new program from the beginning.
3. Decompilation facilitates "hidden" piracy by allowing the reverse engineer to copy a program's functionality.
4. Decompilation is not necessary for interoperability because copyright owners make available the information necessary for interoperability.
5. Decompilation is not necessary because there are non-infringing means of obtaining interoperability information.
6. In the five years since the European Union adopted the Software Directive, no other country has followed its lead on decompilation.
7. A decompilation provision will suggest to the international community that Hong Kong is not serious about copyright infringement.[121]

ACIS responded as follows:

1. Decompilation at most reveals a shadow of the original source code, because it cannot recover the programmer's comments nor restore the original sequence of the code. Additionally, decompilation does not yield

---

121. Presentation of the Business Software Alliance to the Bills Committee (April 18, 1997). As we discussed in subsection 2.2.3, Judge Jackson disagreed with many of these contentions in his decision in *U.S. v. Microsoft*, 84 F.Supp.2d 9 (D.D.C. 1999).

instructions in a high level programming language, but only in assembly language.

2. While the actual act of decompilation is cheap and easy, the engineer using decompilation must still invest significant resources to understand the jumbled, decompiled code.

3. Decompilation does not facilitate hidden piracy because copying a program's functionality, but not its code, does not constitute copyright infringement.

4. While some software developers may be willing to license interface information if doing so is consistent with their business plan, there often are circumstances when a firm may not be willing to license the information on reasonable terms. Moreover, even when a firm does license the information on reasonable terms, the information may be incomplete or untimely.

5. Sometimes other reverse engineering techniques—so called black-box reverse engineering—will reveal the interface information necessary for interoperability, but sometimes decompilation is the only effective method.

6. In addition to the then fifteen members of the EU, eight European countries had adopted a decompilation exception based on article 6 of the Software Directive—Norway, Switzerland, Bulgaria, Estonia, Poland, Romania, Russia, and Slovenia. Further, courts in four different federal circuits in the U.S. had ruled that decompilation constitutes a fair use.[122]

7. Given the lawfulness of decompilation in twenty-four nations, ranging from highly industrialized countries such as the U.S., the U.K., Germany and France, to much less developed countries such as Bulgaria and Romania, the world community would not view Hong Kong's adoption of a decompilation provision as a signal that it did not take copyright seriously. In this context, ACIS noted that BSA's European counsel had described article 6 of the Directive as a "reasonable exception," and that BSA had not objected to its adoption throughout Central and Eastern Europe, where copyright infringement also was a serious concern.[123]

5.3.4 The Imposition of a Fair-Use Approach

When BSA representative Emery Simon testified before the Legislative Council on April 18, he suggested that decompilation be handled case by

122. *Sega Enters. Ltd. v. Accolade Inc.*, 977 F.2d 1521 (9th Cir. 1992); *Atari Games Corp. v. Nintendo of Am., Inc.*, 975 F.2d 832 (Fed. Cir. 1992); *Bateman v. Mnemonics Inc.*, 79 F.3d 1532 (11th Cir. 1996); *DSC Communications v. DGI Techs.*, 898 F. Supp. 1183 (N.D. Tex. 1995), *aff'd*, 81 F.3d 597 (5th Cir. 1996).

123. ACIS Response to BSA's April 18 Presentation to the Bills Committee (April 25, 1997).

case under Hong Kong's fair-dealing exception. The Legislative Council
directed the Board of Trade and Industry to delete section 60 and to pre-
pare amendments to the fair-dealing provisions that would accommodate
decompilation in appropriate circumstances. The staff of the Board of Trade
and Industry's Department of Intellectual Property proposed adding the
following language to section 37 concerning fair dealing: "The incidental
copying by a lawful user of a computer program in the course of research
or private study is fair dealing if it is done for the purpose of studying the
operation of the program under study, or of creating another independent program which is compatible with, but not substantially similar to or
adapted from the program under study." In essence, the proposal imported
the language of section 60 into the fair-dealing provision.

Exactly what happened next is unclear, but it is rumored that when BSA
learned on May 14 of the fair-dealing amendment proposed by the Department of Intellectual Property, it requested that the Office of the U.S. Trade
Representative intervene. A senior official in the Office of the USTR called
the Secretary of Trade and Industry and insisted that the Board of Trade
and Industry replace its fair-dealing amendment with language from the
fair-use provision of the U.S. Copyright Act, 17 U.S.C. § 107. The staff of the
Department of Intellectual Property then prepared the following language
as a new section 37(3):

In determining whether any dealing with a work of any description is fair dealing,
the factors to be considered include—

a. the purpose and nature of the dealing;
b. the nature of the work; and
c. the amount and substantiality of the portion dealt with in relation to the work
as a whole.

Additionally, the Department of Intellectual Property staff proposed a new
section 36(2A): "In determining whether or not an act is permitted, the
primary consideration is whether the act conflicts with a normal exploitation of the work and unreasonably prejudices the legitimate interests of the
copyright owner."

ACIS and BSA agreed to this language. On June 24, when the Secretary
of Trade and Industry submitted the bill—including this language—for its
second reading, she issued a statement explaining that the language was
intended to implement Hong Kong's policy with respect to decompilation.
After describing the decompilation provision in the bill gazetted in March,
she alluded to the concerns raised by ACIS and BSA: "[W]e accept that the
decompilation provision as drafted would be so limited as to be of little
practical help to software companies wanting to decompile. On the other

hand, as an exception to copyright restriction, the provision has aroused serious concerns amongst leading software companies."[124]

The Secretary of Trade and Industry stated that the Board of Trade and Industry had reviewed its policy intention on decompilation, and had concluded that it "would like to encourage competition in the information technology industry by facilitating timely access to information and ideas underlying computer programs." She continued:

> Doing so is necessary for the independent creation of new products that attach to or compete with the programs under study. We accept that the incidental copying of a computer program by a lawful user during the course of decompilation or other reverse engineering performed to understand the operation of the program under study, or to develop a product inter-operable with the program under study, need *not* be absolutely restricted by copyright. Nor should it be completely deregulated. In determining whether the act should be allowed, we believe the overriding test is whether such act conflicts with the normal exploitation of the work by the copyright owner and unreasonably prejudices the legitimate interests of the copyright owner.[125]

The Secretary of Trade and Industry then explained how the modifications to the fair-dealing provisions flowed from these conclusions:

> The object is to allow decompilation to be deemed a fair use provided it does not conflict with the normal exploitation of the rights and legitimate interests of the copyright owner. Drawing from the relevant provisions in the United States, we propose that other factors, including the purpose and nature of the dealing, the nature of the copyrighted work, and the amount and substantiality of the portion dealt with in relation to the copyright work as a whole, will also be taken into account in determining what constitutes "fair use."[126]

The Legislative Council gave the bill its second reading on June 24, 1997, and its third reading on June 27. It took immediate effect on its third reading. Under the turnover agreement with China it will remain in effect for 50 years.

5.3.5   Fair Use vs. Fair Dealing vs. the EU Software Directive

Although the proposed section 60 explicitly permitted decompilation, it did so only for purposes of achieving interoperability, only if there was no other way of obtaining the necessary information, and, most significantly,

---

124. Speech by Secretary of Trade and Industry on Resumption of Second Reading Debate at 10 (June 24, 1997). Under Hong Kong law, such floor statements constitute legislative history upon which courts should rely when interpreting a statute.
125. Id.
126. Id. at 11.

only if it was not prohibited by a license term. By contrast, section 37(3) as enacted by the Legislative Council is far broader. The speech by the Secretary of Trade and Industry makes clear that decompilation could be lawful when conducted "to understand the operation of the program under study" as well as "to develop a product inter-operable with the program under study." Thus, section 37(3) recognizes legitimate objectives beyond achieving interoperability. This expansive reading of section 37(3) is even more compelling when its origins are considered. A Hong Kong court applying this language to a case involving decompilation will understand that it derives from the U.S. fair-use doctrine, and presumably will import the interpretation of the doctrine given by the U.S. courts. The Ninth Circuit ruled in *Sega v. Accolade* that the fair-use doctrine permitted decompilation not only for purposes of learning the information necessary for interoperability, but for any legitimate reason: "[W]here disassembly is the only way to gain access to the ideas and functional elements embodied in a copyrighted computer program and *where there is a legitimate reason for seeking such access*, disassembly is a fair use of the copyrighted work, as a matter of law."[127]

When section 37(3) was enacted, its terms were more expansive than those of the fair-use doctrine codified at 17 U.S.C. § 107.[128] Section 37(3) omitted the phrase "including whether such use is of a commercial nature or is for nonprofit educational purposes" found in section 107(1), thereby eliminating the possibility of a presumption that commercial uses (such as decompilation by a profit-maximizing software firm) are unfair.

Section 37(3) also omitted the phrase "the effect of the use upon the potential market for or value of the copyrighted work" (found in section 107(4)) and inserted in its place language from article 9(2) of the Berne Convention: "whether the act conflicts with the normal exploitation of the work and unreasonably prejudices the legitimate interests of the copyright owner." Both the statute and the statement of the Secretary of Trade and Industry emphasize that this is the primary, overriding test. The inclusion of this language did not signal an intent that section 37(3) had narrower application than article 6 of the EU Software Directive, for article 6(3) itself contains this same language. According to William Cornish of Cambridge University, this language is implicated only if decompilation is

---

127. The terms "disassembly" and "decompilation" have the same meaning in legal parlance, but "disassembly" is commonly used in U.S. court decisions, whereas "decompilation" is used outside the U.S.

128. In 2007, Hong Kong amended its fair-dealing provision to track 17 U.S.C. § 107 more closely.

used to develop a program substantially similar *in expression* to the decompiled program.[129]

Section 37(3) is broader than either of the earlier decompilation provisions (57 and 60) in another significant respect. The earlier provisions
referred to decompilation, but were silent about the lawfulness of the copying that occurs during the course of black-box reverse engineering—for
example, the making of interim copies of the program in RAM when the
program is run for the purpose of observing its operation. Section 37(3), by
contrast, is broad enough to excuse such incidental copying. Once again,
the statement by the Secretary of Trade and Industry confirms this by referring to the incidental copying "during the course of decompilation or *other
reverse engineering.*"

Finally, section 60 specifically permitted contractual limitations on the
decompilation privilege. Section 37, by contrast, is silent on this issue, leaving
open the possibility that a Hong Kong court could determine that enforcing
such a limitation would undermine the "policy intention" of "encourag[ing]
competition in the information technology industry by facilitating timely
access to information and ideas underlying computer programs."

Since the Business Software Alliance had acknowledged that article 6 of
the EU Software Directive was a reasonable compromise in the European
context, and since courts in four circuits had found decompilation to be a
fair use, it is not clear why BSA so strongly preferred fair use to article 6 in
Hong Kong. By all appearances, the BSA gained nothing when it pressured
countries to follow the fair-use model rather than the EU Software Directive
model.

5.4   The Philippines

In 1997, the government of the Philippines proposed a reverse-engineer-
ing exception based on the EU Software Directive. Not surprisingly, that
proposal encountered fierce opposition from the Office of the U.S. Trade
Representative (USTR) and the Business Software Alliance. In response, the
Philippines crafted a hybrid of the fair-use provision of the U.S. Copyright
Act and article 6 of the EU Software Directive:

The fair use of a copyrighted work for criticism, comment, news reporting, teaching including multiple copies for classroom use, scholarship, research, and similar

129. William R. Cornish, "Computer Program Copyright and the Berne Convention," in *A Handbook of European Software Law* (1993). The same language also appears
in article 13 of the TRIPS Agreement.

purposes is not an infringement of copyright. *Decompilation, which is the reproduction of code and translation of the form of the computer program indispensable to obtain the information necessary to achieve the inter-operability of an independently created computer program with other programs may also constitute fair use.* In determining whether the use made of a work in any particular case is fair use, the factors to be considered shall include:

a. The purpose and character of the use, including whether use is of a commercial nature or is for non-profit educational purposes;
b. The nature of the copyrighted work;
c. The amount and substantiality of the portion used in relation to the copyrighted work as a whole; and
d. The effect of the use upon the potential market for value of the copyrighted work.[130]

As was noted above, when the Hong Kong Department of Intellectual Property had proposed a similar grafting of reverse-engineering language onto the fair-use provision, the USTR voiced strong opposition. But there is no public record of the USTR's objecting to the Philippine approach. As with the provision adopted in Hong Kong, it is far from clear that this formulation constrains reverse engineering more than article 6 of the directive; indeed, the opposite may be the case. The provision was enacted in June of 1997 and took effect in January of 1998.

5.5   Korea

Though one may question the wisdom and the propriety of the heavy-handedness of the USTR and the Business Software Alliance in Hong Kong and in the Philippines, those American interventions were far less successful than similar efforts in Japan and Korea. The Japanese Cultural Affairs Agency and the Korean Ministry of Information and Communications suspended consideration of a reverse exception in 1994 and 1995, respectively, in the face of U.S opposition. The history of the Japanese deliberations of this issue is well documented[131] and will not be discussed further here. By contrast, little has been written about the Korean deliberations. What follows is a brief summary.

The Korean episode began in early May of 1995, when the Ministry of Information and Communication of the Republic of Korea (i.e., South

130. Intellectual Property Code of the Philippines, § 185.1 (emphasis added).
131. See Band and Katoh, *Interfaces on Trial* at 297–310. See also Crystal D. Talley, "Japan's Retreat from Reverse Engineering: An Unnecessary Surrender?" 29 *Cornell International Law Journal* 807 (1997).

Korea) proposed consideration of a reverse-engineering exception in the Computer Program Protection Act. The provision would excuse reproductions "where the program is temporarily reproduced or translated within the limits required for purposes of research and analysis necessary for the creation of interoperable programs."

BSA promptly submitted lengthy comments opposing the amendment. Although the proposal by the Ministry of Information and Communication addressed software reverse engineering generally, BSA's comments focused on decompilation. Decompilation, according to BSA, wasn't necessary, because there were other ways to obtain interface information, including other reverse-engineering techniques and licensing; decompilation would facilitate disguised piracy and thereby harm the Korean software industry and prevent foreign investment in Korea; the *Sega* decision was "the view of only one U.S. court on a matter of first impression decided on an incomplete factual record and on a particular set of facts"; the level of protection currently afforded represented a further erosion; and the proposed exception was far broader than that in the EU Software Directive.[132]

The U.S government also strongly protested the Ministry of Information and Communication's proposal. A position paper prepared by the U.S. Patent and Trademark Office made three points that paralleled those of the BSA. First, "Korea's current system of protection is too weak to permit any limitation on protection in the form of a decompilation exception." Second, the EU Software Directive's decompilation provision was far narrower than the proposed Korean exception. In particular, under the directive "[d]ecompilation can never be used to create a program that competes with the program which is being decompiled." Third, the *Sega and Atari* decisions were read very narrowly, with the conclusion that "[d]ecompilation could not be used to create programs which competed with the programs being decompiled."[133]

The American Committee for Interoperable Systems, in letters to the PTO and the USTR, responded sharply to what it called "errors" in the U.S. government's position paper. ACIS first referred to the legislative history of the EU Software Directive and its implementations in the member states to

132. Business Software Alliance Position Paper Submitted to the Ministry of Information and Communications of the Republic of Korean on proposed Exceptions from Protection for Computer Programs Under the Computer Program Protection Act (May 2, 1995).
133. U.S. Government Views on Decompilation Position in Korean Computer Program Law (June 12, 1995).

demonstrate that article 6 of the directive permitted decompilation for purposes of developing both attaching *and* competing programs. Next, ACIS rebutted the U.S. government's parsimonious reading of *Sega* and "improper trivializ[ation]" of *Atari*. Finally, though ACIS explicitly declined to address programs of piracy in Korea, it directly challenged the U.S. government's suggestion that the decompilation could facilitate disguised piracy.[134]

In a letter to the Office of the U.S. Trade Representative, the Computer & Communications Industry Association "object[ed] in the strongest terms possible to the Government's flawed analysis of the EU Directive and the *Sega* decision." "We are," CCIA continued, "especially concerned that the Government is making representations to foreign governments that do not reflect an accurate and balanced analysis of the developing international jurisprudence relating to the permissibility of disassembly."[135]

As ACIS and CCIA corresponded with the U.S. government, the European Committee for Interoperable Systems and the Supporters of Interoperable Systems in Australia communicated directly with the Ministry of Information and Communication. ECIS suggested that "[a] provision permitting reverse engineering for interoperability purposes will facilitate legitimate competition and further consumer welfare without permitting piracy." Likewise, SISA applauded the Ministry of Information and Communication's simple exemption for reverse engineering to achieve interoperability.

In late July of 1995, the president of the Republic of Korea traveled to Washington to participate in the dedication of the Korean War Memorial on the National Mall. Secretary of Commerce Ron Brown used the opportunity to complain to his Korean counterpart about the Ministry of Information and Communication's reverse-engineering proposal. Soon thereafter, the MIC abandoned the proposal.

5.6   Israel

In November of 2007, Israel's legislature, the Knesset, enacted a new copyright law. The law included both a fair-use provision based on 17 U.S.C.

134. Letter from Peter M. C. Choy, Chairman, ACIS, to Bruce Lehman, Commissioner, U.S. Patent and Trademark Office (June 26, 1995); letter from Peter M. C. Choy, Chairman, ACIS, to Thomas Robertson, Assistant General Counsel, Office of the U.S. Trade Representative (June 26, 1995).
135. Letter from Gregory E. Gorman, Government Affairs Manager, CCIA, to Thomas Robertson, Assistant General Counsel, Office of the U.S. Trade Representative (July 5, 1995).

§107, and an exception for software reverse engineering based on the EU Software Directive. Indeed, the reverse-engineering exception in section 24 appears similar to the expanded version of the EU Software Directive that Australia had adopted. It permitted the making of derivative works (i.e., decompilation) for purposes of error correction and security testing, and also for purposes of obtaining the information necessary for interoperability:

(c) Copying of a computer program, or making a derivative work there from, is permitted for a person who possesses an authorized copy of the computer program, for the following purposes and to the extent necessary to achieve said purposes:

(1) Use of the computer program for purposes for which it was intended, including correction of errors in the computer program or making it interoperable with a computer system or with another computer program;

(2) Examination of the information security in the program, correction of security breaches and protection from such breaches;

(3) Obtaining information which is needed to adapt a different and independently developed computer system or program, in such a way that it will be interoperable with the computer program.

(d) The provisions of subparagraph (c) shall not apply with respect to the copying of a computer program or the making of a derivative work there from, as stated in said subparagraph, if the information which has been obtained through the aforementioned means was used in a manner set forth below, or where such information was readily available without use of the aforesaid means:

(1) The said information is transmitted to another person for a purpose different than the purposes set forth in subparagraph (c);

(2) The said information is used to make a different computer program which infringes copyright in the said computer program.

Although in the 1990s the U.S. government urged countries to adopt a general fair-use provision instead of a specific reverse-engineering exception based on the EU Software Directive, it subsequently rejected the requests of U.S. Internet companies to include fair use in bilateral free-trade agreements. Search engines based in the United States rely on fair use to permit the copying they perform to assemble their search databases and to display search results.[136] The copyright regimes of other countries are not as hospitable to search engines; a Belgian court, for example, imposed copyright liability on Google for search activities that would be considered fair use in the United States. To secure the legal environment necessary for them to

136. See Jonathan Band, "Google and Fair Use," 3 *Journal of Business & Technology Law* 1 (2008).

increase their presence overseas, U.S. search-engine companies asked the Office of the U.S. Trade Representative to help "export" fair use to other countries. But in 2007, USTR denied the request that it include fair use in its "template" for future free-trade agreements:

The precise language that is used to achieve our objectives in this area is likely to vary from one trade agreement to another. . . . For example, our assessment of the commitment and capacity of a given trading partner to ensure effective protection and enforcement of the copyright-protected creations may be a factor in shaping our approach in future negotiations. We believe determining the best approach to these issues will continue to require a careful analysis based on each trading partner's copyright system. . . .[137]

Here USTR implied that in most countries a fair-use provision would be abused.

Patrick Leahy, chairman of the Senate Judiciary Committee, had a different view. He stated that the Trade Promotion Authority Act of 2002

instructed the administration to negotiate agreements that provide strong protection for new and emerging technologies and new methods of transmitting and distributing products embodying intellectual property. This, too, is an objective I support. Under our laws, many such new technologies and consumer devices rely, at least in part, on fair use and other limitations and exceptions to the copyright laws. Our trade agreements should promote similar fair use concepts, in order not to stifle the ability of industries relying on emerging technologies to flourish.[138]

In December of 2009, the Obama administration articulated a position similar to Senator Leahy's. At a session of the Standing Committee on Copyright and Related Rights of the World Intellectual Property Organization, Justin Hughes, the head of the U.S. delegation, stated:

We recognize that some in the international copyright community believe that any international consensus on substantive limitations and exceptions to copyright law would weaken international copyright law. The United States does not share that point of view. The United States is committed to both better exceptions in copyright law and better enforcement of copyright law. Indeed, as we work with countries to establish consensus on proper, basic exceptions within copyright law, we will ask countries to work with us to improve the enforcement of copyright. This is part and parcel of a balanced international system of intellectual property.[139]

137. Letter from Stanford K. McCoy, Acting Assistant U.S. Trade Representative, to Duane Webster, Executive Director, Association of Research Libraries (July 19, 2007).

138. Cong. Rec. S14720, December 4, 2007 (Statement of Sen. Leahy).

139. United States of America, Statement on Copyright Exceptions and Limitation for Persons with Print Disabilities, World Intellectual Property Organization, Standing Committee on Copyright and Related Rights, 19th Session (December 15, 2009) at 5.

6   The Road Ahead

As was noted in chapter 1, many factors have contributed to the migration from the locked-in computing environment of the 1970s to today's interoperable world. These factors include consumer demand, business strategy, government policy, and the ideology of technologists. The evolution of copyright law over the past 30 years has also played a critical role. As it became increasingly clear to companies in the information-technology industry that copyright did not facilitate control of interface specifications, companies had less incentive to try to improve their market position by preventing interoperability. If a competitor could lawfully achieve interoperability by reverse engineering and then using the interface specifications developed by a dominant company, the dominant company gained little long-term advantage over its competitor by concealing the interface specifications. In this manner, the evolution of copyright law discussed in this volume and its forerunner has helped encourage the voluntary disclosure of interface information, particularly through open-source software licenses. Although open-source software licenses promote interoperability, patents remain a threat on the horizon.

6.1   Open-Source Software

The interoperability debate arose because some firms attempted to exercise proprietary control over interface specifications. These firms concealed the interface specifications by distributing software only in object code, and they used legal mechanisms (including copyright, contract, and anti-circumvention laws) to prevent the reverse engineering that would be necessary to uncover the interface specifications. In addition, these firms claimed that copyright prevented competitors from complying with these interface specifications. By contrast, open-source developers distribute their software in source code, thereby making reverse engineering unnecessary. Moreover, open-source developers employ license agreements that permit reproduction and distribution of the software and the creation of derivative works. These licenses typically require the licensee to distribute the modified programs to the public only in source code.[1]

As was discussed in chapter 3, proprietary developers have attempted to use software licenses to prevent interoperability. Conversely, open-source developers employ software licenses to mandate interoperability. Among the first entities to use software licenses in this manner was the Free Software Foundation, established in 1985. The label "open source" gained wider acceptance in 1998 with the founding of the Open Source Initiative. The GNU General Public License currently is the most widely used open-source license, but numerous other licenses have been adopted, including the Apache License, the BSD License, the MIT License, the Eclipse Public License, and the Mozilla Public License.

As open-source software has been adopted more widely by major information-technology firms and their corporate customers,[2] the dispersed developers working within particular open-source programming environments have coalesced into networks of varying degrees of formality. In essence, these networks act as standards organizations for the various programming environments. They include a group of developers affiliated with Linus Torvalds (creator of the Linux operating system kernel), the Mozilla Foundation (which supports the Firefox Web browser), the Apache Software Foundation (which supports the Apache Web server), and the Eclipse Foundation (which supports the Eclipse software-development platform).

In August of 2008, the U.S. Court of Appeals for the Federal Circuit provided legal legitimacy to open-source licenses by finding that a person who breaches the terms of an open-source license infringes the copyright in the underlying program.[3] Robert Jacobsen managed an open-source software group for model railroad enthusiasts, the Java Model Railroad Interface (JMRI). JMRI created an application called DecoderPro, which allowed model railroad enthusiasts to program the decoder chips that control model trains. The DecoderPro files were available for free download and use, subject to the terms of the "Artistic License" (one of the many open-source licenses in use). Matthew Katzer offered Decoder Commander, a commercial

---

1. The Open Source Initiative maintains an "Open Source Definition" for determining whether a software license is an open-source license. It is available at opensource.org.

2. See Pamela Samuelson, Open Source and Competition in the Software Industry, available at www.aals.org.

3. *Jacobsen v. Katzer*, 535 F.3d 1373 (Fed. Cir. 2008).

software product for model railroad enthusiasts. One of Katzer's employees included decoder definition files from DecoderPro in Decoder Commander. However, in contravention of the DecoderPro license terms, Katzer did not include in Decoder Commander the names of the DecoderPro authors, the JMRI copyright notices, an identification of JMRI as the original source of the definition files, or a description of how the computer code and the computer file names had been changed from the original source code.

In response to Jacobsen's claim that Katzer had infringed the DecoderPro copyright by copying the program without following all the terms of the license, Katzer argued that the license terms were mere covenants, actionable under contract law, and not conditions on the software license. Katzer's argument was premised on the assumption that Jacobsen's copyright gave him no economic rights because he had made his computer code available to the public at no charge. From this assumption, Katzer argued that copyright law does not recognize a cause of action for non-economic rights.

The Federal Circuit rejected this argument, finding that Jacobsen did receive economic benefit from these terms. The attribution provision directed downstream users to Jacobsen's website, where they could learn about and perhaps join the collaborative efforts of JMRI. Moreover, by requiring that changes made by downstream users be visible to the copyright holder and to others, the copyright holder learned about the uses of his software and gained others' knowledge that could be used to advance future software releases. Thus, the attribution and modification transparency requirements advanced significant economic goals of the copyright holder. Accordingly, the terms were conditions on the software license, and their breach resulted in copyright infringement and in breach of contract.[4]

By holding that the breach of the terms of an open-source license constituted a copyright infringement, the Federal Circuit significantly strengthened the remedies available to an open-source licensor against a breaching licensee. In particular, the licensor can seek statutory damages. This, in turn, will discourage a licensee from attempting to "hijack" an open-source product and render it less interoperable.

6.2 Software Patents

Although copyright law has evolved in a manner that prevents its use to exercise control of interface specifications, and open-source licensing has become widely accepted by both the private and public sectors, Microsoft

---

4. The decision is also notable for its extensive positive dicta on open-source software and Creative Commons licenses.

and other companies continue to pursue proprietary business strategies, with great success. Developers of interoperable software have long feared that companies seeking to exclude competitors will use patent law to prevent interoperability.[5]

Patents implicate interoperability in two respects. First, and most directly, a software developer could receive a patent on a set of interface specifications or on a lockout mechanism. The holder of such a patent could defeat the development of interoperable products by preventing all others from making products that conform to the interface specifications or lockout mechanism.[6] Second, a software developer could receive a patent on a particular function implemented by software. The holder of such a patent could defeat the development of interoperable products by preventing all others from making software products that perform the same function.[7]

Software patents have provoked extensive controversy in their own right. The controversy does not relate specifically to interoperability, however; rather, it concerns the issuance of software patents that do not meet the statutory requirements of the Patent Act and abuses peculiar to patent litigation in the information-technology industry.

6.2.1 Statutory Requirements

6.2.1.1 Statutory Subject Matter

Section 101 of the Patent Act classifies "any new and useful process, machine, manufacture, or composition of matter" as subject matter eligible for patent protection.[8] The Supreme Court suggested in 1972 that an invention involving processes performed by a computer should not receive patent protection, because the invention simply represented unpatentable subject matter (e.g., scientific truths, mathematical expressions, or algorithms).[9] Then, in 1981, the Supreme Court ruled that "a claim drawn to

5. For a comprehensive discussion of this topic, see Pamela Samuelson, "Are Patents on Interfaces Impeding Interoperability?" 93 *Minnesota Law Review* 1943 (2009).

6. For examples of patents on software and telecommunications interfaces, see id. at 1965–1969.

7. Patent law does not contain a "fair-use" provision that permits experimental use. Thus, a developer may infringe a patent if he uses a patented technology in the course of developing software that does not itself infringe. Moreover, unlike copyright law, patent law does not have an independent-invention defense. Accordingly, a person can infringe a patent without ever seeing the patentee's invention.

8. 35 U.S.C. § 101 (2006).

9. *Gottschalk v. Benson*, 409 U.S. 63 (1972).

subject matter otherwise statutory does not become non-statutory simply because it uses a mathematical formula, computer program, or digital computer."[10] Since then, the U.S. Court of Appeals for the Federal Circuit, which has exclusive jurisdiction over most patent appeals, has issued a series of complex and contradictory decisions that attempt to define the statutory subject matter in software and in business methods (which often are implemented by software). For example, the Federal Circuit held in *In re Alappat* that a process satisfied the statutory-subject-matter test if it produced a "useful, concrete, and tangible result."[11] More recently, however, in *In re Bilski*, the Federal Circuit articulated a more restrictive test in an effort to insure that "a process claim is tailored narrowly enough to encompass only a particular application of a fundamental principle rather than to pre-empt the principle itself."[12] Under this test, a claimed process is patent eligible if "(1) it is tied to a particular machine or apparatus; or 2) it transforms a particular article into a different state or thing."[13] The court added that "[p]urported transformations or manipulations simply of public or private legal obligations or relationships, business risks, or other such abstractions cannot meet the test because they are not physical objects or substances, and they are not representative of physical objects or substances."[14]

When the Supreme Court granted Bilski's petition to review the Federal Circuit's decision, the information-technology industry hoped that the Supreme Court would provide much-needed clarity in this area. Unfortunately, the Supreme Court's decision, *Bilski v. Kappos*, 561 U.S. ___, 2010 WL 2555192 (June 28, 2010), increased the uncertainty. All nine justices agreed that Bilski's method for hedging risk in commodities transactions was not eligible for patent protection, but for different reasons. The five justices who joined in the majority opinion rejected Bilski's patent because the concept of hedging was an unpatentable "abstract idea" but provided no guidance for determining when ideas were too abstract. The majority also reversed the Federal Circuit's holding that the "machine-or-transformation test" was the only measure of patentability for a process. Though the test was a useful tool for determining whether claimed inventions were processes under section 101, it was not the exclusive test. Further, the majority

10. *Diamond v. Diehr*, 450 U.S. 175 (1981).
11. *In re Alappat*, 33 F.3d 1526 (Fed. Cir. 1994). Following *Alappat*, the Federal Circuit decided *In re Beauregard*, 53 F.3d 1583 (Fed. Cir. 1995), to allow claims to software so long as reduced to machine-readable format.
12. *In re Bilski*, 545 F.3d 943, 954 (Fed. Cir. 2008) (en banc).
13. Id.
14. Id. at 963.

found that section 101 did not categorically preclude business-method patents. In contrast, four justices, in a concurring opinion written by retiring Justice Stevens, would have held all business methods categorically unpatentable.

6.2.1.2 Nonobviousness

An invention consisting of statutory subject matter must meet the requirements of novelty and non-obviousness before it can receive a patent. The Patent Act provides that an invention's improvement or innovation over the existing technology (termed "prior art") cannot be obvious to "a person having ordinary skill in the art" to which the invention pertains. A patent examiner must determine in the first instance whether an invention meets this non-obviousness requirement. The U.S. Patent and Trademark Office began issuing software patents in the 1980s. In that decade and in the 1990s, many programmers believed that the PTO's examining corps did not have enough familiarity with software technology or enough access to appropriate databases to make such assessments properly. Thus, the PTO granted patents on processes that programmers claimed to have known and used for decades.

In response to concerns about the "quality" of software patents, the PTO revised its internal procedures concerning software patents. Congress revised the reexamination procedure to allow a third party to mount an administrative challenge to the issuance of a patent within the PTO, rather than having to resort to litigation in federal district court. Federal-court litigation typically is more expensive than administrative litigation. Moreover, federal courts must give issued patents a presumption of validity, which makes the patents more difficult to challenge before a court than before the PTO.

Notwithstanding these changes, there is a continuing perception that a patent-quality problem persists with the patenting of software and business methods. Thus, when Congress began to consider patent-reform legislation in 2005, patent quality was one of the major issues on the table. In the 110th Congress, the House passed a patent-reform bill that liberalized the reexamination procedures.[15] One reason why parties are reluctant to use the existing process is that if they initiate a reexamination, they are estopped from raising in district-court litigation "prior art" that they could have raised in the reexamination but did not raise. In addition, under the current process, evidence of public use or sale cannot be used as grounds for requesting a reexamination. The House bill attempted to correct these deficiencies.

15. Patent Reform Act of 2007, H.R. 1908, 110th Cong. (2007).

The legislation encountered significantly more resistance in the Senate.[16] The Senate bill dealt with the issue of patent quality by establishing a new post-grant opposition proceeding before the PTO—a proceeding similar to the opposition proceedings in other countries. Supporters of reform wanted two "windows" for initiating the opposition proceeding: one within twelve months of issuance and one after receipt of a cease-and-desist letter. Information-technology and financial-services companies, among others, asserted that, in view of the broad and often imprecise language used for software and business method claims, they often had no idea that a patent might apply to them until they received a cease-and-desist letter.[17] They might first receive such a letter five or ten years after the issuance of a patent. Hence, they often would not be able to avail themselves of the new post-grant opposition proceeding if they had to initiate the proceeding within twelve months of issuance of the patent. Opponents of the second window said that they needed "quiet title" to their patents—that the possibility of an opposition proceeding should not hang over their patents indefinitely. Of course, no patent owner really has "quiet title" to his patent until a court rules that it is valid, which can occur years after issuance of the patent.[18] In any event, the Senate could not reach agreement on the issue of one or two windows for oppositions, and the 110th Congress ended without enactment of patent-reform legislation.

On March 3, 2009, early in the 111th Congress, identical patent-reform bills were introduced in the House (H.R. 1260) and in the Senate, (S. 515).[19] These bills would establish a post-grant opposition proceeding with one window for the twelve months after issuance. To create a second window for challenging a patent administratively, the bills would strengthen the existing reexamination proceeding. H.R. 1260 and S. 515 as introduced would eliminate estoppel with respect to prior art that could have been raised. They also would allow documentary evidence of public use or sale of prior art. The Senate Judiciary Committee considered S. 515 just a month

16. Patent Reform Act of 2007, S. 1145, 110th Cong. (2007).
17. Under the "doctrine of equivalents," a device or process that does not fall within the literal terms of the patent claims may still infringe if a court finds it "equivalent" to the claimed invention. The doctrine of equivalents creates significant uncertainty with respect to ambiguous software and business-method claims. The patent-reform legislation does not attempt to restrict the doctrine of equivalents, and thus fails to address a major contributor to the patent-quality problem.
18. Moreover, even if one court finds a patent valid with respect to one defendant, a different court can find the patent invalid in a case involving another defendant.
19. Patent Reform Act of 2009, H.R. 1260, 111th Congress (2009); S. 515, 111th Congress (2009).

after its introduction. It approved the post-grant opposition proceeding and the elimination of estoppel in the reexamination proceeding, but it dropped the provision permitting documentary evidence of public use or sale.

The patent-reform legislation remains controversial, and its prospects for enactment remain uncertain. Poor-quality software patents remain a potential threat to interoperability; the more patents there are, the greater is the likelihood of a patent on a critical interface.

6.2.2 Litigation Reform

Information-technology companies have identified a host of problems relating to patent litigation, including venue, the lack of interlocutory appeals from *Markman* hearings on claim construction, the standards for injunctive relief, the standards for measuring damages, the standards for willful infringement, and the standards for inequitable conduct. Attempts to solve these problems have provoked controversy.

Underlying the controversy is the belief that the patent system affects different industries differently. The pharmaceutical and biotech industries generally are satisfied with the status quo; the information-technology and financial-services industries feel burdened by it. One explanation of this disparate impact is that a typical pharmaceutical product is covered by a small number of patents, whereas an IT product may be covered by thousands of patents.

The Pharmaceutical Research and Manufacturers of America (PhRMA) and the Biotechnology Industry Organization (BIO) observe that many of the litigation concerns identified by the information-technology and financial-services industries are rooted in interpretations of the Patent Act by the Federal Circuit, not in the Patent Act itself. Accordingly, the Federal Circuit and the Supreme Court can correct these interpretations. PhRMA and BIO correctly point to several decisions by the Supreme Court and the Federal Circuit since Congress began considering patent reform as demonstrating that the patent system is "self-correcting."

6.2.2.1 *eBay v. MercExchange* (2006)

The most salient example of self-correction is the Supreme Court's decision in *eBay v. MercExchange*. After finding that the auction website eBay had infringed MercExchange's patent, the district court refused to issue an injunction, finding that damages were sufficient to make MercExchange whole. The Federal Circuit reversed, following its "general rule" of granting an injunction when a court has found that a valid patent has been infringed. Some interpreted the Federal Circuit's opinion as holding that an injunction should always issue after a finding of infringement.

A unanimous Supreme Court reversed the Federal Circuit in an opinion written by Justice Thomas.[20] The Court stated that the four traditional equitable factors for issuing injunctive relief apply to patent cases. In each case, a court, in determining whether to issue an injunction, must consider whether the plaintiff suffered an irreparable injury, whether damages are inadequate to compensate for that injury, the balance of hardships between plaintiff and defendant, and the public interest. The Supreme Court based this finding both on the plain language of section 283 of the Patent Act and by analogy on the Copyright Act. The Supreme Court also found that the Patent Act's statements that a patent gave the patentee "a right to exclude" referred to the nature of the right, not the nature of the remedy, and held that the Federal Circuit had been wrong in applying a "general rule" in favor of injunctions. By the same token, the district court had erred in finding categorically that a licensing entity is made whole by money damages alone. The Supreme Court observed that "some patent holders, such as university researchers or self-made inventors, might reasonably prefer to license their patents, rather than undertake efforts to secure the financing necessary to bring their works to market themselves," and that "[s]uch patent holders may be able to satisfy the traditional four-factor test, and we see no basis for categorically denying them the opportunity to do so."[21] Accordingly, the Supreme Court vacated the injunction and remanded the case to the district court for consideration of all four factors.

In addition to the unanimous opinion written by Justice Thomas, there were two interesting concurring opinions. Chief Justice Roberts, joined by Justices Scalia and Ginsburg, observed that courts have a long history of granting injunctions in patent cases. Although this historical practice does not entitle a patentee to an injunction, "[w]hen it comes to discerning and applying those standards, in this area as others, 'a page of history is worth a volume of logic.'"[22] In other words, courts should look to these earlier decisions for guidance, which as a practical matter will mean that patentees usually will receive injunctions.

However, Justice Kennedy, in an opinion joined by Justices Stevens, Souter, and Breyer, noted that times have changed, and "in many instances the nature of the patent being enforced and the economic function of the

20. *eBay, Inc. v. MercExchange, L.L.C.*, 547 U.S. 388 (2006).
21. Id. at 393.
22. Id. at 395.

patent holder present considerations quite unlike earlier cases."[23] Citing a 2003 Federal Trade Commission report on the need for patent reform, the Kennedy concurrence referred to firms' using patents mainly to collect license fees, rather than to produce and sell goods. For such firms, the threat of an injunction "can be employed as a bargaining tool to charge exorbitant fees."[24] In addition, the Kennedy concurrence noted that "when the patented invention is but a small component of the product the companies seek to produce and the threat of an injunction is employed simply for undue leverage in negotiations, legal damages may well be sufficient."[25] Finally, the Kennedy concurrence alluded to the "burgeoning number of patents over business methods, which were not of much economic and legal significance in earlier times" and noted that "the potential vagueness and suspect validity of some of these patents may affect the calculus under the four factor test."[26] This last clause is particularly odd because a court should perform the calculus only after determining that the patent is valid.

The information-technology industry considered the decision a victory, particularly the Kennedy concurrence. At the same time, the decision did not appear to be detrimental to the pharmaceutical industry, because the gloss provided by the Roberts concurrence helps that industry and the Kennedy concurrence doesn't really apply to it. There are few if any patent trolls or business-method patents in the pharmaceutical industry; typically a drug is covered by only a limited number of patents, and the chemical nomenclature usually provides clear notice concerning what those patents cover.

Congress began considering patent reform before the Supreme Court issued the *eBay* decision in 2006, and the issue of the proper standard for injunctive relief in patent cases was very much on the legislative table in the 109th Congress in 2005.[27] When the Supreme Court agreed to review the Federal Circuit's decision, action on patent legislation stopped and Congress waited to see what the Supreme Court would do. Arguably, the Supreme Court's decision was more favorable to defendants than the language in both the House and Senate bills. The Supreme Court clearly stated that the standards for injunctive relief in patent cases were the same as for all other cases; in contrast, the legislative language attempted to forge

23. Id. at 396.
24. Id.
25. Id.
26. Id. at 397.
27. See, e.g., Patent Reform Act of 2005, H.R. 2795, 109th Congress (2005).

a compromise between an automatic injunction rule and the traditional injunction standard in non-patent cases.

The *eBay* decision favors interoperability. It suggests that when an entity infringes on a valid patent on an interface, the court should not enjoin the entity from distributing the interoperable products. Rather, because money damages typically will make the patentee whole and the public interest favors competition, the court usually should allow the entity to remain in the market if it pays a reasonable royalty to the patentee.[28]

6.2.2.2 Determination of Damages

In light of the *eBay* decision, the determination of damages in a case involving a patent on an interface emerges as a critical issue for interoperability. Congress has been considering the proper methodology for determining damages since 2005 but has made little real progress.

The Status Quo[29]

Patent damages are governed by 35 U.S.C. § 284, the relevant portion of which reads as follows: "Upon finding for the claimant the court shall award the claimant damages adequate to compensate for the infringement, but in no event less than a reasonable royalty for the use made of the invention."[30] In awarding damages, courts grant a prevailing plaintiff "lost profits" or a "reasonable royalty" for the infringement.[31] Notably, damages for patent infringement are to be "adequate to compensate for the infringement"[32] and therefore "by definition, make the patentee whole, as opposed to punishing the infringer."[33] In instances of willful infringement, the statute allows courts to "increase the damages up to three times the amount found or assessed."[34]

---

28. See Samuelson, "Are Patents on Interfaces Impeding Interoperability?" at 1983–1984.

29. The section is based on Jonathan Band and Ben Grillot, "The Hobgoblin Argument: An Inconsistent Approach to Intellectual Property Damages," *The Computer & Internet Lawyer*, November 2008, at 1.

30. 35 U.S.C. § 284.

31. Although other types of damages are theoretically possible, courts nearly always adopt one of these two approaches—or both of them, to the extent that it is not duplicative.

32. 35 U.S.C. § 284.

33. *Riles v. Shell Exploration & Prod. Co.*, 298 F.3d 1302, 1312 (Fed. Cir. 2002).

34. 35 U.S.C. § 284.

The debate on damages in patent-reform legislation has centered on the calculation of a reasonable royalty. Courts have interpreted this reasonable royalty award to be the amount that the parties would have agreed to as the result of business negotiations at the time the patent was infringed.[35] In *Georgia-Pacific Corp. v. United States Plywood Corp.*, the district court set out fifteen factors for courts to consider when determining the appropriate amount of a reasonable royalty award.[36] These "*Georgia-Pacific* factors" have become standard in jury instructions for reasonable royalty cases.[37] Factor 13 allows apportionment by separating out the "portion of the realizable profit that should be credited to the invention as distinguished from non-patented elements, the manufacturing process, business risks, or significant features or improvements added by the infringer."[38] The royalty rate then is applied to the portion of the revenue "credited to the invention."

In contrast to apportionment, the entire-market-value rule allows the owner of an infringed patent to recover damages on the basis of value of the entire product in the marketplace. Historically, the entire-market-value rule was applied only when the patentee could show that the entire value of the product was "properly and legally attributable" to the patented improvement.[39] When considering component parts of the same machine in *Marconi Wireless Telegraph Co. v. United States*, the U.S. Court of Claims held that damages were recoverable under the entire-market-value rule if the patented unit was "of such paramount importance that it substantially created the value of the component parts."[40] In several cases in the early 1980s, the Federal Circuit expanded the entire-market-value rule to include

35. See *Georgia-Pacific Corp. v. U.S. Plywood Corp.*, 318 F.Supp. 1116, 1121 (S.D.N.Y. 1970) (citing *Faulkner v. Gibbs*, 199 F.2d 635, 639 (9th Cir. 1952), holding that "the primary inquiry . . . is what the parties would have agreed upon if both were reasonably trying to reach an agreement"), *modified and aff'd*, 446 F.2d 295 (2d Cir. 1971), *cert. denied*, 404 U.S. 870 (1971).
36. See *Georgia-Pacific Corp.*, 318 F.Supp. at 1120 (stating that "[a] comprehensive list of evidentiary facts relevant, in general, to the determination of the amount of a reasonable royalty for a patent license may be drawn from a conspectus of the leading cases.").
37. See Model Patent Jury Instructions § 12.16 (Am. Intellect. Prop. Law Ass'n 2008), available at www.aipla.org. Similar jury instructions are provided by the Federal Circuit Bar Association and the American Bar Association.
38. *Georgia-Pacific Corp.*, 318 F.Supp. at 1120.
39. See *Garretson v. Clark*, 111 U.S. 120, 121 (1884) (finding that the entire-market-value rule did not apply to a patent for a method of attaching a mop head to a mop handle).
40. 53 USPQ 246, 250 (Ct. Cl. 1942), *aff'd in part and vacated in part*, 320 U.S. 1 (1943).

physically separate components when those components "together constituted a functional unit" as long as the patented feature was the "basis for customer demand."[41]

In its 1995 *Rite-Hite* decision, the Federal Circuit clearly articulated a two-step test for applying the entire-market-value rule to the sale of unpatented components along with patented components: the components must function together *and* the patented component must be the basis for customer demand.[42] However, when applying *Rite-Hite*'s two-step test in subsequent cases, courts have relaxed the "customer demand" requirement to allow evidence of marketing or promotion to satisfy the requirement that the patented improvement is "the basis of customer demand."[43]

Furthermore, in *Code-Alarm, Inc. v. Electromotive Technologies Corp.*, an unpublished 1997 decision, the Federal Circuit found that application of the entire-market-value rule was "within the district court's discretion . . . as long as there [was] a functional relationship between these components and the patented invention," thus ignoring the "customer demand" requirement under *Rite-Hite*.[44] Since then, other decisions (e.g. *Lucent Technologies, Inc. v. Gateway*) have similarly mistaken the prongs of *Rite-Hite*'s two-step test as two individual alternative grounds for applying the entire-market-value rule.[45] The jury award in *Lucent* of $1.52 billion for the infringement of a Lucent patent on MP3 technology by Microsoft's

41. *Rite-Hite Corp. v. Kelley Co., Inc.*, 56 F.3d 1538, 1549–1550 (Fed. Cir. 1995) (en banc), *cert. denied*, 116 S. Ct. 184 (1995) (summarizing development of the entire-market-value rule). See also *Paper Converting Machine Co. v. Magna-Graphics Corp.*, 745 F.2d 11 (Fed. Cir. 1984); *Velo-Bind, Inc. v. Minnesota Mining & Mfg. Co.*, 647 F.2d 965 (9th Cir. 1981).

42. *Rite-Hite Corp.*, 56 F.3d at 1550.

43. See *Bose Corp. v. JBL, Inc*, 274 F.3d 1354 (Fed. Cir. 2001) (applying the entire-market-value rule for loudspeaker system based on infringement of enclosure design where there was a functional connection and the improvement wasn't the basis for the demand, but contributed to it); *Micro Chemical, Inc. v. Lextron, Inc.*, 318 F. 3d 1119 (Fed. Cir. 2003) (allowing award based on reasonably foreseeable future sales without requiring patented process to be basis of customer demand); *Fonar Corp. v. General Elec. Co.*, 107 F.3d 1543, 1552–1553 (Fed. Cir. 1997) (upheld jury award based on entire value of MRI machine based on specific imaging feature used to market MRI machine). See also Amy L. Landers, "Let the Games Begin: Incentives to Innovation in the New Economy of Intellectual Property Law," 46 *Santa Clara Law Review* 307, 355–359 (2006).

44. 114 F.3d 1206, 1997 WL 3115542, (Fed. Cir. 1997) (nonprecedential opinion).

45. Post-trial Jury Instructions at 56, *Lucent Technologies, Inc. v. Gateway*, 509 F. Supp 2d 912 (S.D. Cal. 2007) (No. 02-2060). Jury Instruction 62 in *Lucent* instructed jurors

Windows Media Player was based, in part, on the market value of the entire computer system. Although the presiding judge overturned the judgment on other grounds, the award demonstrated the potential scope of damage awards under the entire-market-value rule when courts ignored the "customer demand" requirement.

In addition to receiving either lost profits or reasonable royalty awards, patent owners can receive up to three times the amount of the damages award if a jury or a court finds that the infringement was willful. The patent owner pleads willfulness in 92 percent of patent cases, and willfulness is found in nearly 60 percent of cases.[46] Until recently, an infringer was liable for willful infringement if he had notice of another's patent rights and did not exercise "due care" to determine whether his use was infringing.[47] While patent reform legislation was pending in Congress, the Federal Circuit overturned this standard in *In re Seagate Technology, LLC*, stating that the previous standard was "akin to negligence" and therefore "fail[ed] to comport with the general understanding of willfulness in the civil context."[48] The Federal Circuit then articulated a new, higher standard for willfulness, holding that a patent owner must show, first, that "the infringer acted despite an objectively high likelihood that its actions constituted infringement" and, second, that this risk "was either known or so obvious it should have been known to the accused infringer."[49]

Patent Legislation in the 110th Congress

In April of 2007, against this backdrop, the Patent Reform Act of 2007 was introduced simultaneously in the House (H.R. 1908) and in the Senate (S. 1145).[50] In his statement introducing the legislation, Representative Howard Berman argued that "recent case law has tilted towards overcompensation which works against the primary goal of promoting innovation."[51]

---

to apply the entire-market-value rule if the patented features "were the basis for customer demand *or* that the patented features and the computer function together as a single unit" (emphasis added).

46. See Kimberly A. Moore, "Empirical Statistics on Willful Patent Infringement," 14 *Fed. Cir. B.J.* 227, 232 (2004).

47. *Underwater Devices Inc. v. Morrison-Knudsen Co.*, 717 F.2d 1380 (Fed. Cir. 1983).

48. 497 F.3d 1360, 1371 (Fed. Cir. 2007).

49. Id.

50. Similar bills were introduced in the 109th Congress. See, e.g., Patent Reform Act of 2005, H.R. 2795, 109th Congress (2005); S. 1145, 109th Congress (2005).

51. Statement of Representative Howard Berman on the Patent Reform Act of 2007 (April 18, 2007), available at www.house.gov.

Senator Orrin Hatch, in his introductory remarks, observed that "courts have allowed damages for infringement to be based on the market for an entire product when all that was infringed was a minor component of the product."[52]

The bills proposed several changes to the law regarding reasonable royalty awards.[53] First, H.R. 1908 addressed apportionment by directing a court to "conduct an analysis to ensure that a reasonable royalty. . . is applied only to that economic value properly attributable to the patent's specific contribution over the prior art."[54] Next, the act clarified the entire-market-value rule, stating that "upon a showing . . . that the patent's specific contribution over the prior art is the *predominant basis* for market demand . . . damages may be based upon the entire market value of the products or processes involved."[55] Finally, H.R. 1908 placed explicit limitations on willful infringement, including that "a court may not find that an infringer has willfully infringed . . . for any period of time during which the infringer had an informed good faith belief that the patent was invalid."[56]

The bills' specific reference to apportionment, and their limitation of the entire-market-value rule to the traditional customer-demand test, proved enormously controversial.[57] Supporters of the bills' damages provisions included the Coalition for Patent Fairness (representing a large number of computer and Internet companies),[58] the Business Software Alliance (representing software firms),[59] and the Financial Services Roundtable (representing large financial-services institutions). These entities create and use products and services with many component elements that may rely on thousands of patents. Limiting the entire-market-value rule and codifying apportionment, they argued, would prevent outsized damage judgments such as those awarded in *Lucent*.

---

52. 153 Cong. Rec. S4691 (2007).
53. Lost-profits awards are not affected by the Patent Reform Act.
54. H.R. 1908 § 5(b)(2). The language in the Senate version (S. 1145) was nearly identical.
55. H.R. 1908 § 5(b)(3) (emphasis added).
56. H.R. 1908 § 5(c).
57. The amendment relating to willful infringement, particularly after the *Seagate* decision, was far less controversial.
58. Members of the Coalition for Patent Fairness included Hewlett-Packard, Amazon, and Google.
59. Members of the Business Software Alliance included Adobe, Apple, Corel, and Microsoft.

Proponents of patent damages reform claimed that there were two primary problems in the patent system: first, there was "uncertainty concerning the extent and value of patent rights"; and second, "innovative industry" was forced to pay "high licensing, litigation, and transaction costs" in order to "obtain clear answers."[60] Professor Viet Dinh of the School of Law at the University of California at Berkeley argued that although the reasonable royalty rate was intended to approximate the market rate, "judicially awarded reasonable royalty rates often compensate well above the market rate."[61] Testifying in a hearing held by the House Intellectual Property Subcommittee hearing, Professor John Thomas of the Georgetown University Law Center identified ten cases, in addition to *Lucent*, "awarding damages that may far exceed an individual patent's contribution to an infringing product."[62]

Professor Thomas and other proponents of patent reform argued that these large damage awards had several negative consequences. First, they encouraged patent litigation rather than licensing, thereby increasing the license fees in settlement of this litigation. Professor Thomas termed this a "royalty burden" on innovative companies. Second, the large awards resulted in an increase in "[s]o called trolls—entrepreneurial speculators who prefer to acquire and enforce patents rather than engage in research, development, manufacturing, or other socially productive activity."[63] Third, by failing to apportion damages properly, courts awarded damages for elements taken from prior art, the public domain, and technology patented by third parties, overcompensating plaintiffs unjustly.

Advocates of patent reform pointed to statistical evidence that patent litigation had undergone several shifts in the last 20 years, moving away from bench trials to jury trials and away from lost profits awards to reasonable royalty awards. According to a PricewaterhouseCoopers study, through the 1990s damages for lost profits were awarded in a majority of infringement

60. *Patent Reform Act of 2007: Hearing on H.R. 1908 Before the H. Subcomm. on Courts, the Internet, and Intellectual Property of the H. Comm. on Judiciary*, 110th Cong. 65 (2007) (statement of Professor John R. Thomas, Georgetown University Law Center) (hereafter cited as Thomas Statement).

61. Viet Dinh and William Paxton, Patent Reform: Protecting Property Rights and the Marketplace of Ideas, white paper prepared for Coalition for Patent Reform, December 3, 2007.

62. Thomas Statement at 58.

63. Thomas Statement at 60. See also *eBay Inc.*, 547 U.S. at 396 (2006) (Kennedy, J., concurring), observing that "[a]n industry has developed in which firms use patents not as a basis for producing and selling goods but, instead, primarily for obtaining licensing fees." See also Landers, "Let the Games Begin," at 343–347 (2006).

cases, but after 2000 reasonable royalties were awarded in 65 percent of cases.[64] Since lost profits are available only in cases where the patent holder could have made a sale but failed to do so as a result of the infringement, this rise in reasonable royalty awards reflected an increase in ownership of patents "for the purpose of licensing (or litigation)" by entities that did not have manufacturing or distribution capabilities.[65]

Opponents of the Patent Reform Act included the Coalition for 21st Century Patent Reform (representing major chemical, pharmaceutical, and manufacturing companies[66]), the Innovation Alliance (representing biotechnology, venture capital, and technology research firms[67]), universities, and independent inventors. The products manufactured by some of these entities tend to include fewer patents per product than those manufactured by the supporters of patent reform.

William Rooklidge, an attorney with Howrey LLP and a former president of the American Intellectual Property Law Association, argued in a white paper that although the Patent Reform Act claimed to codify existing law regarding apportionment and the entire-market-value rule, it in fact "would make substantial changes destructive to the patent system."[68] These changes, Rooklidge asserted, included "[f]orcing the courts to conduct an apportionment analysis in every case," which "would be a colossal waste of time" since "apportionment is only occasionally addressed by courts."[69] Further, although historically the burden of proof for apportionment has been on the infringer, the proposed legislation would place it on the court.[70] In addition, by relying on "prior art subtraction," Rooklidge argued, the bill "vastly oversimplifies the analysis of which contributions should be apportioned."[71] Gary Griswold, Chief Counsel of Intellectual Property at 3M, said in testimony before the House Subcommittee on Courts, the Internet and Intellectual Property that "prior art subtraction ignores the reality that at some level all inventions are combinations of old elements,"

64. PricewaterhouseCoopers, Patent and Trademark Damages Study 22, 2007.
65. S. Rep. No. 110-259 (2008).
66. The coalition's members included DuPont, Dow Chemical, Exxon Mobil, AstraZeneca, Merck, 3M, and Corning.
67. The Innovation Alliance included US Nanocorp and Intermolecular, Inc.
68. William C. Rooklidge, "Reform" of Patent Damages: S. 1145 and H.R. 1908 (2007), available at www.patentsmatter.com.
69. Id. at 4.
70. Id., citing *Elizabeth v. Pavement Co.*, 97 U.S. 126, 141 (1877) (holding that the burden of proof for apportionment is on the infringer).
71. Id. at 5.

and that infringement of the patent on Post-It notes would result in minimal damages since both the paper and the adhesive are examples of prior art.[72] These opponents saw no reason for elevating apportionment above the fourteen other *Georgia-Pacific* factors.

Opponents argued that there was "no need for such substantial changes" when "[f]urther judicial development and less-intrusive legislation could solve any problems that truly exist in the patent damages area."[73] In a speech to the Association of Corporate Patent Counsel, Federal Circuit Chief Judge Paul Michel said: "It's an extremely blunt instrument to legislate; it's not a scalpel, it's a hammer."[74] Opponents pointed to *In re Seagate*, in which the Federal Circuit raised the standard for a finding of willful infringement, as an example of the type of judicial reform that made legislation unnecessary.[75]

Moreover, Kevin Sharer, chief executive officer of the biotechnology company Amgen, argued during the House intellectual-property subcommittee's hearing that "the net effect of these provisions is to make it cheaper and easier to infringe a patent," which thereby "discourages innovation and encourages copying."[76] This argument was echoed in a September 6, 2007 Statement of Administration Policy issued by the Office of Management and Budget stating that "the Administration continues to oppose H.R. 1908's limits on the discretion of the court in determining damages" because such a change "is unwarranted and risks reducing the rewards from innovation."[77]

---

72. *Patent Reform Act of 2007: Hearing on H.R. 1908 Before the H. Subcomm. on Courts, the Internet, and Intellectual Property of the H. Comm. on Judiciary*, 110th Cong. 65 (2007) (statement of Gary Griswold, Chief Counsel of Intellectual Property, 3M).

73. Id.

74. Hon. Paul R. Michel, Chief Judge U.S. Court of Appeals for the Federal Circuit, address to the Association of Corporate Patent Counsel, January 28, 2008 (transcript by Federal News Service).

75. S. Rep. No. 110-259 (January 24, 2008), Minority View ("These decisions signify an effort by the Supreme Court and the Federal Circuit to rectify perceived imbalances in the patent system. At a minimum, this recent trend by the courts in the patent field suggests that Congress should exercise extreme caution before tilting the playing field even further towards the interests of potential infringers.")

76. Patent Reform Act of 2007: Hearing on H.R. 1908 Before the H. Subcomm. on Courts, the Internet, and Intellectual Property of the H. Comm. on Judiciary, 110th Cong. 65 (2007) (statement of Kevin Sharer, CEO of Amgen).

77. Office of Management and Budget, Executive Office of the President, Statement of Administration Policy, H.R. 1908—Patent Reform Act of 2007 1 (2007), available at www.whitehouse.gov.

The House of Representatives passed H.R. 1908 on September 7, 2007. In the Senate, the bill encountered fierce resistance centering on the apportionment of damages and the post-grant opposition proceeding. Although the Senate Judiciary Committee favorably reported on the bill with apportionment language on January 24, 2008, it then stalled.

Patent Legislation in the 111th Congress

The identical bills introduced in both chambers of Congress on March 3, 2009[78] contained apportionment of damages language similar to that contained in the House and Senate bills in the 110th Congress. They established the following framework for the calculation of a reasonable royalty:

(1) IN GENERAL- The court shall determine, based on the facts of the case and after adducing any further evidence the court deems necessary, which of the following methods shall be used by the court or the jury in calculating a reasonable royalty pursuant to subsection (a). The court shall also identify the factors that are relevant to the determination of a reasonable royalty, and the court or jury, as the case may be, shall consider only those factors in making such determination.

(A) ENTIRE MARKET VALUE- Upon a showing to the satisfaction of the court that the claimed invention's specific contribution over the prior art is the predominant basis for market demand for an infringing product or process, damages may be based upon the entire market value of that infringing product or process.

(B) ESTABLISHED ROYALTY BASED ON MARKETPLACE LICENSING- Upon a showing to the satisfaction of the court that the claimed invention has been the subject of a nonexclusive license for the use made of the invention by the infringer, to a number of persons sufficient to indicate a general marketplace recognition of the reasonableness of the licensing terms, if the license was secured prior to the filing of the case before the court, and the court determines that the infringer's use is of substantially the same scope, volume, and benefit of the rights granted under such license, damages may be determined on the basis of the terms of such license. Upon a showing to the satisfaction of the court that the claimed invention has sufficiently similar noninfringing substitutes in the relevant market, which have themselves been the subject of such nonexclusive licenses, and the court determines that the infringer's use is of substantially the same scope, volume, and benefit of the rights granted under such licenses, damages may be determined on the basis of the terms of such licenses.

(C) VALUATION CALCULATION- Upon a determination by the court that the showings required under subparagraphs (A) and (B) have not been made, the court shall conduct an analysis to ensure that a reasonable royalty is applied only to the portion of the economic value of the infringing product or process properly attributable to the claimed invention's specific contribution over the prior art. In the case

78. H.R. 1260, 111th Cong. (2009); S. 515, 111th Cong. (2009).

of a combination invention whose elements are present individually in the prior art, the contribution over the prior art may include the value of the additional function resulting from the combination, as well as the enhanced value, if any, of some or all of the prior art elements as part of the combination, if the patentee demonstrates that value.

(2) ADDITIONAL FACTORS- Where the court determines it to be appropriate in determining a reasonable royalty under paragraph (1), the court may also consider, or direct the jury to consider, any other relevant factors under applicable law.[79]

In short, the bills stated that if the evidence showed that the invention's specific contribution over the prior art was the predominant basis for market demand for an infringing product, damages were to be based on the entire market value of the product. If there was evidence of license fees for use of the invention, then the fees were the standard for a reasonable royalty. The court would apportion damages only if the plaintiff could meet neither of these tests.

The information-technology industry felt that this language provided courts with sufficient guidance as to when they should apply which test. The opponents of reform, however, convinced a group of senators on the Judiciary Committee to oppose significant reform. These senators forced a compromise with Senator Leahy, the chairman of the Senate Judiciary Committee, that weakened the bill substantially. This weakened bill was reported out of the Senate Judiciary Committee on April 2, just a month after the bill's introduction.

With respect to apportionment of damages, S. 515 as reported replaced the language quoted above with the following:

(1) IN GENERAL- The court shall identify the methodologies and factors that are relevant to the determination of damages, and the court or jury, shall consider only those methodologies and factors relevant to making such determination.

(2) DISCLOSURE OF CLAIMS- By no later than the entry of the final pretrial order, unless otherwise ordered by the court, the parties shall state, in writing and with particularity, the methodologies and factors the parties propose for instruction to the jury in determining damages under this section, specifying the relevant underlying legal and factual bases for their assertions.

(3) SUFFICIENCY OF EVIDENCE- Prior to the introduction of any evidence concerning the determination of damages, upon motion of either party or sua sponte, the court shall consider whether one or more of a party's damages contentions lacks a legally sufficient evidentiary basis. After providing a nonmovant the opportunity to be heard, and after any further proffer of evidence, briefing, or argument that the court may deem appropriate, the court shall identify on the record those method-

79. H.R. 1260 § 284(c).

ologies and factors as to which there is a legally sufficient evidentiary basis, and the court or jury shall consider only those methodologies and factors in making the determination of damages under this section. The court shall only permit the introduction of evidence relating to the determination of damages that is relevant to the methodologies and factors that the court determines may be considered in making the damages determination.[80]

This language is completely procedural and does not contain any substantive standards. It simply specifies that the parties must propose to the court the methodologies they believe are appropriate, and the court must then decide the sufficiency of the evidentiary record for each methodology. To be sure, the provision directs the court to perform a "gatekeeper" function, enabling it to keep the entire-market-value rule away from juries when there is not enough evidence to warrant this methodology. Nonetheless, the language represents a significant defeat for proponents of patent litigation reform, because it does not provide courts with any guidance as to what constitutes a legally sufficient evidentiary basis for apportionment or application of the entire-market-value rule.

The bill as reported did, however, retain the language in the bill as introduced concerning willful infringement. In essence, that language codified the standards articulated by the Federal Circuit in *Seagate*.

Five months after the Senate Judiciary Committee passed the compromise patent bill, the Federal Circuit arguably engaged in self-correction when it reversed application of the entire-market-value rule in *Lucent Technologies v. Gateway, Inc.*[81] (a separate case from the *Lucent* case discussed above). Here, the Federal Circuit considered a $350 million patent-infringement judgment against Microsoft for the date-picker tool and other features of a version of Microsoft Outlook. Writing for the court, Judge Michel emphasized that "[f]or the entire market value rule to apply, the patentee must prove that the 'patent-related feature is the basis for customer demand.'"[82] Referring to articles by Mark Lemley and Amy Landers, Judge Michel acknowledged that "[s]ome commentators suggest that the entire market value rule should have little role in reasonable royalty law."[83] He responded by arguing that "[t]here is nothing inherently wrong with using the market value of the entire product, especially when there is no established market value for the infringing component or feature, so long as

80. S. 515 § 284(b) (as reported by S. Comm. on the Judiciary, April 2, 2009).
81. 580 F.3d 1301 (Fed. Cir. 2009).
82. Id. at 1336 (citations omitted).
83. Id. at 1339.

the multiplier accounts for the proportion of the base represented by the infringing component or feature."[84] In other words, if a product includes ten components, only one of which infringes, the defendant should be indifferent as to whether the damages are a 10 percent royalty on the component or a 1 percent royalty on the entire product. For Judge Michel, the key is that the multiplier—the royalty rate—account for the proportion of the base represented by the infringing component. This, however, sounds like apportionment. Judge Michel, therefore, appears to have blurred the distinction between apportionment and the entire-market-value rule. Judge Michel then rejected application of the entire-market-value rule in this case because there was no evidence that the infringing component was the basis for consumer demand for Outlook. Moreover, the evidence did not support the royalty rate Lucent's damages expert applied to Outlook.

To the extent that the entire-market-value rule survives Judge Michel's opinion in *Lucent*, restoration in the patent legislation of meaningful standards for the application of the apportionment and entire-market-value rules would promote interoperability. Basing the reasonable royalty only on the value of the infringed interfaces, rather than on the value of the entire interoperable product, will encourage the development of interoperable products by reducing the risk of draconian damages. Similarly, rigorous standards for claims of willful infringement will diminish the exposure of developers of interoperable products to ruinous damages.

Even if copyright does not protect a program's interface specifications, and even if the interface's implementation is distributed in source code that is subject to an open-source license, a patent that applies to the program's interface or basic functionality can frustrate interoperability with that program. This is particularly the case when the patent is held by a third party who does not participate directly in the market for the program or related products. Such a patentee simply seeks to maximize revenue by charging the highest possible toll for the use of the patented invention, without the countervailing need to cross-license patented technologies from its competitors. For this reason, resolution of the central issues in the patent-reform debate—patent quality and patent damages—could have a significant effect on the development of interoperable software products in the future.

84. Id. Judge Michel added that entire-market-value rule reflects the realities of patent licensing: "[S]ophisticated parties routinely enter into licensing agreements that base the value of the patented invention as a percentage of the commercial products' sales price." Id.

Statutory Appendix

U.S. Copyright Act (1998)

§ 107 Limitations on exclusive rights: Fair use

Notwithstanding the provisions of sections 106 and 106A, the fair use of a copyrighted work, including such use by reproduction in copies or phonorecords or by any other means specified by that section, for purposes such as criticism, comment, news reporting, teaching (including multiple copies for classroom use), scholarship, or research, is not an infringement of copyright. In determining whether the use made of a work in any particular case is a fair use the factors to be considered shall include—

(1) the purpose and character of the use, including whether such use is of a commercial nature or is for nonprofit educational purposes;
(2) the nature of the copyrighted work;
(3) the amount and substantiality of the portion used in relation to the copyrighted work as a whole; and
(4) the effect of the use upon the potential market for or value of the copyrighted work.

The fact that a work is unpublished shall not itself bar a finding of fair use if such finding is made upon consideration of all the above factors.

§ 1201 Circumvention of copyright protection systems

(a) Violations regarding circumvention of technological measures.

(1) (A) No person shall circumvent a technological measure that effectively controls access to a work protected under this title. The prohibition contained in the preceding sentence shall take effect at the end of the 2-year period beginning on the date of the enactment of this chapter [enacted October 28, 1998].

(B) The prohibition contained in subparagraph (A) shall not apply to persons who are users of a copyrighted work which is in a particular class of works, if such persons are, or are likely to be in the succeeding 3-year period, adversely affected by virtue of such prohibition in their ability to make noninfringing uses of that particular class of works under this title, as determined under subparagraph (C).

(C) During the 2-year period described in subparagraph (A), and during each succeeding 3-year period, the Librarian of Congress, upon the recommendation of the Register of Copyrights, who shall consult with the Assistant Secretary for Communications and Information of the Department of Commerce and report and comment on his or her views in making such recommendation, shall make the determination in a rulemaking proceeding for purposes of subparagraph (B) of whether persons who are users of a copyrighted work are, or are likely to be in the succeeding 3-year period, adversely affected by the prohibition under subparagraph (A) in their ability to make noninfringing uses under this title of a particular class of copyrighted works. In conducting such rulemaking, the Librarian shall examine—

(i) the availability for use of copyrighted works;

(ii) the availability for use of works for nonprofit archival, preservation, and educational purposes;

(iii) the impact that the prohibition on the circumvention of technological measures applied to copyrighted works has on criticism, comment, news reporting, teaching, scholarship, or research;

(iv) the effect of circumvention of technological measures on the market for or value of copyrighted works; and

(v) such other factors as the Librarian considers appropriate.

(D) The Librarian shall publish any class of copyrighted works for which the Librarian has determined, pursuant to the rulemaking conducted under subparagraph (C), that noninfringing uses by persons who are users of a copyrighted work are, or are likely to be, adversely affected, and the prohibition contained in subparagraph (A) shall not apply to such users with respect to such class of works for the ensuing 3-year period.

(E) Neither the exception under subparagraph (B) from the applicability of the prohibition contained in subparagraph (A), nor any determination made in a rulemaking conducted under subparagraph (C), may be used as a defense in any action to enforce any provision of this title other than this paragraph.

(2) No person shall manufacture, import, offer to the public, provide, or otherwise traffic in any technology, product, service, device, component, or part thereof, that—

(A) is primarily designed or produced for the purpose of circumventing a technological measure that effectively controls access to a work protected under this title;

(B) has only limited commercially significant purpose or use other than to circumvent a technological measure that effectively controls access to a work protected under this title; or

(C) is marketed by that person or another acting in concert with that person with that person's knowledge for use in circumventing a technological measure that effectively controls access to a work protected under this title.

(3) As used in this subsection—

(A) to "circumvent a technological measure" means to descramble a scrambled work, to decrypt an encrypted work, or otherwise to avoid, bypass, remove, deactivate, or impair a technological measure, without the authority of the copyright owner; and

(B) a technological measure "effectively controls access to a work" if the measure, in the ordinary course of its operation, requires the application of information, or a process or a treatment, with the authority of the copyright owner, to gain access to the work.

(b) Additional violations.

(1) No person shall manufacture, import, offer to the public, provide, or otherwise traffic in any technology, product, service, device, component, or part thereof, that—

(A) is primarily designed or produced for the purpose of circumventing protection afforded by a technological measure that effectively protects a right of a copyright owner under this title in a work or a portion thereof;

(B) has only limited commercially significant purpose or use other than to circumvent protection afforded by a technological measure that effectively protects a right of a copyright owner under this title in a work or a portion thereof; or

(C) is marketed by that person or another acting in concert with that person with that person's knowledge for use in circumventing protection afforded by a technological measure that effectively protects a right of a copyright owner under this title in a work or a portion thereof.

(2) As used in this subsection—

(A) to "circumvent protection afforded by a technological measure" means avoiding, bypassing, removing, deactivating, or otherwise impairing a technological measure; and

(B) a technological measure "effectively protects a right of a copyright owner under this title" if the measure, in the ordinary course of its operation, prevents, restricts, or otherwise limits the exercise of a right of a copyright owner under this title.

(c) Other rights, etc., not affected.
(1) Nothing in this section shall affect rights, remedies, limitations, or defenses to copyright infringement, including fair use, under this title.
(2) Nothing in this section shall enlarge or diminish vicarious or contributory liability for copyright infringement in connection with any technology, product, service, device, component, or part thereof.
(3) Nothing in this section shall require that the design of, or design and selection of parts and components for, a consumer electronics, telecommunications, or computing product provide for a response to any particular technological measure, so long as such part or component, or the product in which such part or component is integrated, does not otherwise fall within the prohibitions of subsection (a)(2) or (b)(1).
(4) Nothing in this section shall enlarge or diminish any rights of free speech or the press for activities using consumer electronics, telecommunications, or computing products.

(d) Exemption for nonprofit libraries, archives, and educational institutions.
(1) A nonprofit library, archives, or educational institution which gains access to a commercially exploited copyrighted work solely in order to make a good faith determination of whether to acquire a copy of that work for the sole purpose of engaging in conduct permitted under this title shall not be in violation of subsection (a)(1)(A). A copy of a work to which access has been gained under this paragraph—
(A) may not be retained longer than necessary to make such good faith determination; and
(B) may not be used for any other purpose.
(2) The exemption made available under paragraph (1) shall only apply with respect to a work when an identical copy of that work is not reasonably available in another form.
(3) A nonprofit library, archives, or educational institution that willfully for the purpose of commercial advantage or financial gain violates paragraph (1)—
(A) shall, for the first offense, be subject to the civil remedies under section 1203; and
(B) shall, for repeated or subsequent offenses, in addition to the civil remedies under section 1203, forfeit the exemption provided under paragraph (1).
(4) This subsection may not be used as a defense to a claim under subsection (a)(2) or (b), nor may this subsection permit a nonprofit library,

archives, or educational institution to manufacture, import, offer to the public, provide, or otherwise traffic in any technology, product, service, component, or part thereof, which circumvents a technological measure.

(5) In order for a library or archives to qualify for the exemption under this subsection, the collections of that library or archives shall be—

(A) open to the public; or

(B) available not only to researchers affiliated with the library or archives or with the institution of which it is a part, but also to other persons doing research in a specialized field.

(e) Law enforcement, intelligence, and other government activities.

This section does not prohibit any lawfully authorized investigative, protective, information security, or intelligence activity of an officer, agent, or employee of the United States, a State, or a political subdivision of a State, or a person acting pursuant to a contract with the United States, a State, or a political subdivision of a State. For purposes of this subsection, the term "information security" means activities carried out in order to identify and address the vulnerabilities of a government computer, computer system, or computer network.

(f) Reverse engineering.

(1) Notwithstanding the provisions of subsection (a)(1)(A), a person who has lawfully obtained the right to use a copy of a computer program may circumvent a technological measure that effectively controls access to a particular portion of that program for the sole purpose of identifying and analyzing those elements of the program that are necessary to achieve interoperability of an independently created computer program with other programs, and that have not previously been readily available to the person engaging in the circumvention, to the extent any such acts of identification and analysis do not constitute infringement under this title.

(2) Notwithstanding the provisions of subsections (a)(2) and (b), a person may develop and employ technological means to circumvent a technological measure, or to circumvent protection afforded by a technological measure, in order to enable the identification and analysis under paragraph (1), or for the purpose of enabling interoperability of an independently created computer program with other programs, if such means are necessary to achieve such interoperability, to the extent that doing so does not constitute infringement under this title.

(3) The information acquired through the acts permitted under paragraph (1), and the means permitted under paragraph (2), may be made available to others if the person referred to in paragraph (1) or (2), as the case may

be, provides such information or means solely for the purpose of enabling interoperability of an independently created computer program with other programs, and to the extent that doing so does not constitute infringement under this title or violate applicable law other than this section.

(4) For purposes of this subsection, the term "interoperability" means the ability of computer programs to exchange information, and of such programs mutually to use the information which has been exchanged.

(g) Encryption research.

(1) Definitions. For purposes of this subsection—

(A) the term "encryption research" means activities necessary to identify and analyze flaws and vulnerabilities of encryption technologies applied to copyrighted works, if these activities are conducted to advance the state of knowledge in the field of encryption technology or to assist in the development of encryption products; and

(B) the term "encryption technology" means the scrambling and descrambling of information using mathematical formulas or algorithms.

(2) Permissible acts of encryption research. Notwithstanding the provisions of subsection (a)(1)(A), it is not a violation of that subsection for a person to circumvent a technological measure as applied to a copy, phonorecord, performance, or display of a published work in the course of an act of good faith encryption research if—

(A) the person lawfully obtained the encrypted copy, phonorecord, performance, or display of the published work;

(B) such act is necessary to conduct such encryption research;

(C) the person made a good faith effort to obtain authorization before the circumvention; and

(D) such act does not constitute infringement under this title or a violation of applicable law other than this section, including section 1030 of title 18 and those provisions of title 18 amended by the Computer Fraud and Abuse Act of 1986.

(3) Factors in determining exemption. In determining whether a person qualifies for the exemption under paragraph (2), the factors to be considered shall include—

(A) whether the information derived from the encryption research was disseminated, and if so, whether it was disseminated in a manner reasonably calculated to advance the state of knowledge or development of encryption technology, versus whether it was disseminated in a manner that facilitates infringement under this title or a violation of applicable law other than this section, including a violation of privacy or breach of security;

(B) whether the person is engaged in a legitimate course of study, is employed, or is appropriately trained or experienced, in the field of encryption technology; and

(C) whether the person provides the copyright owner of the work to which the technological measure is applied with notice of the findings and documentation of the research, and the time when such notice is provided.

(4) Use of technological means for research activities. Notwithstanding the provisions of subsection (a)(2), it is not a violation of that subsection for a person to—

(A) develop and employ technological means to circumvent a technological measure for the sole purpose of that person performing the acts of good faith enc1ryption research described in paragraph (2); and

(B) provide the technological means to another person with whom he or she is working collaboratively for the purpose of conducting the acts of good faith encryption research described in paragraph (2) or for the purpose of having that other person verify his or her acts of good faith encryption research described in paragraph (2).

(5) Report to Congress. Not later than 1 year after the date of the enactment of this chapter [enacted October 28, 1998], the Register of Copyrights and the Assistant Secretary for Communications and Information of the Department of Commerce shall jointly report to the Congress on the effect this subsection has had on—

(A) encryption research and the development of encryption technology;

(B) the adequacy and effectiveness of technological measures designed to protect copyrighted works; and

(C) protection of copyright owners against the unauthorized access to their encrypted copyrighted works.

The report shall include legislative recommendations, if any.

(h) Exceptions regarding minors.

In applying subsection (a) to a component or part, the court may consider the necessity for its intended and actual incorporation in a technology, product, service, or device, which—

(1) does not itself violate the provisions of this title; and

(2) has the sole purpose to prevent the access of minors to material on the Internet.

(i) Protection of personally identifying information.

(1) Circumvention permitted. Notwithstanding the provisions of subsection (a)(1)(A), it is not a violation of that subsection for a person to

circumvent a technological measure that effectively controls access to a
work protected under this title, if—

(A) the technological measure, or the work it protects, contains the capability of collecting or disseminating personally identifying information
reflecting the online activities of a natural person who seeks to gain access
to the work protected;

(B) in the normal course of its operation, the technological measure, or
the work it protects, collects or disseminates personally identifying information about the person who seeks to gain access to the work protected,
without providing conspicuous notice of such collection or dissemination
to such person, and without providing such person with the capability to
prevent or restrict such collection or dissemination;

(C) the act of circumvention has the sole effect of identifying and disabling
the capability described in subparagraph (A), and has no other effect on the
ability of any person to gain access to any work; and

(D) the act of circumvention is carried out solely for the purpose of preventing the collection or dissemination of personally identifying information about a natural person who seeks to gain access to the work protected,
and is not in violation of any other law.

(2) Inapplicability to certain technological measures. This subsection does
not apply to a technological measure, or a work it protects, that does not
collect or disseminate personally identifying information and that is dis-
closed to a user as not having or using such capability.

(j) Security testing.

(1) Definition. For purposes of this subsection, the term "security testing" means accessing a computer, computer system, or computer network,
solely for the purpose of good faith testing, investigating, or correcting, a
security flaw or vulnerability, with the authorization of the owner or operator of such computer, computer system, or computer network.

(2) Permissible acts of security testing. Notwithstanding the provisions of
subsection (a)(1)(A), it is not a violation of that subsection for a person to
engage in an act of security testing, if such act does not constitute infringement under this title or a violation of applicable law other than this section,
including section 1030 of title 18 and those provisions of title 18 amended
by the Computer Fraud and Abuse Act of 1986.

(3) Factors in determining exemption. In determining whether a person
qualifies for the exemption under paragraph (2), the factors to be considered shall include—

(A) whether the information derived from the security testing was used
solely to promote the security of the owner or operator of such computer,

computer system or computer network, or shared directly with the developer of such computer, computer system, or computer network; and

(B) whether the information derived from the security testing was used or maintained in a manner that does not facilitate infringement under this title or a violation of applicable law other than this section, including a violation of privacy or breach of security.

(4) Use of technological means for security testing. Notwithstanding the provisions of subsection (a)(2), it is not a violation of that subsection for a person to develop, produce, distribute or employ technological means for the sole purpose of performing the acts of security testing described in subsection (2), provided such technological means does not otherwise violate section (a)(2).

(k) Certain analog devices and certain technological measures.
(1) Certain analog devices.

(A) Effective 18 months after the date of the enactment of this chapter, no person shall manufacture, import, offer to the public, provide or otherwise traffic in any—

(i) VHS format analog video cassette recorder unless such recorder conforms to the automatic gain control copy control technology;

(ii) 8mm format analog video cassette camcorder unless such camcorder conforms to the automatic gain control technology;

(iii) Beta format analog video cassette recorder, unless such recorder conforms to the automatic gain control copy control technology, except that this requirement shall not apply until there are 1,000 Beta format analog video cassette recorders sold in the United States in any one calendar year after the date of the enactment of this chapter [enacted October 28, 1998];

(iv) 8mm format analog video cassette recorder that is not an analog video cassette camcorder, unless such recorder conforms to the automatic gain control copy control technology, except that this requirement shall not apply until there are 20,000 such recorders sold in the United States in any one calendar year after the date of the enactment of this chapter; or

(v) analog video cassette recorder that records using an NTSC format video input and that is not otherwise covered under clauses (i) through (iv), unless such device conforms to the automatic gain control copy control technology.

(B) Effective on the date of the enactment of this chapter, no person shall manufacture, import, offer to the public, provide or otherwise traffic in—

(i) any VHS format analog video cassette recorder or any 8mm format analog video cassette recorder if the design of the model of such recorder has been modified after such date of enactment so that a model of recorder that previously conformed to the automatic gain control copy control technology no longer conforms to such technology; or

(ii) any VHS format analog video cassette recorder, or any 8mm format analog video cassette recorder that is not an 8mm analog video cassette camcorder, if the design of the model of such recorder has been modified after such date of enactment so that a model of recorder that previously conformed to the four-line colorstripe copy control technology no longer conforms to such technology.

Manufacturers that have not previously manufactured or sold a VHS format analog video cassette recorder, or an 8mm format analog cassette recorder, shall be required to conform to the four-line colorstripe copy control technology in the initial model of any such recorder manufactured after the date of the enactment of this chapter, and thereafter to continue conforming to the four-line colorstripe copy control technology. For purposes of this subparagraph, an analog video cassette recorder "conforms to" the four-line colorstripe copy control technology if it records a signal that, when played back by the playback function of that recorder in the normal viewing mode, exhibits, on a reference display device, a display containing distracting visible lines through portions of the viewable picture.

(2) Certain encoding restrictions. No person shall apply the automatic gain control copy control technology or colorstripe copy control technology to prevent or limit consumer copying except such copying—

(A) of a single transmission, or specified group of transmissions, of live events or of audiovisual works for which a member of the public has exercised choice in selecting the transmissions, including the content of the transmissions or the time of receipt of such transmissions, or both, and as to which such member is charged a separate fee for each such transmission or specified group of transmissions;

(B) from a copy of a transmission of a live event or an audiovisual work if such transmission is provided by a channel or service where payment is made by a member of the public for such channel or service in the form of a subscription fee that entitles the member of the public to receive all of the programming contained in such channel or service;

(C) from a physical medium containing one or more prerecorded audiovisual works; or

(D) from a copy of a transmission described in subparagraph (A) or from a copy made from a physical medium described in subparagraph (C).

In the event that a transmission meets both the conditions set forth in subparagraph (A) and those set forth in subparagraph (B), the transmission shall be treated as a transmission described in subparagraph (A).

(3) Inapplicability. This subsection shall not—

(A) require any analog video cassette camcorder to conform to the automatic gain control copy control technology with respect to any video signal received through a camera lens;

(B) apply to the manufacture, importation, offer for sale, provision of, or other trafficking in, any professional analog video cassette recorder; or

(C) apply to the offer for sale or provision of, or other trafficking in, any previously owned analog video cassette recorder, if such recorder was legally manufactured and sold when new and not subsequently modified in violation of paragraph (1)(B).

(4) Definitions. For purposes of this subsection:

(A) An "analog video cassette recorder" means a device that records, or a device that includes a function that records, on electromagnetic tape in an analog format the electronic impulses produced by the video and audio portions of a television program, motion picture, or other form of audiovisual work.

(B) An "analog video cassette camcorder" means an analog video cassette recorder that contains a recording function that operates through a camera lens and through a video input that may be connected with a television or other video playback device.

(C) An analog video cassette recorder "conforms" to the automatic gain control copy control technology if it—

(i) detects one or more of the elements of such technology and does not record the motion picture or transmission protected by such technology; or

(ii) records a signal that, when played back, exhibits a meaningfully distorted or degraded display.

(D) The term "professional analog video cassette recorder" means an analog video cassette recorder that is designed, manufactured, marketed, and intended for use by a person who regularly employs such a device for a lawful business or industrial use, including making, performing, displaying, distributing, or transmitting copies of motion pictures on a commercial scale.

(E) The terms " VHS format," "8mm format," "Beta format," "automatic gain control copy control technology," "colorstripe copy control technology," "four-line version of the colorstripe copy control technology," and "NTSC" have the meanings that are commonly understood in the consumer electronics and motion picture industries as of the date of the enactment of this chapter.

(5) Violations. Any violation of paragraph (1) of this subsection shall be treated as a violation of subsection (b)(1) of this section. Any violation of

paragraph (2) of this subsection shall be deemed an "act of circumvention" for the purposes of section 1203(c)(3)(A) of this chapter.

EU Software Directive (1991)

Article 1 Object of protection
1. In accordance with the provisions of this Directive, Member States shall protect computer programs, by copyright, as literary works within the meaning of the Berne Convention for the Protection of Literary and Artistic Works. For the purposes of this Directive, the term 'computer programs` shall include their preparatory design material.
2. Protection in accordance with this Directive shall apply to the expression in any form of a computer program. Ideas and principles which underlie any element of a computer program, including those which underlie its interfaces, are not protected by copyright under this Directive.
3. A computer program shall be protected if it is original in the sense that it is the author's own intellectual creation. No other criteria shall be applied to determine its eligibility for protection.

Article 2 Authorship of computer programs
1. The author of a computer program shall be the natural person or group of natural persons who has created the program or, where the legislation of the Member State permits, the legal person designated as the rightholder by that legislation. Where collective works are recognized by the legislation of a Member State, the person considered by the legislation of the Member State to have created the work shall be deemed to be its author.
2. In respect of a computer program created by a group of natural persons jointly, the exclusive rights shall be owned jointly.
3. Where a computer program is created by an employee in the execution of his duties or following the instructions given by his employer, the employer exclusively shall be entitled to exercise all economic rights in the program so created, unless otherwise provided by contract.

Article 3 Beneficiaries of protection
Protection shall be granted to all natural or legal persons eligible under national copyright legislation as applied to literary works.

Article 4 Restricted acts
Subject to the provisions of Articles 5 and 6, the exclusive rights of the rightholder within the meaning of Article 2, shall include the right to do or to authorize:

(a) the permanent or temporary reproduction of a computer program by any means and in any form, in part or in whole. Insofar as loading, displaying, running, transmission or storage of the computer program necessitate such reproduction, such acts shall be subject to authorization by the rightholder;

(b) the translation, adaptation, arrangement and any other alteration of a computer program and the reproduction of the results thereof, without prejudice to the rights of the person who alters the program;

(c) any form of distribution to the public, including the rental, of the original computer program or of copies thereof. The first sale in the Community of a copy of a program by the rightholder or with his consent shall exhaust the distribution right within the Community of that copy, with the exception of the right to control further rental of the program or a copy thereof.

Article 5 Exceptions to the restricted acts

1. In the absence of specific contractual provisions, the acts referred to in Article 4 (a) and (b) shall not require authorization by the rightholder where they are necessary for the use of the computer program by the lawful acquirer in accordance with its intended purpose, including for error correction.

2. The making of a back-up copy by a person having a right to use the computer program may not be prevented by contract insofar as it is necessary for that use.

3. The person having a right to use a copy of a computer program shall be entitled, without the authorization of the rightholder, to observe, study or test the functioning of the program in order to determine the ideas and principles which underlie any element of the program if he does so while performing any of the acts of loading, displaying, running, transmitting or storing the program which he is entitled to do.

Article 6 Decompilation

1. The authorization of the rightholder shall not be required where reproduction of the code and translation of its form within the meaning of Article 4 (a) and (b) are indispensable to obtain the information necessary to achieve the interoperability of an independently created computer program with other programs, provided that the following conditions are met:

(a) these acts are performed by the licensee or by another person having a right to use a copy of a program, or on their behalf by a person authorized to do so;

(b) the information necessary to achieve interoperability has not previously been readily available to the persons referred to in subparagraph (a);

and (c) these acts are confined to the parts of the original program which are necessary to achieve interoperability.

2. The provisions of paragraph 1 shall not permit the information obtained through its application:

(a) to be used for goals other than to achieve the interoperability of the independently created computer program;

(b) to be given to others, except when necessary for the interoperability of the independently created computer program; or (c) to be used for the development, production or marketing of a computer program substantially similar in its expression, or for any other act which infringes copyright.

3. In accordance with the provisions of the Berne Convention for the protection of Literary and Artistic Works, the provisions of this Article may not be interpreted in such a way as to allow its application to be used in a manner which unreasonably prejudices the right holder's legitimate interests or conflicts with a normal exploitation of the computer program.

Article 7 Special measures of protection

1. Without prejudice to the provisions of Articles 4, 5 and 6, Member States shall provide, in accordance with their national legislation, appropriate remedies against a person committing any of the acts listed in subparagraphs (a), (b) and (c) below:

(a) any act of putting into circulation a copy of a computer program knowing, or having reason to believe, that it is an infringing copy;

(b) the possession, for commercial purposes, of a copy of a computer program knowing, or having reason to believe, that it is an infringing copy;

(c) any act of putting into circulation, or the possession for commercial purposes of, any means the sole intended purpose of which is to facilitate the unauthorized removal or circumvention of any technical device which may have been applied to protect a computer program.

2. Any infringing copy of a computer program shall be liable to seizure in accordance with the legislation of the Member State concerned.

3. Member States may provide for the seizure of any means referred to in paragraph 1 (c).

Article 8 Term of protection

1. Protection shall be granted for the life of the author and for fifty years after his death or after the death of the last surviving author; where the computer program is an anonymous or pseudonymous work, or where a legal person is designated as the author by national legislation in accordance with Article 2 (1), the term of protection shall be fifty years from the

time that the computer program is first lawfully made available to the public. The term of protection shall be deemed to begin on the first of January of the year following the abovementioned events.

2. Member States which already have a term of protection longer than that provided for in paragraph 1 are allowed to maintain their present term until such time as the term of protection for copyright works is harmonized by Community law in a more general way.

Article 9 Continued application of other legal provisions

1. The provisions of this Directive shall be without prejudice to any other legal provisions such as those concerning patent rights, trade-marks, unfair competition, trade secrets, protection of semi-conductor products or the law of contract. Any contractual provisions contrary to Article 6 or to the exceptions provided for in Article 5 (2) and (3) shall be null and void.

2. The provisions of this Directive shall apply also to programs created before 1 January 1993 without prejudice to any acts concluded and rights acquired before that date.

Article 10 Final provisions

1. Member States shall bring into force the laws, regulations and administrative provisions necessary to comply with this Directive before 1 January 1993.
When Member States adopt these measures, the latter shall contain a reference to this Directive or shall be accompanied by such reference on the occasion of their official publication. The methods of making such a reference shall be laid down by the Member States.

2. Member States shall communicate to the Commission the provisions of national law which they adopt in the field governed by this Directive.

Article 11

This Directive is addressed to the Member States.
Done at Brussels, 14 May 1991. For the Council The President J. F. POOS

Australian Copyright Act (2006)

Section 47D Reproducing computer programs to make interoperable products

(1) Subject to this Division, the copyright in a literary work that is a computer program is not infringed by the making of a reproduction or adaptation of the work if:

(a) the reproduction or adaptation is made by, or on behalf of, the owner or licensee of the copy of the program (the original program) used for making the reproduction or adaptation; and

(b) the reproduction or adaptation is made for the purpose of obtaining information necessary to enable the owner or licensee, or a person acting on behalf of the owner or licensee, to make independently another program (the new program), or an article, to connect to and be used together with, or otherwise to interoperate with, the original program or any other program; and

(c) the reproduction or adaptation is made only to the extent reasonably necessary to obtain the information referred to in paragraph (b); and

(d) to the extent that the new program reproduces or adapts the original program, it does so only to the extent necessary to enable the new program to connect to and be used together with, or otherwise to interoperate with, the original program or the other program; and

(e) the information referred to in paragraph (b) is not readily available to the owner or licensee from another source when the reproduction or adaptation is made.

(2) Subsection (1) does not apply to the making of a reproduction or adaptation of a computer program from an infringing copy of the computer program.

Section 47E Reproducing computer programs to correct errors
(1) Subject to this Division, the copyright in a literary work that is a computer program is not infringed by the making, on or after 23 February 1999, of a reproduction or adaptation of the work if:

(a) the reproduction or adaptation is made by, or on behalf of, the owner or licensee of the copy of the program (the original copy) used for making the reproduction or adaptation; and

(b) the reproduction or adaptation is made for the purpose of correcting an error in the original copy that prevents it from operating (including in conjunction with other programs or with hardware):

(i) as intended by its author; or

(ii) in accordance with any specifications or other documentation supplied with the original copy; and

(c) the reproduction or adaptation is made only to the extent reasonably necessary to correct the error referred to in paragraph (b); and

(d) when the reproduction or adaptation is made, another copy of the program that does operate as mentioned in paragraph (b) is not available to the owner or licensee within a reasonable time at an ordinary commercial price.

(2) Subsection (1) does not apply to the making of a reproduction or adaptation of a computer program from an infringing copy of the computer program.

Section 47F Reproducing computer programs for security testing
(1) Subject to this Division, the copyright in a literary work that is a computer program is not infringed by the making of a reproduction or adaptation of the work if:
(a) the reproduction or adaptation is made by, or on behalf of, the owner or licensee of the copy of the program (the original copy) used for making the reproduction or adaptation; and
(b) the reproduction or adaptation is made for the purpose of:
(i) testing in good faith the security of the original copy, or of a computer system or network of which the original copy is a part; or
(ii) investigating, or correcting, in good faith a security flaw in, or the vulnerability to unauthorised access of, the original copy, or of a computer system or network of which the original copy is a part; and
(c) the reproduction or adaptation is made only to the extent reasonably necessary to achieve a purpose referred to in paragraph (b); and
(d) the information resulting from the making of the reproduction or adaptation is not readily available to the owner or licensee from another source when the reproduction or adaptation is made.
(2) Subsection (1) does not apply to the making of a reproduction or adaptation of a computer program from an infringing copy of the computer program.

Section 47H Agreements excluding operation of certain provisions
An agreement, or a provision of an agreement, that excludes or limits, or has the effect of excluding or limiting, the operation of subsection 47B(3), or section 47C, 47D, 47E or 47F, has no effect.

Section 116AO Manufacturing etc. a circumvention device for a technological protection measure
(1) An owner or exclusive licensee of the copyright in a work or other subject-matter may bring an action against a person if:
(a) the person does any of the following acts with a device:
(i) manufactures it with the intention of providing it to another person;
(ii) imports it into Australia with the intention of providing it to another person;
(iii) distributes it to another person;
(iv) offers it to the public;

(v) provides it to another person;

(vi) communicates it to another person; and

(b) the person knows, or ought reasonably to know, that the device is a circumvention device for a technological protection measure; and

(c) the work or other subject-matter is protected by the technological protection measure.

Exception—interoperability

(3) Subsection (1) does not apply to the person if:

(a) the circumvention device will be used to circumvent the technological protection measure to enable the doing of an act; and

(b) the act:

(i) relates to a copy of a computer program (the original program) that is not an infringing copy and that was lawfully obtained; and

(ii) will not infringe the copyright in the original program; and

(iia) relates to elements of the original program that will not be readily available to the person doing the act when the circumvention occurs; and

(iii) will be done for the sole purpose of achieving interoperability of an independently created computer program with the original program or any other program.

Singapore Copyright Act (2004)

Fair dealing in relation to works

35.—(1) Subject to this section, a fair dealing with a literary, dramatic, musical or artistic work, or with an adaptation of a literary, dramatic or musical work, for any purpose other than a purpose referred to in section 36 or 37 shall not constitute an infringement of the copyright in the work.

(1A) The purposes for which a dealing with a literary, dramatic, musical or artistic work, or with an adaptation of a literary, dramatic or musical work, may constitute a fair dealing under subsection (1) shall include research and study.

(2) For the purposes of this Act, the matters to which regard shall be had, in determining whether a dealing with a literary, dramatic, musical or artistic work or with an adaptation of a literary, dramatic or musical work, being a dealing by way of copying the whole or a part of the work or adaptation, constitutes a fair dealing with the work or adaptation for any purpose other than a purpose referred to in section 36 or 37 shall include—

(a) the purpose and character of the dealing, including whether such dealing is of a commercial nature or is for non-profit educational purposes;

(b) the nature of the work or adaptation;

(c) the amount and substantiality of the part copied taken in relation to the whole work or adaptation;

(d) the effect of the dealing upon the potential market for, or value of, the work or adaptation; and

(e) the possibility of obtaining the work or adaptation within a reasonable time at an ordinary commercial price.

(3) Notwithstanding subsection (2), a dealing with a literary, dramatic or musical work, or with an adaptation of such a work, being a dealing by way of the copying, for the purposes of research or study—

(a) if the work or adaptation comprises an article in a periodical publication, of the whole or a part of that work or adaptation; or

(b) in any other case, of not more than a reasonable portion of the work or adaptation,

shall be taken to be a fair dealing with that work or adaptation for the purpose of research or study.

(4) Subsection (3) shall not apply to a dealing by way of the copying of the whole or a part of an article in a periodical publication if another article in that publication, being an article dealing with a different subject-matter, is also copied.

Decompilation

39.A.—(1) Subject to subsection (2), the copyright in a literary work, being a computer program expressed in a low level language, is not infringed by a lawful user of the computer program decompiling it if—

(a) it is necessary to decompile the computer program to achieve the objective of obtaining the information necessary to create an independent computer program which can be operated with the computer program decompiled or with another computer program (referred to in this section as the permitted objective); and

(b) the information so obtained is not used for any purpose other than the permitted objective.

(2) Subsection (1) shall not apply if the lawful user—

(a) has readily available to him the information necessary to achieve the permitted objective;

(b) does not confine the decompiling to such acts as are necessary to achieve the permitted objective;

(c) supplies the information obtained by the decompiling to any person to whom it is not necessary to supply the information in order to achieve the permitted objective; or

(d) uses the information—

(i) to create a computer program which is substantially similar in its expression to the computer program decompiled; or

(ii) to do any act restricted by copyright.

(3) Where an act is permitted under this section—

(a) it shall be irrelevant whether or not there exists any term or condition in an agreement which purports to prohibit or restrict the act; and

(b) any such term or condition shall, insofar as it purports to prohibit or restrict the act, be void.

(4) For the avoidance of doubt, this section is without prejudice to the generality of section 35 and does not limit the operation of that section.

(5) For the purposes of this section and sections 39B and 39C, a person is a lawful user of a computer program if he has a right to use the computer program, whether under a license to do any act restricted by the copyright in the computer program or otherwise.

(6) In this section, "decompiling," in relation to a computer program expressed in a low level language, means—

(a) converting the computer program into a version expressed in a higher level language; or

(b) incidentally in the course of so converting the computer program, copying the computer program,

and "decompile" shall be construed accordingly.

Observing, studying and testing of computer programs

39.B.—(1) The copyright in a literary work, being a computer program, is not infringed by a lawful user of the computer program observing, studying or testing the functioning of the computer program in order to determine the ideas and principles which underlie any element of the computer program, if he does so while performing any of the acts of loading, displaying, running, transmitting or storing the computer program which he is entitled to do.

(2) Where an act is permitted under this section—

(a) it shall be irrelevant whether or not there exists any term or condition in an agreement which purports to prohibit or restrict the act; and

(b) any such term or condition shall, insofar as it purports to prohibit or restrict the act, be void.

(3) For the avoidance of doubt, this section is without prejudice to the generality of section 35 and does not limit the operation of that section.

Other acts permitted to lawful users

39.C.—(1) Subject to subsection (3), the copyright in a literary work, being a computer program, is not infringed by a lawful user of the computer program copying or adapting the computer program, if such copying or adapting is necessary for his lawful use.

(2) For the avoidance of doubt, it may be necessary for the lawful use of a computer program to copy or adapt the computer program for the purpose of correcting errors in the computer program.

(3) Subsection (1) shall not apply to any copying or adapting permitted under section 39 or 39A.

Hong Kong Copyright Ordinance (2007)

Section 38 Research and private study

(1) Fair dealing with a work for the purposes of research or private study does not infringe any copyright in the work or, in the case of a published edition, in the typographical arrangement.

(2) Copying by a person other than the researcher or student himself is not fair dealing if-

(a) in the case of a librarian, or a person acting on behalf of a librarian, he does anything which regulations under section 49 would not permit to be done under section 47 or 48 (articles or parts of published works: restriction on multiple copies of same material); or

(b) in any other case, the person doing the copying knows or has reason to believe that it will result in copies of substantially the same material being provided to more than one person at substantially the same time and for substantially the same purpose.

(3) In determining whether any dealing with a work is fair dealing under subsection (1), the court shall take into account all the circumstances of the case and, in particular-

(a) the purpose and nature of the dealing, including whether the dealing is for a non-profit-making purpose and whether the dealing is of a commercial nature;

(b) the nature of the work;

(c) the amount and substantiality of the portion dealt with in relation to the work as a whole; and

(d) the effect of the dealing on the potential market for or value of the work.

Intellectual Property Code of the Philippines (1997)

Section 185.1 Fair Use of a Copyrighted Work

The fair use of a copyrighted work for criticism, comment, news reporting, teaching including multiple copies for classroom use, scholarship, research, and similar purposes is not an infringement of copyright. Decompilation, which is the reproduction of code and translation of the form of the computer program indispensable to obtain the information necessary to achieve the inter-operability of an independently created computer program with other programs may also constitute fair use. In determining whether the use made of a work in any particular case is fair use, the factors to be considered shall include:

The purpose and character of the use, including whether use is of a commercial nature or is for non-profit educational purposes;
The nature of the copyrighted work;
The amount and substantiality of the portion used in relation to the copyrighted work as a whole; and
The effect of the use upon the potential market for value of the copyrighted work.

Israeli Copyright Act (2007)

Section 19 Fair Use

(a) Fair use of a work is permitted for purposes such as: private study, research, criticism, review, journalistic reporting, quotation, or instruction and examination by an educational institution.

(b) In determining whether a use made of a work is fair within the meaning of this paragraph the factors to be considered shall include, inter alia

(1) The purpose and character of the use;

(2) The character of the work used;

(3) The scope of the use, quantitatively and qualitatively, in relation to the work as a whole;

(4) The impact of the use on the value of the work and its potential market.

(c) The Minister may make regulations prescribing conditions under which a use shall be deemed a fair use.

Section 24 Computer Programs

(c) Copying of a computer program, or making a derivative work there from, is permitted for a person who possesses an authorized copy of the computer program, for the following purposes and to the extent necessary to achieve said purposes:

(1) Use of the computer program for purposes for which it was intended, including correction of errors in the computer program or making it interoperable with a computer system or with another computer program;

(2) Examination of the information security in the program, correction of security breaches and protection from such breaches;

(3) Obtaining information which is needed to adapt a different and independently developed computer system or program, in such a way that it will be interoperable with the computer program.

(d) The provisions of subparagraph (c) shall not apply with respect to the copying of a computer program or the making of a derivative work there from, as stated in said subparagraph, if the information which has been obtained through the aforementioned means was used in a manner set forth below, or where such information was readily available without use of the aforesaid means:

(1) The said information is transmitted to another person for a purpose different than the purposes set forth in subparagraph (c);

(2) The said information is used to make a different computer program which infringes copyright in the said computer program.

Korea-U.S. Free Trade Agreement (2007)

Footnote 11

Each Party shall confine limitations or exceptions to the rights described in paragraph 1 to certain special cases that do not conflict with a normal exploitation of the work, performance, or phonogram, and do not unreasonably prejudice the legitimate interests of the right holder. For greater certainty, each Party may adopt or maintain limitations or exceptions to the rights described in paragraph 1 for fair use, as long as any such limitation or exception is confined as stated in the previous sentence.

Article 18.4.7

(d) Each Party shall confine exceptions and limitations to measures implementing subparagraph (a) to the following activities, which shall be applied to relevant measures in accordance with subparagraph (e):

(i) noninfringing reverse engineering activities with regard to a lawfully obtained copy of a computer program, carried out in good faith with respect to particular elements of that computer program that have not been readily available to the person engaged in those activities, for the sole purpose of achieving interoperability of an independently created computer program with other programs. . . .

World Intellectual Property Organization Copyright Treaty (1996)

Article 11 Obligations concerning technological measures
Contracting Parties shall provide adequate legal protection and effective legal remedies against the circumvention of effective technological measures that are used by authors in connection with the exercise of their rights under this Treaty or the Berne Convention and that restrict acts, in respect of their works, which are not authorized by the authors concerned or permitted by law.

World Intellectual Property Organization Performances and Phonograms Treaty (1996)

Article 18 Obligations concerning technological measures
Contracting Parties shall provide adequate legal protection and effective legal remedies against the circumvention of effective technological measures that are used by performers or producers of phonograms in connection with the exercise of their rights under this Treaty and that restrict acts, in respect of their performances or phonograms, which are not authorized by the performers or the producers of phonograms concerned or permitted by law.

Index